The March to
MADNESS

Nelson Dacier

NEWMAN SPRINGS PUBLISHING
320 Broad Street
Red Bank, NJ 07701

First originally published by Newman Springs Publishing 2019

ISBN 978-1-64531-841-5 (Paperback)
ISBN 978-1-64531-839-2 (Digital)

Printed in the United States of America

To My Brother, My Hero

"Because brothers don't let each other
wander in the dark alone."
—Jolene Perry

Contents

CHAPTER 1

Jailhouse Rock

Wednesday, April 8th, 2015

APRIL 8TH WAS AS GOOD a day as any to accept my fate. Though spring had arrived, it was a cool, damp, windy morning surrounding the county courthouse. It was approaching 9:00 a.m., and the activity around the dreary government buildings was frenetic as always. The ride over was not long, and I decided to drive in order to ease my overactive mind. Ann looked nervously out the window while she fidgeted with her fingernails, her usual stress-relieving activity. Not much was spoken throughout the trip; there was truly nothing left to say.

Upon parking the car and obtaining the requisite receipt from the newly installed and invariably fickle Muni Meter device, Ann and I lowered our heads and began the long walk toward the halls of justice. My trial part was in the smaller of the two worn-down structures. We knew the drill by heart now as we had had the pleasure of being there several times in the past few months. Today, however, was different. Today Ann would be leaving alone.

I had surrendered to the authorities just over five months ago, but the wheels of justice turn ever so slowly, and it took all that time for my case to finally be docketed. Thankfully, a plea deal had been bargained for and arranged with prosecutors at the district attorney's office; however, it was still up to the judge to make the final determination and to give the deal his seal of approval. While we were all confident that the proposed outcome would be reached, I still planned to take my Higher Power into the courtroom with me just for good measure.

Once upstairs and situated, we sat and waited in the corridor for my esteemed counsel to arrive. Ben Kraft was a prominent local attorney with a thriving practice and a reputation which preceded him. I had known Ben for nearly a quarter of a century and had seen him regularly when I first began my now tarnished legal career as a real estate associate back in the early '90s. He was arrogant, brash, and often somewhat of a prick, the perfect mouthpiece. Ann had retained Ben's services after I was hospitalized, and the incredible string of events began to unravel piece by piece. In fact, his office was the first stop on our trip home from the psychiatric center. After being an inpatient there for over two weeks, I was just happy to be going anywhere. Today, however, Ben's role was to just to reassure us, to confirm all the procedures which would follow, and to keep both Ann and me as relaxed as humanly possible. After all, we were not expecting surprises, and we both knew that I was in very capable hands.

Ben bounded upstairs moments later with his briefcase in one hand and his cell phone in the other. As he approached us, he made the call. We were all present and accounted for, and the assistant district attorney was on his way. While I appeared calm in my outward demeanor, inside, my stomach began to churn, and I had to make several trips to the men's room prior to the ADA's arrival. Upon his entrance, the impeccably clad older gentleman, scholarly in both his appearance and tone, addressed Ben privately and then had the court officers usher us into the trial part. The room was small and dingy and was by no means the dramatic poetic bastion of truth and justice that is portrayed in the legal crime dramas seen on television. Ann and I were seated in the rear and waited for the litany of court personnel—bailiffs, stenographers, clerks, and officers—to take their official places. Once the legal craftsmen had taken their assigned seats at the respective tables, all rose in anticipation of the judge's arrival from chambers.

Judge Vincent Scalabrini has been appointed to the District Court only four years earlier and was being forced into retirement at the year's end when he turned age seventy. The elder honorable justice was known as a fair and reasonable man, and as Ben had previously informed me early on, "We could have done a lot worse." I had never met Judge Scalabrini but pictured him as a tall, distinguished, gray-haired type with ruggedly chiseled features, almost like Don Barzini of *The Godfather* fame. Instead, a frail short undistinguished-looking chap wearing glasses and seeming almost disinterested by the upcoming proceedings appeared almost out of nowhere. "Please be seated," he barked as he gestured toward the attorneys and climbed up onto the bench.

After the preliminary procedures, some introductions, and a brief sidebar with counsel, all eyes turned toward me as one of the court officers graciously escorted me over to the defense table so that I could sit beside Ben. Apparently, the charges levied against me were going to be read aloud, followed by a series of questions directed at me from Judge Scalabrini. I was to respond to these inquiries either by saying *yes*, *no*, *guilty*, or *not guilty*, and Ben had written those choices down on a piece of scrap paper to guide me to answer appropriately. As each query was spelled out by the judge, Ben would point his pen toward the correct retort, and I would then reply accordingly, ensuring that no mistakes were made. It all seemed quite long and drawn out for a decision that was previously agreed to, but when you are facing six various felony charges and up to fifteen years behind bars, you act humbly and do as you're told. Once Justice Scalabrini had completed his inquisition and I had plead guilty to all six of the indictments, two armed corrections officers from the Sheriff's Department came up behind me, told me to stand, to place my hands behind my back, and then proceeded to cuff me right there in the courtroom. I glanced back at Ann, who had tears in her eyes, and then I turned and faced Ben, who appeared to be both simultaneously relieved and depressed. He had done all that he possibly could, and the sentence of twelve months in the county lockup was truly the best result that I could have hoped for. Even so, it was quite a somber few minutes as I said my goodbyes and was led out of courtroom and down to the bowels of the pens below.

My initial lesson regarding jail, and the entire prison system for that matter, was learned very quickly. Nothing, and I mean absolutely nothing, takes only a few minutes. Sure, they may tell you that it will "just take a second" or "to hang on a minute," but inevitably, you will always be waiting for something or someone. I asked one of the officers who had taken me into custody if we were going straight over to the county facility, and he replied, "It should only be a couple of minutes, and then we will make our way over." Some two hours later, most of which I spent praying and trying not to make eye contact with any of the other thirty or so convicts who were surrounding me, I was recuffed to another inmate and led from the holding cells outside to the awaiting vans for the twenty-minute ride over to the correctional center. I tried to stay internally at ease while appearing outwardly cocky, but inside my heart was racing, and my blood pressure was rising. It was my first sense of penitentiary life, and the pungent odor and the foul interplay virtually smacked me in the face. Unfortunately, this was just the beginning, and patience and serenity were soon to become my two best friends.

As the vehicles rumbled through the prison entrance, I noticed a tall three-story building looming off in the distance. Its outer walls were covered with soot and decaying stone, and its windows were all secured with metallic mesh guards and iron gratings. Still shackled in twos, we were led out of the transports, and I could almost taste the murky and depressing flavor as we approached the ominous, run-down dungeon. While it now served only as a simple barracks for the almost two thousand prisoners, both men and woman alike, in its heyday, it had been viewed as a modem marvel of the corrections world with all the newest bells and whistles that money could buy. As we were being ushered toward the doorway of what would be my new abode for the next twelve months, I had a frightening flashback visualizing where I was just a single year ago compared to where I was now. The situations couldn't have been more at odds with each other. It was a truly poignant and paralyzing moment in my journey and one that I would never forget.

It had certainly been a wonderful and miraculous turnaround for me, and while I knew that the upcoming 365 days would be yet another difficult chapter in my life, I was hopeful that that it would be the closing leg in my trip back to sanity. That may seem like an odd statement, as not many people welcome their stay in a house of detention, but I was at peace with my penance and, even more importantly, at peace with myself. In addition, I knew that I was taking my Higher Power in along with me and that He would never leave my side. I recalled the small square medallion that my mentor Francis had given me after we had first met. It read, "Do not be afraid, I am with you always," and I took that message to heart and through the doors inside to the cellblock with me.

Today I am still a firm believer, and not only do I have absolute faith in God as I understand Him, but more importantly, I have an unrelenting trust in Him as well. "FAITH" for me stands for "Fully Assured I Trust Him," and when friends and family members wished me luck prior to my final court date, I would comfortably reply, "I do not need luck. I am taking God into the courthouse with me." I was a changed person, a better person, a spiritual person, and I knew that God had both guided me and provided for me during my complete and total metamorphosis. Accordingly, my daily responsibility was simply to just continue doing the "next right thing" and to continue to align my will with that of my Higher Power. As long as I sought that out as my ongoing goal, I knew that I would always be able to witness and experience His grace and His favor.

A few days prior to my imprisonment, I returned the medallion back to Francis, certain that I would be unable to take it in with me. He looked at me surprisingly and then peered down at the symbol in his hand. After flipping it over and back again several times, he looked up and said, "No, it's yours, but I will hold on to it for you until you get out, and then you can decide to pass it on to whomever you choose." I nodded back, understanding the meaning in his emotional words and the message that they conveyed. The main purpose of our "program" was to try and help others who were still sick and suffering and to pass on to them all that was so freely given to us. To aid and encourage those who were desperately seeking a solution to their addiction and self-destruction was not only key to their survival but was also paramount to my own freedom and recovery.

My thoughts got interrupted by the deafening clang as the motorized iron gates slammed shut behind me. This stop on the jailhouse entry tour was yet another holding cell where me and my five other colleagues would remain until we could be officially processed into the county's computer system. Of course, this "processing" would take several hours to both begin and then to complete, so I tried to find a comfortable place to rest among the rock walls and steel benches. One particular young black man with braided locks of hair, several tattoos on his arms and neck, and an impressively muscular build caught my attention right away. Perhaps a gangbanger and almost certainly a recidivist, he seemed very knowledgeable regarding all the events and procedures that were about to unfold. Unfortunately, however, as a prison novice myself, I found it quite difficult to either comprehend or decipher what he was saying. It was neither due to an accent nor a stutter but rather due to his language and the usage of a seemingly foreign vocabulary, which was piecemeal combination of part "hood" and part "jailhouse" lingo. Junior, as he was referred to by all who knew him, spouted out words and expressions like *bid*, *72*, *MO*, *the count*, and *the bubble*, which were clearly new to my refined background. In addition, the way that he carelessly sprinkled in the slang curse words and racial epithets throughout his commentary was also extremely intimidating. It was a dialect of the streets, but obviously not one of the picturesque lanes or avenues that I had become accustomed to.

I had grown up in a nice suburban upper-middle-class hamlet some twenty-five miles east of the greatest city in the world. Many of the towns in the local vicinity, while not openly racist, were often segregated by their social-economical classes or by explicit and precise choices. There were also a few areas that were specifically known for their religious demographics as either Jewish or goyish locales. And while still others mixed their religious and ethnic denominations into the Jewish/Italian or so-called matzah/pizza communities here and there, predominantly most of the races, creeds, and colors did not cohabitate together, and the municipalities were generally either all white or all black; mine was the former. In fact, I believe that there were only two African-American families living within our entire city population of about thirty thousand residents. Accordingly, I neither encountered nor had my first real personal interaction with young African-American teenagers until I arrived at college.

My freshman year at the university, I had a suite mate named "LJ," who was a flamboyant, outgoing individual with an endearing ear-to-ear smile and an engaging personality. We quickly became friends, and I can recall many occasions when we stayed up late and exchanged stories with each other relating to our vastly different upbringings. I learned what a "dew rag" was and what all its varied uses were, and LJ learned that "chicken soup" was not just a food but rather the magic elixir that would cure all human suffering. He was smart and eager to gain as much knowledge as possible, whether it was from his textbook or from some strange white kid from the country.

Unfortunately, LJ relocated and transferred out of dormitory hall after the first semester. I got the feeling that while many people like myself were friendly to him, others were not, and his comfort level had greatly diminished. He moved to another quad with a much larger minority base, and I only saw him briefly once in a while and on a very rare occasion thereafter. I missed my friend and all the good times that we had shared together, but when we did happen to bump into each other around the campus center, we always reminisced about those early carefree days and how much they meant to us both. They were times that neither of us would ever forget.

As the decibel level continued to rise inside the cramped enclosure, the tension began to escalate as well. The hours sluggishly crept by as if time had stopped. Yet, thankfully, I was able to keep my composure by quietly praying and meditating internally. I knew that, eventually, someone was going to address me directly, so my thoughts turned toward concentrating on what my necessary response would be. Just then, Junior strutted over to where I was seated, looked down at me, and asked, "Yo, my brother, what's your trip, not drugs?" I glanced up quickly and replied, "No, bro, not drugs, but I am facing six felony raps, and I plan to be here for a while." He stared at me for a moment in total amazement, shook his head, and then said out loud to no one specific, "Whoa, white boy here be trippin'! You into some serious shit, huh? Who would have guessed." And with that, he stuck out his hand, and we commenced to do a finger shake and a fist bump, and I felt my heart return to my chest from my throat. I had passed my first test. But this was not the time to get overconfident or cocky, so I remained still after that and just continued to listen and to pick up whatever tiny bits of information that were being passed on. I thought to myself, *Damn, if I only understood the language.*

As I struggled to a find a somewhat comfortable position among the steel slabs, the guards began to call us one by one over to the intake area. I anxiously awaited my name to be announced and tried to remain cool until it was my turn. Finally, the "CO," correction officer, bellowed out my new moniker, and the heavy metal gate clicked, automatically opened, and then crashed shut behind me after my exit into the dank hallway. I was shuffled over to one the heavily secured information desks which conjured up notions of the betting windows at the racetrack as thick plexiglass dividers separating you from the person with whom you where communicating. In addition, there was a large metal handrail which jutted out in front of the glass and which prevented any inmate from getting too close to either the window itself or the officer seated on the other side. There were also several clearly posted warning signs—"Do Not Touch or Tap on the Glass," "Do Not Lean on the Bar," and finally, "Do Not Use Profanity."

My discussion with the CO began with him asking me a series of questions ranging from my name, age, and Social Security number, to what my current mental state was and what, if any, medications I was presently taking. After a few minutes of him entering the requisite data, he passed a tiny piece of notepaper through the small slot at the bottom of the window and explained that it contained my personal prison identification number and that I should not share this information with anyone else under any circumstance. I nodded in acknowledgment and then quickly folded up the paper and put in my pocket for safekeeping. Once our session was completed, the officer printed out my lowdown and statistics, told me to sign in all the appropriate places, and then nonchalantly directed me to the next station, "Fingerprinting and Photography."

I proceeded down the dingy, dimly lit long passageway until I found a room which read on the door "PHOTO LAB/IDENTIFICA-TION." The gentleman inside offered me a friendly greeting and asked for my paperwork. After checking and rechecking my information, he guided me to the back wall of the room and started to take a series of snapshots both straight on and from the side. Next came the fingerprinting portion of the exercise. The state-of-the-art computer-enhanced printing machine was quite sophisticated and utilized no ink whatsoever. Rather, just a few drops of water were placed onto my fingertips, thereby enhancing the natural oils in my skin. I was then instructed to rest my hand gently on a set of clear plastic tiles and told to delicately roll my digits first left then right to elicit the desired image. Ten smaller squares were then produced, one for each finger and thumb on both hands, and the computer then read the impressions and forwarded them on for viewing to an attached flat-screen monitor located above my head. The final print would appear thereon in a much more magnified condition and would be examined carefully to ensure that it could pass the usage test, which was based on both the quality and legibility of the image. While the device was somewhat temperamental and often rejected the initial readings even when they appeared nice and clear, the process was fascinating to witness, though it did prove a bit tedious. Unfortunately, it seemed as if entirely all the county's prison budget must have gone into that one apparatus as the other surrounding areas and gizmos were all decidedly old and antiquated. Unbelievably, they still had manual typewriters and rotary phones!

After my encounter at the photo lab, there were still various stops at medical, clothing, and psych that needed to be completed before my processing could be finalized. It was a never-ending circle of scurrying here and there only to be told continuously to "wait in line" or to "go back where you came from" because they already had too many people lingering about. Two things became quite clear to me at this point: first, that there was a ton of "red tape" in the correctional system and that protocol and decorum were the keys to a prisoner's success; and second, that no task or assignment was to be rushed or done in a hurry. Accuracy took the place of speed, and complacency took the place of everything else. The officers, nurses, and staff walked around like emotionless zombies who had been reawakened from the dead. That, along with the dreary catacombs that you had to navigate your way through, projected a scene that you find in a bad "B" horror flick or silent movie from the olden days. It was truly a very unfamiliar and unsettling atmosphere that made me feel like an outcast—or, I guess in the alternative, to remind me that I was a criminal.

With the intake procedures finally concluded, I was sent back to the holding pen and told to "sit tight" until they were ready and had organized my transfer over to the housing block. The introductory three-day stay, "72" as it was nicknamed, stood for the seminal period that all inmates would spend under quarantine with the rest of the newbies to ensure that no one would carry either TB or any other infectious diseases along with them into the general population. I had been told that 72 was by far the worst time of your "bid," slang for your sentence or jail time, and that once I was cleared from that hellhole, things would improve dramatically. In hindsight, those three days were absolutely one of the bleakest and depressing stretches that prison has to offer. But facing adversity usually only makes us stronger, and the harrowing experience prepared me for what was yet to come.

A multitude of voices and laughter echoed all around the lockup as a shift change was occurring, and there was a lot of traffic and activity in and about the area. Subsequently, two of the new guards approached our cage and informed the group that they would be transporting us to our assigned destinations. What I did not know at the time was that due to my recent history and the time that I had spent the previous year in a local psychiatric ward, I was going to the "MO," or mental observation wing of the dormitory rather than the standard location. MO was a special section of the 72 residential housing block where the inhabitants' mental states were reviewed daily and inmates were frequently taken for evaluations to ensure that they were neither harmful to themselves nor to others. Upon arriving at my alternative quarters, I was immediately furnished with my own "Inmate Survival Kit," which included a plastic coffee mug and spoon, a roll of toilet paper with a bar of soap hidden in the center, and a small tube of toothpaste along with a tiny brushlike thimble item which was worn on your finger and which was supposedly utilized as a toothbrush. "Open 8," barked one of the COs, and before I even realized what was happening, I was led down the narrow alleyway to my pristine six-foot-by-eight-foot chamber.

The foul stench of unwashed bodies, stale urine, and damp mildew permeated every inch of the confines. My suite consisted of a rectangular steel framed slab for a bed and a decaying, soiled, and stained sink-and-toilet-combination unit which appeared to be constructed of some type of concrete and metal compound. Over the bed was a mounted placard which read, "ALL INMATES MUST SLEEP WITH THEIR HEADS TOWARDS THE BARS," and another on the far wall added "DISORDERLY CONDUCT WILL NOT BE TOLERATED." Sounds simple, I thought, as I repositioned the two blankets on the bed in the hopes of cushioning my sore and aching back. Just as I was about to sit down, I heard some footsteps, and I saw a blur go streaking past my cage.

As I looked up, Junior whirled around and shouted, "Yo, CO. Cell number 8 needs a mattress. Get cell 8 a mattress." *A mattress in here, really?* Then, from out of nowhere, an officer appeared and told me that there was an air mattress in cell 5 that I could grab, so I quickly hurried over, retrieved the mattress, and deposited it carefully into the metallic bedframe. *What a find,* my thoughts raced on. *I wonder when the two-hundred-threat-count sheets and soft cotton towels will show up?* It was then that I realized that I probably would need a towel at some point, so I sheepishly asked the next CO who walked by if I could possibly get one. "Sure," he replied. "I will check the supply room on my way back." Well, now we were really getting someplace, both a towel and a mattress in a matter of minutes. Maybe this place wouldn't be so bad after all. I let my mind hold on to that idea as I lay down, closed my eyes, and drifted off tacitly to sleep.

It was just after six o'clock in the morning when I was startled by the rhythmic clanging of the heavy steel doors opening and closing. Bleary eyed, I made my way over to the sink and pushed the button to obtain some water to wash the fog from my face. Apparently, breakfast was to be served, ready or not. And while the accommodations were far less than what I was normally accustomed to, the board was initially much more bearable than the room. Each mealtime, one of the inmate workers who served on the tier's "food cart" would pass by my cubicle and leave a plain square Styrofoam container between the bars of my gate. That meal was usually accompanied by two pieces of bread and, depending on the daily fare, either a small container of skim milk or "prison juice." This so-called prison juice, which was distributed from some sort of old decrepit slop bucket, was certainly not squeezed from any type of fruit known to man. Rather, it was a weak, bland Kool-Aid-like liquid which had considerably less flavor than it did color. Breakfast was generally comprised of cold cereal with a small sampling of fruit, and once in a blue moon, it would contain a hard-boiled egg as an added bonus. For lunch, more often than not, I received a mysterious cold-cut product which always looked as if it had seen better days. The dinner selections did vary somewhat more than the other daily grub; however, undoubtedly there would be a side dish of either starchy rice or pasta smothered in gravy, beans, or jailhouse chili. Later, I was introduced to the indistinguishable thin oblong breaded patty which was supposedly sometimes fish and supposedly sometimes veal, but either way was a definite pass for me.

During the daily feasts, the only available eating implement that was at my disposal was the standard-issued plastic prison spoon which I had received on my initial arrival. Sometimes, as I sawed my way through whatever chow had been cast in front of me, I hearkened back to the days spent at my favorite family-style Italian restaurant where I would watch the waiter cut the veal parmigiana with the side of his spoon before he doled out the cuisine. While it was a far cry from the present, it was a happy recollection, and any positive visualizations that would assist me in getting through the mundane drudgery was gladly welcomed.

Unfortunately, while confined in the 72 wing, convicts were unable to access the jailhouse "commissary," which, for all intents and purposes, was like the "canteen" provided at summer camps or on military bases. At the commissary, one could purchase food, snacks, toiletries, clothing, and various other essentials. Funds needed to be deposited into an individual's institution account, and once a week, inmates were given a requisition sheet where they would log desired selections. Barring any unforeseen event, which seemed to occur frequently, delivery of the purchased goods was scheduled for a few days thereafter. Invariably, some requested item would be missing, out of stock, or just forgotten due to laxness, and your plain, nondescript brown paper sack would come back lighter than normal. Prior to my incarceration, I had been tipped off by Paulie, one of my outpatient cohorts who had just recently served a four-month bid, to order the brownies and the black-and-white cookies as they were not only the best-tasting items but also were the best value available. Regrettably, it was still only Thursday, and my anticipated Saturday departure date out of 72 seemed light-years away.

The afternoon passed by surprisingly fast as I was fortunate enough to corral a newspaper from one of the COs when he left his shift for the day. Prior to prison, when I read the paper, I would just glance at the cover and then turn directly to the sports pages; but in this case, each page and tiny morsel of information was like mental gold, and I eagerly devoured every word, even reading most of the articles twice. In addition, I spent hours trying to solve the jumble and the crossword puzzle merely to spark my brain and to focus my thoughts on anything else but my surroundings. The other veritably bone-chilling part of my prison orientation was the constant cold that permeated every inch of the cellblock. Even wearing multiple undershirts and socks, along with the traditional jailhouse "oranges," the bright V-neck top, and pajama-like bottoms the county called a uniform, it was impossible to warm up for any extended period of time. There were no hot liquids to heat my interior, and I had been duly warned to avoid the foul-smelling and filthy communal hole of a shower that was located near the entranceway, therefore preventing any chance of warming my exterior either. The best option to keep my blood flowing was to continually stay in some kind of motion.

Later, when I was permitted to vacate my cage for an hour, I paced the length of the hundred or so odd feet of the corridor in the hopes of stretching my legs and enhancing my circulation. Distressingly, I felt myself becoming quickly overwhelmed by the vile stench emanating from several of the other enclosures. It was evident that many of my fellow cons had also passed on utilizing the shower facilities, and as such, it became very difficult to vanquish the repulsive smell of body odor and excrement. Finally, when my gag reflex could no longer be controlled, I covered my nose and mouth and retreated to less putrid air surrounding my abode. Hygiene was obviously not high on the priority list for much of the inmate population, and that became simply another reason for me to stay in my box and stick to myself. I then realized that it was probably a good thing that the temperature was maintained at such a frigid level as I could not even imagine the alternative or how truly unbearable it would have been if it was sweltering and if odors were allowed to percolate. Thank goodness for small comforts and gratitude for the little things. I crawled under the covers, closed my eyes, and prayed that my new digs, wherever they assigned me, would be better.

CHAPTER 2

Go West, Young Man

One year earlier

THE SUN WAS STILL TRYING to appear this early spring morning, and the streets were enveloped with a calm and wispy fog. Several of my neighbors were out walking their purebred dogs, poop bags in hand, and I recalled the old joke that said if aliens ever landed on earth they would have to assume that the dogs ruled the planet and that the humans worked for them. After all, why else would one species be cleaning up after another and carrying away their waste? My mind continued to drift and wander. Perception—that is, the primary aspect of our lives that not only allows us to comprehend and conceive what is taking place around us but also enables us to function within society based on our own notions and impressions. How we perceive ourselves and others is the only true way to evaluate our character, motives, and actions appropriately. Are we hiding behind some false facade? Are we portraying a role for the world to see like an actor upon the stage, or are we real, honest, and genuine? Do we continually lie to ourselves over and over again about our shortcomings, utilizing rationalizations and blaming circumstances as the fall guys for our failures? The answers to these questions presently escaped me, and it would be quite some time until the haze was actually lifted from my head, and I permitted God's light to enter my being and to restore my sanity. For now, however, I was in the throes of preparing to embark on yet another week of self-centered fun; amusement and total mayhem. It was tournament time. The NCAA Men's College Basketball Tournament—or, as it was more fondly nicknamed, "March Madness"—was upon us. The so-called "Big Dance" was scheduled to kick off later that evening, and by then I would be some twenty-five hundred miles away, eagerly awaiting the pandemonium to commence.

The limousine pulled up to the house at 5:45 a.m., and I informed the driver that I would be out shortly as I was still making last-minute preparations. My bags had been customarily packed the night before, and I had already reviewed their contents numerous times. I only needed to finish dressing, secure the necessary funds into my carry-on bag, and make one last pit stop in the john. My favorite traveling outfit consisting of black Adidas sweats, a solid-black polo shirt, immaculate Nike sneakers, and an oversized black windbreaker, which I had purchased on a recent cruise, were all perfectly laid out on the bed. The "drug-courier profile look" was not only quite comfy, but it also evoked an air of cockiness, which was required for this type of venture. This chic fashion statement allowed me to comfortable with myself and yet maintain that certain outward perception and portrayal that was paramount to my existence. After all, who was more notable or affluent than me?

I tried to be silent so as to not awaken either Ann or "The Prince," my only son and heir to the throne, but unfortunately my scurrying about must have stirred Ann as she sat up in bed and stared bleary-eyed in my direction. Weakly, she mumbled, "Have a safe flight. Say hi to Jack for me and don't forget to call when you get settled in." I blew a kiss in her direction and then hurriedly headed for the door. The driver was lingering just outside, and he promptly grabbed the larger of my two suitcases and started toward the curb. At no time did I ever authorize anyone to either touch or handle my black leather satchel, and it was permanently tattooed to my right side at all times. That case contained all of my personal valuables, as well as my vast, intricate research regarding each and every one of the sixty-eight teams who had been selected to compete in the upcoming competition. It was only recently that four "play-in" games had been added to the schedule, enlarging the field from the usual sixty-four participants to the present-day number of sixty-eight competitors, who were now vying for the elusive championship crown. These extra contests did nothing except to create just another unnecessary revenue scheme for both the television networks and the NCAA alike.

Two games were to be played each of the next two nights, and the four winning teams that survived would be added to the sixty remaining qualifying schools, thereby returning us to the magic number of sixty-four squads that purists like myself had been accustomed to. These initial battles were basically incidental in nature as they pitted the eight weakest platoons in the tourney who hailed from either the bottom portion of one of the "power conferences" or from an otherwise obscure conference championship finale. The two winners from each contest advanced as either eleven seeds or sixteen seeds respectively. However, most people would fill in their "brackets" well before these games were even decided as none of the victors were predicted to advance much further anyway. As I approached the long black stretch limo, I paused, closed my eyes, and took in a long, deep breath. The air truly smelled sweet and was also filled with the aroma of tension and expectation that I had learned to love.

The true beauty of the early-morning flight was that I really did not lose any time to my day. The departure was scheduled for 8:10 a.m., and the landing out west was slated for 9:45 a.m. as the four-and-half-hour trip was offset by the three-hour time difference. While the plane was packed to the rafters, I was fortunately able to procure an "extra-space seat" which allowed me to stretch out and to sleep for most of the excursion. I knew that Jack would want me fresh and alert when I arrived, and I was certain that he had planned a busy day of activities. After touching down, taking the shuttle tram to the terminal, and locating the proper baggage carousel, I turned on my cell phone and found three messages from Jack already waiting. They explained that he was in transit and where I was to meet him so that he would neither have to park the car nor foolishly waste any precious time. I gathered myself together and proceeded to the meeting point with my bags in hand and a whimsical smile on my face.

Jack and I had been friends for almost thirty years, and while we lived virtually across the entire country from each other, our relationship was stronger now than it had ever been. His dark-black usually unkempt hair, warm eyes, bushy overgrown eyebrows, and round-shaped face made his appearance almost cartoonlike, as if he was mobster from the old days that one would see in the comics or the funny papers. While he never smoked, seldom drank, and possessed only one real vice, gambling, he was far from the picture of health. He had a stocky build, which was nowadays closer to portly, and an unorthodox stutter in his gait from a series of recent illnesses and accidents. The only solace that he seemed to enjoy and which helped him to alleviate the unrelenting stress from his daily exploits was found in his one constant love: food.

His celebrity status within the gaming community and the fact that he could eat gratis at just about every restaurant west of the Mississippi, allowed Jack to relish in the ceremony of dining as it became more of a social event and less of just a meal. Whether he liked it or not, Jack was a well-known and prominent figure around town, and most folks were more than happy to roll out the red-carpet treatment just for him. Upon his arrival, the persistent pomp and circumstance along with the initial ingratiation could alone take several minutes as a parade of maître d's, servers, cooks, and even restaurateurs themselves would come out to welcome Jack and make his acquaintance. And while he did, on occasion, get a kick out of the preferential behavior conveyed, he was really a very humble man at heart and was often at times embarrassed by all the fuss. He was more apt to have a casual conversation with one of the busboys than with one of the higher-ups or even with the other clientele. But that was Jack. Even years ago back in college, he kept an extremely low profile and led a less-than-assuming lifestyle. His concern was at all times focused on others and how he could possibly improve the quality of life of those around him. Friends and family needed to be taken care of first and foremost even at the expense of himself, for otherwise he would be incapable of appeasement.

One somewhat odd yet consistent tidbit of information about Jack was that while he had virtually every door in the city open to him, he often frequented many small out-of-the-way joints where the grub was barely edible and the cleanliness and decor even worse.

Perhaps it was that his taste and palate were truly unrefined, or perhaps it was a conscious choice to again partake in a simple and moderate lifestyle among all the bright lights and the endless action. Either way, I have had the opportunity of feasting with Jack at his full spectrum of eateries, and even though the food was not always up to par, the company and the conversation were compensating factors. Thankfully, we had already had dinner reservations for both Thursday and Friday nights when my posse would be in town, but for tonight and tomorrow, it would be just Jack and me, and the final destinations would be up to him.

Thursday night's venue was, in my opinion, the best Italian restaurant on the planet. In addition to the food being five-star quality, the ambiance, atmosphere, and picturesque views entirely heightened the experience. It was by far my first choice. Friday night was steak night, and we had made plans to dine at a recently opened chophouse that was located directly adjacent to our hotel. Jack had made a hefty investment in the new contemporary lounge and grill and therefore was also able to arrange for us to have cocktails and appetizers outside under the lights in the exclusive VIP patio area as a special treat prior to dinner. Since the games would still be underway, I questioned him about the early 7:00 p.m. booking. He assured me that he had everything covered and that we would not miss any of the action. As all of these images went racing through my mind, my thoughts came back to the present. I began to have a panic attack thinking about all that still needed to be accomplished in the next thirty or so hours. Then faintly in the distance, I heard a familiar voice cry out, "Hello, my boy! Hello, my boy!" It was Jack, and as I eagerly approached my lifelong friend, it hit me like a bolt of lightning that this would be my last trip out to visit my old pal and the last few days that we would ever spend together again.

It was approximately 10:45 a.m. local time, and Jack said that we had an hour to kill before our lunch appointment and that afterward he would drive me over to the hotel to meet up with our other college buddy Romeo, who would finalize the necessary lodging arrangements. Due to both my fragile mental state and my inability to commit to anything over the past few months, I had grievously delayed in acquiring the usual block of suites at my favorite secluded casino, and consequently, Romeo had to scramble somewhat just to get us a set of rooms in an appropriate setting. And while I was positive that Romeo would produce a first-rate result, I was still quite antsy since I was in charge of that aspect of my clique's itinerary, and I was picking up the tab for everyone as well. My trepidation was not unfounded either because whereas Romeo was by far one of the greatest schmoozers of all time, he was also quite forgetful and oftentimes managed to omit the most important of details. That fact, coupled with the fact that I had only given him the final room count a few days earlier, was certainly enough reason for my concern.

The car slowed down, and Jack pulled into a supermarket parking lot and said, "Hang out here for a minute, my boy. I just have to take care of something quickly." Unfortunately, Jack's idea of quickly was all too similar to that of the county prison's, and neither meant anytime soon. I lowered the window, found a good station on the radio, and reclined the seat back to soak up some of the warm desert sunshine. Jack returned about a half an hour later to find me speaking with Ann, who I had promised to call upon my arrival. More importantly, I had also spoken to Romeo to ensure that he was, in fact, going to meet us at the hotel around 2:00 p.m. Thankfully, he confirmed that he would be there at 2:00 p.m. sharp, that he had my requested package in hand, and that he was working on the rooms as we spoke. All good news, I thought, as Jack started the car and headed out for the anticipated lunch date.

The meeting was scheduled for high noon, and while normally that was a bit early for my liking, my stomach did not seem to mind as I was truly famished. We entered a small strip mall just off the main drag, and I immediately noticed that an Italian restaurant basically took up the entire plaza. Upon entering the majestic eatery, Jack was instantly greeted by a handsome young Sicilian gentleman who looked as if he just stepped out of a recent issue of Mr. Italy 2014. Later on, I learned that Dom was the son of Giuseppe Carbone, the owner and proprietor of the ristorante, and that he and the rest of the staff were all deliberately dressed to the nines because they were just starting to film a new reality television series featuring the best authentic Italian cuisine west of the Mississippi. Dom escorted us to our table and after introducing me to the other various personnel as a friend of both his and Jack's, I was showered with greetings and salutations. Once seated, the waitress brought over a large blackboard which listed the "specials of the day," and Jack insisted that we both order the veal Italiano with baked pasta, his personal favorite.

After getting settled in and surveying my surroundings, I realized that we were the only patrons in the entire restaurant. I was not really sure why this was the case, but perhaps it was the early noon hour or perhaps the "family"-like atmosphere. Either way, it certainly added to the unadulterated enjoyment of the moment. Then, almost out of nowhere, appeared Don Carbone himself. He was followed closely by a gigantic camera crew which was headed by a gorgeous slim olive-skinned belladonna who was interviewing the don as he made his entrance. Giuseppe paused momentarily, and the camera light clicked off almost simultaneously with his slight hesitation. As the workers all exhaled and relaxed, the dapper smiling paisano gracefully made his way over to our table. Jack and I both hurriedly stood to greet our host and after he and Jack exchanged hugs and then kisses on both cheeks, I was introduced to the godfather. He extended his hand and said graciously, "Ah, mio amico. I have heard great things about you. Let's hope we all make some real money this weekend." I nodded respectfully, shook his hand, and then replied, "That's why I am here, my friend. That's why I am here."

After sharing a laugh and several other jovial pleasantries, Giuseppe pulled Jack aside privately, and I took the opportunity to review the most recent betting lines and all the latest pre-tourney news of the day on my cell phone. I was still perusing the odds and information when Jack returned unaccompanied and explained to me how Giuseppe had asked him if he could film us having lunch for the television spot as he wanted some footage of normal, every-day diners enjoying their meals. In addition, he conveyed that he would greatly appreciate our involvement in the piece, and that all we needed to do was to "act natural" and say a few words for the camera. It sounded much like an offer that could not be refused, and anyway, who was I to argue? So after the enormous smorgasbord had been served and we had begun to indulge in the various delicacies, Don Carbone, with team alongside, made their approach.

As he sauntered across the room, all the while continuing his loud and intense dialogue with the scrumptious show host, the don stopped abruptly in disbelief and turned directly toward Jack. "Unbelievable," he bellowed out. "Here is one of our best friends and most valued customers Jack Whitlock, along with his associate from New York, Mr. Stefano." He continued, "You see, Maria, people come from all over this great country of ours and from around the globe to dine with me and my family at our little ristorante. It has become quite a tradition." Maria and the cameraman then quickly shifted themselves next to Jack, and while she was asking him a series of obviously prescripted questions, I was able to get a really good look at her spectacular figure, sparkling brown eyes, and full red lips. Unfortunately, my ogling did not get to last long as their exchange ended quickly, and Maria sped off toward the kitchen with her troupe in tow. "You see, my boy, you never know when you will be discovered." Jack chuckled. I smiled back and quipped, "True. You can become famous when you least expect it." I still wasn't sure if Jack knew beforehand or not about the whole television show, but it really did not matter one way or the other. What did matter was that I was able to meet and greet Don Carbone in person and, even more importantly, that he had the opportunity to meet me and size me up. After all, I was Jack's basketball guru who was going to make him rich this weekend.

The remainder of the meal, which by the way was outstanding, was consumed over serious discussions of game analysis, point spreads, and several detailed inquiries from Jack regarding specific teams and their anticipated game plans. From time to time, he pulled out a small set of crib notes from his shirt pocket and either stared or crossed out certain entries as we furthered our conversation. We had narrowed down the first day's sixteen contests to only nine which were playable, and I had already determined my final seven selections, which I had cemented in the back of my mind. Luckily, there were only a couple of games that Jack and I vehemently disagreed upon. Usually, when this occurred and we each possessed a strong and differing opinion, we would simply "pass" on that particular betting option and often just enter a small friendly wager between ourselves. This year, however, Jack continued to impress upon me that he was unequivocally counting on me and my extraordinary knowledge and NCAA basketball expertise and that he would ultimately yield to any decision that I felt firmly enough about. As our review session continued, I felt the pressure starting to mount somewhat; and when a large lump began to form in the back of my throat, I leaned back, took a long swig of my Diet Coke, and tried to reassure myself, *I've got this covered. I am prepared, and I am as ready as I will ever be. No worries.*

Jack took care of the bill—my money was never good when I came to town—and we said our farewells to Giuseppe, Dom, and the rest of staff as we exited and made our way out to the car. While he clearly could afford any vehicle on the market today, including the latest Bentley or Ferrari, Jack was still puttering around in the same old Mitsubishi that he purchased some dozen years prior. Again, that was Jack. He was perfectly happy and content driving his aged good friend and often remarked that it still got him where he needed to go. This humility, the essence of being humble, was just another of the wonderful traits that Jack possessed and gratefully one which would later become the central and most integral component of my metamorphosis and complete lifestyle change. Modesty had never been my strong suit, yet when I was around Jack and witnessed his daily demeanor, I would recognize that I could learn a great deal from emulating his behavior and utilizing him as a role model. With all of his talents, his mathematical genius, and the vast fortune that he had accumulated, he always managed to stay "right sized." It was truly the "simple things in life" that Jack enjoyed the most. All he really needed was a game to watch, some food to eat, and some close friends to share it all with, and he was "good."

In that light, and in order to try and avoid some of the noise and hype that always seemed to surround him, Jack had recently relocated into a newly built but moderately priced gated community on the outskirts of town. Although the house was quite spacious inside and included two massive den/living-room areas, one of which had been converted into a fully equipped "war room"—complete with several different computer feeds, monitors, and a television wall containing four sixty-inch plasma screens—from the outside, it was very unassuming and actually almost sparse. Due to the current water restrictions throughout the area, no freshly completed lots possessed either large lawns or expansive landscaping. However, this particular home did have a small fenced-in backyard with a tiny square patch of green grass, which enabled him to allow his two most precious possessions to run free: his dogs, Cuff and Link. And while this splendid "man cave" was certainly sufficient for a bachelor such as Jack, it was a far cry from the opulent mansions closer to the action which he could easily have afforded.

As we continued onward toward the hotel, I felt my head continue to bob up and down as I started to doze off. Luckily, Jack had a few "quick stops" to make on the way over, so I was able to grab a power nap while he was off conducting business.

When we finally arrived at the pavilion, the dashboard clock read exactly 2:03 p.m. Amazingly, we had managed to stay on schedule. As I struggled to remove my tired and aching body from the car, a hand reached out to help me, and a voice rang out, "Hey, old-timer, you need some help?" I knew that voice, and it could only be one person: Romeo.

Similar to Jack, Romeo and I had been close friends since our early college days. While we had only seen each other a handful of times since graduation, we had that special kind of relationship, a mutual admiration and respect, which is shared with only a few select people on this earth. Over the past several years, we had become even closer as my trips out west became more frequent and as we spoke quite often during the summer months when Romeo would travel back east to spend time carousing around Manhattan. His suave manner and laid-back style truly made him hard to resist. He was also the quintessential ladies' man, as the name suggests. I had been informed, however, that Romeo was his actual given name rather than a concocted nickname or alias given to him by some wise guy. To me, he was simply a true ally, confidant, and someone whom I could share my deepest thoughts, emotions, and desires with. Furthermore, it was totally inconsequential that our conversations generally occurred when we were consuming mass quantities of drugs and alcohol as that only added to the already spicy flavor of the dialogue. We spoke about all things: gambling, drugs, women, politics, our daily lives, and where we currently were and where we wanted to be. Most importantly, we spoke without reservation and with an honesty that was truly palpable.

Jack's one and only rule, which needed to be adhered to at all times, was the strict moderation of alcohol and any other "substances" for the initial thirty-six hours of my visit. Romeo was also familiar with this restriction, and rather than feel Jack's wrath, he would not allow me to engage in any overindulgences until after the forbidden period had elapsed. Comically, prior to my arrival, I was given the itinerary for the first two days, along with a pep-talk from Jack which invariably featured a lecture on both moderation and the need to stay focused on our ultimate plan. In addition, he always reminded me not to bring illegal contraband along with me as I would be of no help to him if I got stopped prior to my arrival. "We can provide you with whatever you require, my boy," he would say adamantly, continuing by reiterating that "Romeo is at your disposal, and you know that he will have your usual package waiting." It was all pretty simple: relax and take care of business; after that, the sky was the limit.

Never an active user of any mind-altering matter, Jack only imbibed when either Romeo or I insisted or if there was some special occasion that warranted a celebratory toast. Even going back to college, he was never one for the bar scene nor the late-night "after" party. Back then, his typical Saturday night was comprised of dinner, watching sports, and trying to create novel ways to mathematically conquer the world, or at least the Sunday spreads. Romeo, on the other hand, was more like myself. He was a social butterfly who reveled in the nighttime action and all that it had to offer. We spent many an evening barhopping together until 4:00 a.m. when the pubs closed and the early-morning soirees commenced. Of course, Jack was fully aware of this prior history—hence, the thirty-six-hour rule—as he knew that left to our devices, neither of us would be functioning for long, nor useful in any manner.

While I was able to leave certain aspects of those wild younger years behind me, my alcohol and drug abuse continued to thrive. On occasion, it was mild and sporadic; but more often than not, it was totally out of control. The previous five years of my life had not gone according to plan, and both my marriage and my business were crumbling down around me. The only substantial comfort that I could find was either out of a bottle or through some sort of narcotic haze. I began to spend more and more time at the local watering hole and less and less time at my house and my office. The bar was the only location where I truly felt safe, protected, at ease with myself and my surroundings. Likewise, I had numerous friends among the "regulars," and Timmy, the bartender, had become one of my closest friends and conspirators.

Accordingly, my random jaunts for "happy hour" become a daily occurrence, and I began lying to Ann about my whereabouts almost as frequently. As things continued to progress, I began showing up for lunch or a quick snack in the afternoon as an excuse to drown my sorrows and to get my needed buzz on. Work became an afterthought, and I would just "phone in" many days rather than making an actual appearance. The ruse of meeting clients, bringing in new business, or investigating other possible opportunities was quite plausible, and in addition, I was the boss, and no one was going to question my authority.

The hours at the pub soon turned into full days, and the little white lies turned into a pattern of pathological deceit and deception. It truly neither mattered who confronted me nor what the situation was at hand. Rather, all that counted was that I was able to achieve my "mental escape," and I would do whatever was necessary in order to reach that goal. So long as I was able to get my seat at the bar, acquire my necessary fix, and sink into my "comfort zone," I thought that all would be fine and that I could survive anything and everything. It was not until much later on that I gained the knowledge and realization that these constant indulgences, which I believed were keeping me alive and functioning, were actually methodically and painfully killing me day by day. This horrific discovery was truly the "unkindest cut of all." Armed with this sickening fact, I contemplated about what I was going to do next.

All of my life, as far back as I can remember, I always had the need to be a people pleaser. Being the "go-to guy" whenever the chance arose was a role that I savored. The feeling of importance that it conveyed satisfied my alarming inner need for both acceptance and approval. Unfortunately, however, this type of behavior can very often lead to unhealthy patterns of activity which literally harm the individual who is trying to be helpful. Consistently being there for others, devoting all of my time to doing favors, and not taking care of myself mentally or physically contributed greatly to my demise. Furthermore, this psychological component and compulsion to be liked by all elicited a personality trait which frequently appeared flirtatious and inviting. And while I did enjoy chatting it up with just about anyone who would listen, invariably, my bark was far worse than my bite.

During our many years of marriage I had been forever faithful to Ann and through thick and thin, I had maintained the wedding vows that I had pledged. But as time moved along, the relationship seemingly fell into oblivion. The mundane routines continued to persist, and the apathetic aura that encompassed our lives intensified to such a degree that we barely even associated with each other. Yet there was still a sense of responsibility and even some love and devotion that I would experience from time to time. Notwithstanding those fleeting emotions, the ever-expanding cavernous hole inside of me incessantly beckoned to be satiated. All the alcohol, drugs, gambling, and other assorted vices could not fill the gaping void that existed within. I helplessly grasped for anything and everything in order to calm my inner demons, and while I did intermittently find some gratification through a brief "rush" or "high," that temporary solution was a just a Band-Aid on a much more serious wound. As my ongoing struggles steadily grew and festered, so did my levels of anxiety and paranoia. This mind-set of indescribable fear, disgust, and instability began to consume me round the clock. The only solace that I presently possessed was the fact that, pills in tow and the plan in hand, I would enjoy my last few days with the people that I cherished the most.

After a brief conference with Romeo, Jack said his farewell, and Romeo and I proceeded to the hotel lobby and the main reception located therein. The scene resembled Penn Station amid a Friday night's rush hour. The entrance was mobbed with weary patrons, and the dozens of customer service representatives were having trouble maintaining both the crowd and any sense of decorum. Romeo directed me out the fracas and over to a less-crowded check-in facility where I noticed the overhead sign which read, "VIP GUESTS / PLATINUM MEMBERS ONLY." He then nodded and declared, "Don't worry, kid. I got this." I just grinned and watched him maneuver his way through security until he was face-to-face with the casino's reservation manager. The two exchanged some pleasantries, shook hands, and then disappeared through a door which read "HOTEL STAFF ONLY / NO GUESTS ALLOWED."

Almost simultaneously, I received a text message from Romeo which stated, "Go to the bar off to left. I will be there in a minute." I turned to my left and saw a large lounge area adorned with picturesque palm trees and other assorted foliage, which looked quite inviting. As I made my way over to the warm, welcoming watering hole, I anxiously rationalized that one drink would not be a problem. But before I could even get situated and order my first cocktail, Romeo trotted over and plopped down on the barstool next to me. "There may be an issue," he said sheepishly, continuing, "But I am working on it."

Apparently, the resort was way overbooked, and as a result, they were having a hard time piecing together the four rooms which I had requested. "Tough time of the year," Romeo quipped. "Besides the basketball tournament getting underway, there is also a big technology convention in town this week, and that is throwing a wrench into the works." While I could feel my blood pressure rising by the second, outwardly I remained cool, calm, and collected as I certainly didn't want Romeo to sense either my displeasure or my dissatisfaction of how things were proceeding. Still, in my head, I knew that my mental wellness was beginning to deteriorate and that I needed some type of elixir in order to quell the unease. Fortunately, Romeo had already called over the bartender Vanessa, whom he cordially addressed as "Van," and instructed her to "get my friend here whatever he desires and put it on my tab." With that, he downed two quick shots of bourbon, wiped off his mouth, and started back toward the reservation kiosk. Halfway there, he stopped and yelled back, "Remember, kid, moderation until tomorrow night." Although I had tried to hide it, it was apparent that Romeo had observed my present discomfort and that he also knew that I could easily overindulge in just a few minutes as I tried to settle my nerves. So there I sat, tired, worried, and worst of all, on a very short leash. At least "Van" was still there and at my disposal. Her sheer beauty, seductive voice, and ample attributes did manage to assuage my aggravation somewhat, but it was not until the liquor hit the back of my throat that I truly began to relax. She left the freshly opened bottle of Basil Hayden's right in front me, and with my true friend now with me, all I could say was, "Cheers."

It was common knowledge for all those in the "gaming community" to understand that each and every gambling establishment set aside a certain number of suites which were to remain unoccupied so that "high rollers," or "whales" as they were known, who decided to visit at the last minute could be easily accommodated. Armed with this fact, and also since the booze had yet to soothe my stress, I texted Romeo and asked him if I should get Jack involved in our little situation. My phone bleeped, and the return message conveyed, "Just chill, kid. We are almost home. Have another drink and try to relax." I sat pondering, One more couldn't hurt. After all, Jack and I had just consumed a bountiful brunch, and my stomach would be able to stand at least another spirit and perhaps even a few shots. "Hit me again," I bellowed at Vanessa. "And make it a double." She sashayed over, gave me a scintillating smile, and filled my glass to the top. "Good luck." She laughed as she motioned toward the lobby. "You're going to need it." I swung around casually and saw Romeo heading our way with an ear-to-ear grin and look of satisfaction in his eyes. I breathed a sigh of relief and awaited the news of his seeming success.

The rooms had been secured until Friday, and while this was not the best result imaginable, it was progress. Once Friday morning came, I was to go see the head of the Platinum Club, mention Romeo's name, and then coordinate the rest of our stay. I removed the last remnants of my neurotic frame of mind by downing a few more celebratory shots with Romeo and "Van" and then started for the elevators in order to inspect my new digs. I was still desperately in need of some solid nap time, and I knew that I had at least a couple of hours to myself. As I approached the first security checkpoint between me and my high-rise destination, my cell phone started to vibrate again. This time, the message read, "Go get some rest, kid. Call me around 6:00. Jack should be here around 7:30 for dinner. Oh, and let me know how you like the room. Romeo." The plan was really starting to take shape, and a broad smile crossed my face as I reached into my wallet for my access card and my photo ID.

Upon clearing the second stringent surveillance stop, all guests were constantly monitored throughout the facility, and the luxury towers had an even greater patrol presence. I let out a huge sigh of relief, took a deep cleansing breath, and entered the private lift for the ride up to the twenty-sixth floor. When I arrived at suite 2602, the senior concierge was already standing outside awaiting my appearance. In his possession was my luggage, a bountiful fruit basket, and a room-service cart with several covered plates. He greeted me cheerfully and asked how my trip had been thus far. "All going to plan as of now," I replied and then gestured toward the dolly. "What's all of this nonsense?" "These are all compliments of the house. We hope you enjoy them, sir," he answered back graciously as he guided me inside to the prodigious parlor. The overly opulent penthouse or "businessman's mélange," as it was billed, contained a very nice mix of a classic corporate boardroom with the affluence of a lavish living space. There was an enormous kitchen area, living room, dining room, separate conference room with a communications network, and two bedrooms each with full spa-like steam baths. I perused the surroundings and nodded. "This should work," I said and then thanked him for his service, handed him a generous gratuity, and showed him out. Before the door even closed behind him, and without investigating or rearranging anything further, contrary to all of my OCD tendencies, I collapsed onto the gigantic king-sized bed and closed my eyes. I still had a couple of hours until the next round of nighttime activities commenced.

The ringing of the house phone snapped me back into consciousness as I had fallen into a delightful doze. Of course, it was Jack, and his first words were, "Hello, my boy. Hope all has worked out and that you are unwinding." Just as I was about to respond, he continued on by informing me that the "committee meeting" was all set for the next day at noon and that he would be over at 8:00 that evening to meet Romeo and me for dinner and to discuss the strategy for tomorrow's roundtable. "Sounds wonderful, my boy," I replied enthusiastically. "See you then." I hung up the receiver, stretched my aching body, and gathered up my wits about me.

It was only 5:30, and consequently, I had plenty of time to review all of my notes, grab a quick shower, and still hook up with Romeo prior to Jack's entrance. I messaged Romeo to find out both his whereabouts and his course of action, and he answered back that I should meet him outside by the taxi stand promptly at 7:15. While clearly well aware that I was currently under the rigorous restrictions of the "thirty-six-hour rule," I was "Jonesing" for a smoke and therefore asked Romeo if he would be kind enough to roll a couple of "spliffs" for me. I was genuinely elated when the phrase "Way ahead of you, kid" appeared on my blackberry. I knew that I loved him for a reason.

All prepped and freshened up, I left my new makeshift residence and hurriedly headed for the elevators and my encounter with Romeo. My cell phone read only 7:02 a.m., but I knew that it would take several minutes to negotiate the long corridors, the elevator ride, and the throngs of people swarming in the casino. The joint was literally buzzing with excitement, and I thought to myself that it was only Tuesday and that I couldn't even imagine what the atmosphere and theatrics would be like come Thursday, Friday, and the weekend. I navigated my way through the hip crowd, which I noticed was both extremely young and good-looking.

As I approached the foyer, I saw Romeo standing outside and conversing with one of the gorgeous "greeters" who were strategically stationed in front of the marquee. He looked stoked and ready for action, and while I understood that I had to keep myself in check due to the upcoming meeting with Jack, both Romeo and I knew that we could get a nice "game face" on prior to Jack's arrival. It was a typical crystal-clear spring evening in the desert, and dusk had begun to fall, illuminating all the lights of the city. The scene was perfect.

Romeo sauntered toward me and quipped, "Hey, kid, you look good. You clean up nice." "Thanks," I replied, "just trying to do my best to keep with you." He patted me on the back and steered me toward the steakhouse, which was conveniently positioned right between the hotel and the high-rise condominium where Romeo was currently living. That apartment was actually one of the dozen or so units which Jack owned in the vicinity and one of the perks Romeo was afforded, along with a car and a hefty expense account. After all, a person had to portray a certain kind of nouveau-riche persona in order to survive in this community, and Romeo virtually oozed an aura of success and splendor. He had been working for Jack since the turn of the century and, at this point, had worked himself up to be Jack's number one right-hand man. Not a bad position to hold and one both well-known and well coveted in the gaming industry.

We slipped into the exclusive restaurant via a secluded side entrance, which led us directly to a staircase accessing the building's top floor. This upper level was generally utilized as a platform for bands and other live shows but was apparently now undergoing full-scale renovations and was in a state of total disarray. There were also several offices located behind the stage, and after sifting our way through the rubble of old props and scenery, we emerged at a large workplace. "Sorry for taking the scenic route, kid," Romeo whispered. "But I figured we could have some privacy and spark one up back here." I smiled and said, "You read my mind, dude. You read my mind." He nodded, professing, "Age before beauty, old-timer," and he handed me a perfectly rolled cigar-sized joint along with a metallic gas filled Jack Daniels lighter. The smoke cloud quickly infiltrated the entire area as we smoked that "dube" down to a tiny "roach," and after tapping it out in the ashtray, Romeo carefully placed the remains into a cigarette box and then handed it to me for safekeeping. "Just a little taste until your restrictions break." He grinned. I opened the box, and inside were three more joints and a minilighter carefully hidden among the cigarettes. "Bless you." I gestured to him, my hands clasped together in prayer, and then asked, "What is this place anyway, just more perks of the business?" "Nah," he grumbled, "this one's more personal." He continued, "I used to date one of the hostesses downstairs, and we would often sneak up here during her breaks for some quiet time." Then he stood up, gave me a broad stoner's smile, and said, "We're actually still good friends. You'll meet her later." I just shook my head, let out a chuckle, and replied, "That's my Romeo."

Somehow we were able to escape from the loft by taking the service elevator down to the main dining room, and when the doors opened, we were greeted by a scene buzzing with excitement. The bar was totally packed, and the outdoor veranda was also brimming with activity. Romeo explained that the place had recently become one of the hottest new happy-hour spots and that it also specifically catered to the twenty-five and older crowd in order to keep out the young riffraff. While the crowd was smartly dressed and properly behaved, there was an air of naughtiness which permeated the backdrop. We were pleasantly greeted by many of the staffers and some of the most breathtaking bartenders and well-endowed waitresses that I had ever seen. A path to the end of the bar miraculously opened up, and I caught a glimpse of two open barstools with cocktails in front them covered with coasters. Romeo darted over to the space, picked up one of the glasses, and then turned to me and inquired, "Bourbon and ginger ale, I presume?" "Why mess with a good thing?" I joked back, adding, "Shaken, not stirred, of course." And from that moment on, we were on our way.

It was obvious that Romeo had thought of everything and also that no expense would be spared. I was like a kid in candy store. Unfortunately, my sheer delight was soon tarnished as images of Jack shaking his head in disdain kept popping into my mind. I was cognizant that I needed to stay composed and under control, but the really pathetic part was that my tolerance had grown so high that I no longer even knew where the line to cross was. I was sure of one thing, however: I was still unquestionably miles away from it. After downing numerous bourbons and several shots, Romeo pulled me aside and muttered, "When Jack gets here, we will set up shop outside and find a more serene spot. You know he can't deal with all of this commotion." "You're right about that," I answered, punctuating, "And you know that he will want talk business first." We raised our glasses, toasted to Jack, and quickly ordered another round before it was too late.

Jack made the scene some twenty minutes or so later and was already quite aggravated by the time he engaged us. He immediately went off on a lengthy tirade about how he hated this week and all the incessant favors and courtesies that he was required to grant. After ranting on for several minutes, he abruptly stopped and asked us if we would do a shot with him. Romeo and I glanced at each other in amazement and then almost simultaneously replied, "Sure, Jack, if *you* need one." "Just one!" Jack roared back. "Remember, tonight is a work night." Sternly, I reiterated, "Of course, my boy. We are fresh and ready to go." With that, Romeo ordered up another round of liquid refreshments. We all eagerly gulped them down, and then we departed for the outdoor patio to begin the real conversation. The festival of food and strategic discussion lasted for hours, and I was genuinely glad that Romeo and I had found the time to meet up prior and take our necessary comfort. The "Selection Committee" was looming tomorrow, and all of a sudden, things got significantly more serious.

CHAPTER 3

The Selection Committee

The next day (Wednesday)

I WAS AWAKENED BY A loud muffled voice followed by a faint knocking on my suite-room door. "Just a minute," I called out as I sat up on the edge of the bed and tried to gather my thoughts. I barked, "Who is it?" and then stumbled drowsily from the bedroom and out into the living-room area. Upon reaching the foyer and peering through the peephole, I could see that it was a waiter with a pushcart and a steaming carafe, which I was praying was filled with coffee. After opening the door, I was greeted cheerfully by the young uniformed gentleman. "Good morning, sir. Breakfast, sir," he declared as he raced past me and began to organize the assortment of trays and accouterments. "Did I order breakfast?" I replied inquisitively. "Just following my instructions," he explained. "Where would you like me to set everything up?" I pointed toward the round table in the parlor and instructed him to place it anywhere in the neighboring vicinity. "Piping hot coffee, scrambled eggs, home-fried potatoes, wheat toast, crisp bacon, fresh fruit, cream, and various sweeteners," he explained as he poured the steaming black liquid gold from the boiling percolator, adding, "Shall you require anything else, sir?"

As I glanced over at the smorgasbord of delicacies being presented, I could not imagine that I could possibly need anything else, but then thought to myself, *Sweetener, there is never ever enough sweetener.* "Just some additional sugar-substitute packets, my good man, either the blue or the yellow." "Very good, sir. Right away, sir." And just as quickly as he had first appeared, the footboy shot out of the room and disappeared behind the closing door. Breakfast had been served.

I was a bit surprised by all the early pomp and circumstance, and when I glanced over at the handsome twinkling Tiffany wall clock, it read 9:52 a.m. Prior to retiring last night, I had arranged for a 10:00 a.m. wake-up call, so I was happy to be up, relatively awake, and on time. While I was totally excited to delve into the lavish breakfast banquet, first I needed to wash my face and take care of some other important business. Accordingly, I headed toward the bedroom and the pretentious powder room located therein. Once my freshening was completed, I returned to the salon, shook the remaining cobwebs from my head, and ruminated more about the fanciful food service. Was it just the hotel being polite, or did Jack somehow have a hand in this? Perhaps it was just his way to ensure that I was properly fed and functioning? After all, today was our big day, "Selection Wednesday," the eve of the "Big Dance," and the most important day of the week for Jack and his many cohorts.

Now, if you are confused by the "Selection Wednesday" terminology, you should be. Every sports fan knows that the NCAA Basketball Selection Committee meets regularly throughout the last few weeks of the regular season and the conference championships until the culmination of its research concludes with the airing of the CBS Sunday-night "Tournament Selection Special" at 6:00 p.m. eastern standard time. It is only then that the tournament's participants are officially announced, along with the team's seeding, initial first-round opponent, and specific geographical location. These complex "brackets" are what the frenzied fans are chomping at the bit for, and upon the dissemination of this information to the public at large, the real serious analysis and prognostication can begin. The wild anticipation and speculation that builds up prior to the "Selection Sunday Show" is just a precursor to the total mayhem that commences once the ball is dropped and the games begin. And while most of the schools can forecast their fate—and if they will, in fact, be included in the March Madness— there are always surprises in the art of "bracketology."

Our round-robin forum was scheduled for high noon, and while there would be both food and refreshments served, no alcohol would be permitted. Due to the number of invitees, ten in all including Jack and myself, this year's event was to be held in the Sonata Ballroom, which was centrally located on the promenade level next to the spa and fitness center. I knew most of the other committee members personally except for the two new guys Vinnie and Charlie, who were flying in from Chicago. The regulars. Carmine, Sal and Joey were part of Jack's local cartel, and the Jersey Boys who helped run the northeast corridor Fat Tony and Paulie, I had met on several different occasions both here in town and also back east when Jack would visit over the summer. The final and most senior member of the group, "El Gato," was looking to give up the "business" and to retire after a career which spanned over half a century. As such, it was Jack's intention to send him off in style with one last grand score.

I had known El Gato for over a decade now, and I also knew that he and Jack had a very long and close relationship. It turned out that when Jack first moved out West after college, it was El Gato who got him up and running and whom Jack relied upon in those early days if he ran into roadblocks or difficulties. The elder statesman had been in the gaming industry since the early '60s, and now, at seventy-three years young, was finally ready to call it quits. The fun had dissipated for him long ago. And with the advent of the internet, computerized wagering, and all the recently enacted IRS tax regulations, the old-fashioned bookmaker had virtually disappeared from the desert and was facing extinction. Yet for seventy-three, the old goat was still in great physical shape. He spoke often about his younger days and how he used to train with the great and world-famous Jack LaLanne. Unfortunately, a recent illness, coupled with his continued and long-term steroid usage, was starting to affect him mentally, and his aptitude and intensity for odds making had greatly waned. Yet to look at him, one would never know. The best picture that I could paint for you is a shorter, older, and more grizzled "Nature Boy" Ric Flair of World Wrestling Federation fame, with a bright-red face, a few strands of silver hair slicked back, and muscles bulging everywhere as if he had just been "pumped up."

My relationship and dealings with El Gato had always been both respectful and cordial even though 99 percent of them took place over the phone. Often we would speak of friends and family prior to conducting our business transactions, and he would always wish me good luck even though he was personally taking my action. We initially met several years into our friendship while Jack and I were sharing a casual lunch together at an outdoor cafe. He strolled over to our table, exchanged a few friendly pleasantries with Jack, picked up the tab, and then hurried off. I remember that I had no idea who he was at the time but that something did seem very familiar about him. After a couple of minutes, as we were getting up to leave, Jack asked if I recognized the mysterious stranger who had stopped by. I told him I did not but that something had struck a chord within me. "Well put, my boy," Jack replied coyly. "He should have sounded quite recognizable." And there it was. The familiarity was the voice. The deep, gravely, fatigued-sounding, raspy voice that was chronically irritated about something. There was only one man who possessed such dulcet tones: it had been El Gato.

The afternoon symposium was going to be a veritable who's who of the prognosticator's world. Even the infamous Jimmy "The Greek" Snyder would have been proud of this assemblage. Thankfully, I still had a couple of hours to prepare, and since the meeting was being held just downstairs from me, I knew that time was a nonissue. As I began to devour the sumptuous spread that had been unfurled before me, my mind began to critically assess the seven selections which I had previously formulated and which I would be presenting later for discussion. I was quite confident about five of the picks, but Jack wanted seven, so seven it was. I strolled back and forth between the buffet table and the conference room where all my personal research, notes, and data were scattered about. It was overwhelming just looking at the array of newspapers, statistical printouts, and line sheets that littered the massive work surface.

Before I could even think about delving into the assortment of information at my fingertips, I picked out a nice, fat joint from the package that Romeo had given me the previous night and slowly inhaled the magic reefer into my lungs. The soothing vapor immediately calmed my mind while also facilitating my thinking process. It has become more and more apparent, whether real or fictitious, that I required that first smoke in the morning to get my day underway. While stretching and a good hot shower stimulated me physically and got my juices flowing, the "pot" was necessary to restore me mentally and to help me find my comfort zone. The essential and inescapable need to ease my mind into action and to allow myself to cope with daily trials and tribulations that would ultimately rear their ugly heads was patently obvious. I had become dependent on the various chemical substances at my disposal and was unable to function without them. These compensating factors, the yin and yang of life, as I liked to call them, brought me both the balance and stability which permitted me to proceed productively and to carry on with my life.

I poured another cup of coffee, joint in hand, and then sat down to review my preferences one final time. There was nothing at this point that I was going to change, and the exercise was more of a "psyche session" and pep talk than anything else. I was more than ready. So after cranking up the air-conditioning unit—I usually ran warm, and the coffee had made me even warmer—I located an '80s station on the Bose Radio and proceeded to get dressed. While belting out the words to "Bette Davis Eyes" and "Come on Eileen!" I assembled a casual ensemble and made sure that I was comfy since I knew that we would be in conference for quite some time. Though the summit always had a definite strict formality to it, the dress code was very informal. If you looked presentable and neat, you were fine. Accordingly, I of course chose another version of my "drug-courier profile look," this time displaying a bright-white polo shirt and my crispest and cleanest white baseball hat. I was almost certain that Jack would be donning his standard outfit comprised of jeans and some kind of designer-label golf shirt which invariably would look like he had slept in it the previous night. The rest of the crew would be clad in various campy costumes ranging from silk T-shirts to stylish thousand-dollar suits. It was going to be a real medley of misfits, and as the keynote speaker, I was the one who had to bring it all together. I knew that I had my work cut out for me.

The clock approached 11:30 a.m., and after tidying up and ensuring that all the goods had been properly stashed away, I carefully packed my briefcase and headed downstairs for the ballroom. On the walk over to the elevator bank, my cell phone rang; and upon answering the call, I heard Jack cry out excitedly, "Good morning, my boy. Ready for the big day?" "Ready as I'll ever be," I answered. "Oh, and thanks for the fabulous breakfast too." "Breakfast?" he said, half-heartedly laughing. "I have no idea what you are talking about, but I hope you enjoyed it nonetheless." He then continued, "I almost forgot, make sure that you ask El Gato how he is feeling. He hasn't been doing well lately, and I am sure that he would greatly appreciate it, especially coming from you." "Of course," I responded. "It will be my pleasure. You know that the old curmudgeon means the world to me." "Yes, my boy, I know. Now get a move on and meet me at the Juice Bar in the lobby so that we can concur further. I'm pulling up to the valet now."

Jack was already sipping on some cranberry juice and chatting on his phone by the time that I arrived at the Juice Bar. He looked more gussied up today than usual, and it was clear that he had shaved and that he also had picked out a relatively clean and unwrinkled shirt. As he saw me approaching, he quickly finished his drink and motioned me toward the front reception area. "Greetings," I said cheerfully, a broad smile on my face. "Greetings, my boy," Jack reiterated, and then asked, "Any issues or problems with the rooms or the amenities that I should know about?" I explained all that occurred with Romeo yesterday and told him that we were all set for the time being. "Really? Romeo did a good job?" he blurted inquisitively. He shook his head in amazement and continued, "He has your package as well, my boy, I did not forget." "Ah yes, my package," I muttered nonchalantly. "I had almost forgotten myself."

Jack at that point glanced over at the manager who was working the counter and as they began to surreptitiously chat with each other, I noticed an occasional gaze cast in my direction. It was as if Jack was subliminally informing me that all was, in fact, fine and that the proper parties now knew for certain who I was. Once they shook hands and the manager departed into the back office, Jack returned and informed me that all the "right" people were aware of my presence and that if any inconvenience should arise, it would be solved immediately and appropriately. I nodded graciously, thanked him, and we proceeded to make our way out of the lobby and up to the Sonata Ballroom for our long-awaited rendezvous.

The auditorium was a medium-sized room which was generally utilized for intimate corporate gatherings. Today, however, the chairs were not arranged in rows facing toward a central viewing area, but rather, they were strategically located behind four tables which were positioned in the center of the room in a rectangular-shaped manner. There were ten individual workstations that had been set up each containing a leather desk blotter, pads, pens, personal laptops, and two bottles of water. At the far end of the salon was a lavish brunch buffet which offered just about anything and everything that one could desire. It was clear that Jack had gone all out and had spared no expense. When I inquired what he had "dropped" for this arrangement, he winked and whispered, "It's all on the house, my boy. They owe me a favor or two." Then after a pat on the back and a hand gesture toward where I was assigned to sit, next to him at the head of the dais, Jack cleared his throat, took a sip a water, and bellowed, "Gentlemen, it is time to begin."

There were neither name tags nor place settings on the tables, but it was more than apparent that all involved knew both where to be seated and where their place was in the hierarchy. The two new guys from Chicago sat at the far end of the table across from Jack and me, El Gato was just off to Jack's right with Paulie and Fat Tony, and opposite them to my left were Jack's "three amigos." As I surveyed the group, it became obvious to me that someone was missing. I leaned over to ask Jack about this situation, but before I could even get the words out of mouth, he turned and said, "Romeo's out minding the store, and besides, he is out of his league here anyway." I thought to myself in amazement, *Out of his league, really? He dealt with these guys every day of his life.* However, that was just it. Romeo was seen more as a worker and an employee than an active member or participant in the game. Regardless of his years of service and often insightful commentary, he was neither someone who was respected nor someone who would be listened. Therefore, he was not considered worthy to partake in the festivities.

Following the strict etiquette of the proceedings, Jack opened with a few perfunctory words, and then the platform was handed off to each member one at a time in a counterclockwise fashion. Accordingly, El Gato would have his allotted time first, and I was going to be bringing up the rear. I assumed that this was not a coincidence but instead was carefully orchestrated by Jack to ensure that both El Gato commanded the proper respect by commencing the dialogue, and I would be given my moment to shine by culminating the discussions. I began to feel flushed and warm inside as it dawned on me that I was the keynote speaker and that all eyes would be concentrated upon me and my guidance regarding the specific plays or passes on the upcoming contests. Trying to focus and to gather my composure, I methodically sipped on my water wishing the whole time that it would magically turn into bourbon and ease my ever-building anxiety. I fantasized about excusing myself for a moment and heading off to the men's lounge for a quick toke of reefer or a cool inhaling drag on the bong but immediately realized that was impossible. No, I just had to grin and bear. I had yet to acquire either the necessary spiritual tools or the vital knowledge of prayer and meditation to calm my inner demons. These assets and principles were still light-years away from my awareness.

After almost two hours and now approaching the left-hand flank's turn to speak, Jack called for a break in the action so that we could all rejuvenate ourselves, have a bite to eat, and use the facilities if needed. I'm sure he also would have said, "Smoke 'em if you got 'em"; but with this crowd, that was entirely unnecessary as the room was already encompassed in a dense fog of cigar fumes. I then felt a tug on my arm as Jack pulled me aside for a brief conference. He wanted to get my take on the prior presentations and to see if I was all set to go. I reached up, stretched my arms toward the ceiling, and reassured him that I felt confident and that nothing that was conveyed so far had overly impressed me. He nodded in agreement and then excused himself, so I took the opportunity to head over to the buffet and find myself a snack.

When I reached the massive array of edible enticements, I noticed El Gato filling a plate with fruit and assorted raw vegetables. He looked up, smiled wryly, and said, "Hey, buddy, how've you been?" Not wanting to alert him to any of my current maladies, I lied and replied, "Never better," continuing, "But what's with you? I've heard that you haven't been your usual cheerful self lately?" He laughed in his deep, halting, throaty way and grumbled, "I'm okay, just a little older and a little crabbier. What do those freakin' doctors know anyway? They're all just overpaid morons in white jackets. I'm strong as an ox. Jack LaLanne would be proud. You know we used to work out together."

"Really?" I responded inquisitively, trying to sound shocked, and then followed up, "Well, you look great to me. Is it true that you're hanging up your gambling garments?" He joked, "I'm calling it semiretired, but not for you, my friend. I expect to hear from you regularly as always." We smiled, shared a quick hug, and then I departed over to the deli and salads station to prepare a hefty sandwich before the roundtable reconvened. Jack's voice resonated throughout the low murmur in the room, "Gentlemen, please find your seats. We still have quite a way to go."

The "three amigos," just like their namesakes, proved to be little more than comic relief, and their uninspiring rantings were a complete waste of time. I watched as most of the other members either daydreamed or doodled on their pads until finally the incessant babbling had ended. Jack, who was always the proper host, thanked the amigos for their contributions and then segued over to my formal introduction. "And finally," he began, "without further ado, please welcome my good friend and our foremost authority and expert on all things NCAA basketball, the Maestro of March Madness himself." As all eyes turned toward me, an eerie feeling of calmness and composure came upon me. I had prepared for this my entire life, and now that my time had come, I totally relished the moment. After all, if I picked all winners, and I certainly thought I had, money would be made by all in attendance, and I would be praised for days on end. The concept or thought of losing never even entered my mind.

My research was top notch, my selections were solid, and since everyone was still 0-0 right now, it was absolutely the correct time to be brash and cocky. I stated my opinions clearly and concisely and backed up each one of them with the painstaking statistics and trends that I had compiled over the last few months. Seven stellar picks comprised of three "totals" or "over/unders" and four "sides" with the current point spreads, just as Jack had requested. When asked by Chicago Charlie what my top three choices were, as seven was too large a number for him to fathom, I glanced back at Jack for his approval; and once receiving the sign to proceed, I revealed my three favorite "five-star" plays.

My part of the presentation was now finished. Accordingly, after a few final words of encouragement from Jack, all the other participants stood up, gave the customary salutes of respect to one another, and then hurried out of the conference room feverishly dialing their cell phones. The meeting was officially over, and I had passed my initial test. As I reached down to grab my water bottle, I felt a strong hand land upon my shoulder. "Great job, my friend," a voice crackled. "You're a real natural at this." As I turned around to see who it was, I was face-to-face with El Gato. Smiling, he extended his hand and whispered, "Unfortunately, you just gave me a ton of work to do. If I don't move my lines by tomorrow, you're gonna take me to the cleaners." I responded somewhat jokingly, "Let's just hope that we all end up in the black so the crew won't have anything to complain about." "Oh, they'll find something to bitch about. It's the nature of the game," he countered. And with that, he released my hand, patted me on the cheek, and flexed his way all the way to the exit.

By the time I turned back to survey my surroundings, the place was a virtual ghost town. Only Jack and Carmine remained. It was apparent, even from afar, that Jack was delivering some last-minute instructions to his entrusted operative. Carmine frantically took down notes as Jack rattled off his instructions, and then they departed company with Carmine scurrying out the door and Jack purposefully striding over toward me. "We did well today, my boy," he said confidently, continuing, "How do you feel after your big day?" Weary and somewhat depleted from all the excitement, I managed a quick comeback and then sagged down into an awaiting chair. Jack pulled up a chair next to mine, and after allowing a moment for silent reflection, he began to explain to me his real hidden agenda.

The configuration of Jack's master plan was, to quote the great Looney Toons' character Wile E. Coyote, "Brilliance—sheer, unadulterated brilliance." As Jack proceeded to reveal the specific details, I began to fully understand what had actually transpired over the last few hours. It was a true tactical lesson not only on how to create a winning advantage but also on how to position yourself properly, a lesson which I would never forget. The soliloquy began, "It's all about going back to the basics, my boy, gaming 101 so to speak." He went on to tell me that prior to today's meeting, he had placed action on all seven of my selections at various casinos around town. Some wagers were naturally larger than others. Obviously, the elusive five-star plays received more attention, and still others were tinkered with a bit based upon the odds and possible payouts rather than just the final results. The whole key to his chicanery, however, was the notion that I alone held the answer to the biggest questions of the day. Who would win the games? By how much? And what would the final score add up to? With this premise seemingly already confirmed, coupled with Jack's patronizing pontifications toward my ability to determine the correct outcomes, none of the attending guests dared to take their eyes off me during my entire presentation. They just nodded their heads, puffed on their expensive stogies, and stared blankly as if they were in some kind of trance. After all, I was the proverbial goose that was going to lay their golden eggs; and therefore, I commanded their undivided attention.

Jack glanced down at his watch, smirked, and then professed, "By now the boys have already made numerous calls to their clients and benefactors, and the wheels have been placed in motion." I mumbled to myself, "What wheels? What is he talking about?" I just wasn't getting it. Then suddenly, as if I had been struck by a bolt of lightning, the entire picture came through bright and clear. He had already placed our bets! We had gotten the numbers we wanted on every game, and our tickets were already punched! Therefore, whatever happened now didn't matter. We could just sit back, relax, and watch as all the lines moved in our favor. In total shock and awe of both what I had just learned and also of what had just transpired before me, all I could do was gaze upon Jack admiringly and try to comprehend his utter genius.

It was an extremely simple recipe for success, yet one that had to be calculated ever so precisely. In order to pull off this magnificent machination, timing was everything, and Jack had worked it out almost to the minute. Once the crew had advised their clientele which side to play and all those wagers came pouring in from around the nation, the betting lines naturally would have to adjust. The numbers would shift based on the amount of incoming action being taken by the bookies and the sports books. Unlike the pooled parimutuel wagering systems which are utilized in horse racing, jai alai, and many other lottery-type games, sports gambling is based solely on a fixed-odds scenario. The major difference between these two gaming factions is that in parimutuel betting, the final odds and payouts are not determined until the pool is closed while in fixed-odds betting, the odds and payouts are agreed to at the time the bet is consummated. Therefore, even if the lines moved drastically, once the news of my picks circulated, the tickets that Jack had previously purchased were already locked in, and his numbers could not fluctuate. The chain of events played out exactly as he predicted, and the subsequent movements not only created a huge advantage for our side, but they also established various "middle" opportunities that we could explore as well. It was like getting in on the ground floor of a new stock option or IPO and then having the SEC, market analysts, and trading experts all extol the company's potential future earnings the next morning. The buzz generated would get more people to invest, the price would soar, and there you would be holding the veritable bag containing all the cash. The design, strategy, and forethought necessary to draw up this blueprint for success was a true masterpiece of manipulation. My favorite type of risky venture has always been the one where the chance of making a profit totally outweighs the chance for loss. That is what Jack manufactured for us today.

Now to further clarify things for the novices out there, let me expound upon the typical "total" or "over/under" wagering proposition. Each individual game is assigned a number or "total," and the betting public must determine whether the combined total number of points scored by both teams will be either over or under that posted number. For example, in Duke University's opening round game of the tournament, 142.5 was the listed "total." Therefore, you, the player, could choose to bet over the 142.5 and hope that the combined final scores of the two teams landed on 143 or higher; or on the other hand, you could bet under the 142.5 and hope that the combined scores landed on 142 or lower. While this concept is so easy that a child could understand it, forecasting the correct outcome is an entirely different matter. The oddsmakers today, due to their savvy and expertise, can almost always formulate a number which will make the perspective bettor somewhat weary one way or the other. Obviously, the goal of any good bookmaker is to create a magic number where an equal amount of money is wagered on each side. If they can elicit that result from the gambling population, then they will guarantee themselves a profit on every game due to their standard piece of the action, or "vig," as it is commonly referred to. This "transaction fee" is only collected by the bookies on the losing wagers.

Accordingly, if you placed a $100 bet on a particular interest and you were victorious, then you would get back $200; your initial $100 wagered plus the additional $100 which you won. Alas, if you lost your bet, you would lose not only the initial $100 cast but an additional $10 as a brokerage allowance. It should be apparent then that if the "line" is properly positioned, and therefore induces an equal amount of wagers on each side, the bookmaker cannot lose. While the winners will receive their 100 percent payout, the losers must pay 110 percent, thereby netting a 10 percent profit or stipend regardless of the outcome of the contest! Advantage to the "house," as they always say. Unless, of course, you could somehow find a way to gain the upper hand. That, invariably, was what Jack was always trying to achieve.

Since I had predicted that the Duke game would be a high-scoring affair, Jack had placed a very significant wager over the proposed

142.5 total. The hope was that once the public began to bet the "over" as well, and an overwhelmingly large number of wagers were lodged in that direction, the final line would move higher to 145 or 146. As more and more money would continue to come in on the "over," the casinos would be forced to jump up the number until the public finds it unbettable and is enticed to start betting the "under." Remember, the ultimate goal of all sports books is to level off the amount of incoming action with a view toward collecting their percentage, limiting their liability, and not getting taken to the cleaners. For us, the objective was to have the number rise as high as possible so that we would be sitting in the catbird's seat by game time. Contradictory positions, to say the least, but all part of the moving dance. Our 142.5 interest would certainly be much more attractive if the closing figure turned out to be in the mid or upper 140s. The smallest deviation could be the difference between winning and losing, and then here were still the possibilities of the elusive "middles."

The art of "middling" games is a strategic and specific money-making proposition wherein the bettor can both limit his potential liability while at the same time exponentially enhancing his possible payout. This technique, along with his innate ability to perceive and deduce the perfect percentage plays, allowed Jack to flourish, prosper, and amass a vast fortune during the decade of the '90s. Let me elaborate. In our earlier example, Jack initially had wagered $10,000 on "over" 142.5 in the Duke game. After all the gossip and buzz was leaked that the "smart money" was all on the "over," the line climbed four points and sat at 146.5 just prior to tip-off. Because of that significant increase, Jack's next ploy was to bet another $10,000; but this time, not on "over" as he did previously, but instead on "under," the newly revised 146.5 number, thereby creating two separate and seemingly opposing alternatives. While this may appear to be the case at first glance, upon further review, it doesn't take a mathematical wizard to realize that it is impossible to lose both of those bets regardless of the final outcome. However, it is still quite possible to win both of those bets, if the breaks go your way and that the combined final scores tally up to either 144, 145, or 146. In a nutshell, on every "middle" where you wager the exact same amount on each side, you will receive a 20–1 payout if the game falls on one of the proposed middle figures. It works every time and in every situation. Pretty fucking cool.

Let's now turn back to the Duke game and utilize actual dollar amounts and figures to clarify this illustration. If the game ended 80–70, a combined total score of 150 points, then we would win our original "over" 142.5 and $10,000, but we would lose our subsequent "under" 146.5 and $11,000 including the "vig," creating a net loss of $1,000. If the game ended 70–60, a combined total score of 130 points, then we would lose our original "over" 142.5 and $11,000 including the "vig," but we would win our subsequent under 146.5 and $10,000, creating the same net loss of $1,000. But if the game ends 77–67, a combined total score of 144 and one of our magical middle numbers, we would win both our initial "over" 142.5 and our ensuing "under" 146.5, and $10,000 on each for a total net profit of $20,000. Therefore, it is plain to see that when the "middle" is "hit," we collect not only once but twice and receive a total payout of $20,000. And when the "middle" is missed, either way, you win one and lose one, bringing about a $1,000 loss and thereby confirming our 20–1 proposition.

Unfortunately, as I alluded earlier, due to the advent of all the modern technology, computer software, and the internet, many of the old gaming techniques that were present back in the day are no longer feasible today. In the '80s and '90s, there were far more available options for the knowledgeable and skilled player due to the wider variations in the odds that existed at the different sports books. Nowadays, if one of the betting house's numbers are off even the slightest degree from the rest of the community, a red flag will go up, and the correction will be made immediately. Prior to the development of our newfangled up-to-the-minute "information highway," it took much longer for the line makers to remedy their nonconformance.

Due to that fact, Jack, in his infinite wisdom, devised a way to exploit those delays by placing "runners" manned with long-distance walkie-talkies at each of the major casinos. The ability of the "runners" to relay all the frequent line changes back to Jack at any given moment was the real key to mastering the market. For instance, if the Mirage was using a figure of JETS-2, and Caesars was using a figure of JETS-4, Jack could instruct his operatives to lay the two points with the JETS and to take back the four points with the *underdog*, thereby fashioning a beautiful middle on the number 3, a very popular winning margin for an NFL game. The upcoming NCAA Basketball Tournament presented a variety of different opportunities due to the greater point spreads and the higher totals that existed in basketball rather than football. Naturally, there were also several contests that appeared so tempted and so attractive that even if the lines moved in our favor, we would still stand pat and stick with our initial impressions and wagers. But if we could navigate the muddy waters and hit just a couple of "middles" along the way, then all of our hard work would be worthwhile.

While Jack's plans and actions did afford us an undeniable upper hand, please do recognize that they in no way harmed anyone else. In fact, the other committee members were also handed a clear-cut and decided dominance by being exposed to the information which we provided to them. El Gato, being the sly fox that he was, was the only other participant who truly got the picture and sympathized with our cause. My two closest allies were certainly sharp and experienced gamesmen, and they had virtually seen it all. Thankfully, they shared their experience and knowledge freely and taught me many valuable lessons. Of course, if I had predicted the games correctly, then none of this fancy footwork would amount to much anyway. It was all in *God's* hands now, so there was nothing left to do but let the real partying begin.

CHAPTER 4

Moving Day

Saturday, April 11, 2015

JUST LIKE A SUMMERTIME SATURDAY on the PGA Tour, this Saturday was "moving day" for me and several of my fellow cons. Unfortunately, while I had no idea where we were moving to, I did know that it had to be better than where we were moving from. We were instructed to quickly gather up our belongings and head up to the front gate for our relocation assignments. I anxiously secured my valuables and other assorted jailhouse accessories inside my towel, making sure that they were neatly tucked away, only to have them minutes later carelessly dumped out onto the floor and aggressively rummaged through by the CO who was overseeing the "movement." He barked in my direction, "You, you're okay," and then continued by telling me to pick up my stuff and to face the wall. The full-body search or "pat down," as it was affectionately known, was next, and it was moving along just fine until an object was located in the pocket of my orange pullover. "What's this shit, asshole?" was the cry from behind me. "What's this shit in your pocket?" Startled by the loud and indignant shouting, all I could manage to squeak out was, "I don't know, CO, I don't know." Upon further examination, the foreign object was nothing more than a prison-issued plastic spoon that I had inadvertently put in pocket after breakfast. Accordingly, with the security breach now quelled and tempers assuaged, we continued the stroll down the dank hallway to our new home.

The convoy was ushered forward through another long laby-rinth of cold corridors and pee-stained portals until we approached a doorway ahead which read "Transport Unit." A voice from behind bellowed, "Hold it right there, gentlemen." The CO opened the door, exchanged some paperwork with another officer inside, and then lead us outside into the courtyard where a police van was awaiting our arrival. It was still early in the morning, and the cloud cover kept the air damp and cool. A group of officers were congregated near the van, making small talk as they sipped their steaming 7-Eleven cof-fees. The smell of the coffee gave me a warm comforting feeling for a moment. However, the moment was fleeting. Once I glanced up at the thirty-foot-high walls clad with barbed wire and razor-sharp curls of steel, I immediately snapped back into reality.

We entered through the rear of the van, were forcibly placed into our seats, and after being handcuffed to the prisoner next to us, proceeded to the E block on the other side of the compound. The rough, bumpy ride reminded me of the airport's park and ride shuttle bus that I always took from the car drop area over to the terminal whenever I traveled. Unfortunately, the current trip that I was about to embark upon surely was not going to be as pleasant.

Once we arrived at the E block's grounds, we slowly disem-barked the vehicle and awaited further instructions. A guard appeared through a vestibule on the side of the building, and the ever-present sound of iron doors slamming shut and locking behind him echoed throughout the pen. Our chaperone walked toward the other officer raising his hand in greeting and shouting, "Three nice newbies fresh out of 72 for your pleasure, Charlie." "Thanks Joe," came back the reply, followed by, "They're just what the sheriff ordered. I'll be sure to make them feel right at home." And with that, our new captor steered us over to the entryway and accompanied us within.

As the next set of metallic partitions methodically began to open, I was immediately blinded by a sea of orange. Prisoners were scattered all about the vast L-shaped dormitory, and my eyes were frantically scanning the scene faster than my brain was able to com-pute all the images. The ceiling was at least twenty feet high, and the two-tiered setup surrounded by catwalks on the upper level produced an even more spacious feel. Everything was zooming past me at lightning speed, but when I did manage to catch the eye of one of the other convicts, the picture froze for a second, allowing me to view their lifeless and sullen faces. There was quite a mix of inhabitants ranging from black to white to Hispanic; yet being white, middle-aged, and a virgin to the prison system certainly had me in the minority. There was also something else that struck me as being odd about this place, and as I stood there contemplating the situation, I felt a nervous twinge in the pit of my stomach. Just then, a voice barked from behind me, "Hey you, new guy, head upstairs to cell 31 and make sure you have a mattress." Nodding affirmatively, I gathered myself, turned around to locate the staircase, and then marched upward to find my cell.

In this particular barracks, there were fifty-two cages in all; and while it was very busy in the valley down below, my area up top was unoccupied. I later found out that during "free time," no one was allowed to roam about the upper level unless they had received permission from one of the guards, hence the inactivity surrounding my cell. As I entered my new digs, I noticed right away that it was both bigger and cleaner than where I had previously resided. There was a wood desk-like structure along the far wall accompanied with a securely fastened rusty stool in front. The slab bedframe was positioned off to my left, and it fit snugly up against the wall and next to the desk projecting outward toward me. The luxurious combination sink-and-toilet vanity was located off to my right. Upon retrieving my mattress and making up the bed accordingly, I sat down and tried to comprehend my new surroundings.

Images continuously flashed through my mind as I began to doze in and out of consciousness. The sunken faces of the other inmates, the array of dank and dark corridors and passageways, and the towering fortress walls kept flickering in my head. Startled, I awoke in a sweaty frenzy and immediately displaced the eerie scenes from my memory. I thought of my Beth, her smiling face, her sparkling eyes, and her contagious laugh. The vision became so strong and intense that I could almost feel her by my side. I couldn't help but smile as I got down on my knees and thanked my Higher Power for clearing my mind and refreshing my soul. It reminded me that not only was He always right there beside me, but also that as long as I continued to seek out His guidance, grace, and favor, everything would turn out fine. A calm, peaceful feeling entered my body; and as a wave of warmth soothed and steadied my heartbeat, I knew that I was blessed.

A blaring static-filled communication was the next thing to permeate my awareness. Apparently, all convict directives and commands were to be broadcast over an archaic public-address system and disseminated throughout the ward. These inaudible announcements were harder to distinguish than the subway platform notifications that one tries to decipher while catching a train in Penn Station. The biggest difference, of course, was that if you failed to heed an order here and didn't follow your proscribed instructions, the consequences would be much worse than just missing your train.

The exact penalties for inmate infractions were clearly set forth in the "Inmate Handbook," a guide manual which was issued to each prisoner upon his arrival, and were classified by the letters A–C, with an A violation being the most severe. A first offense for insolence or insubordination, a class C violation, could get you as much as fourteen days of lock-in time. That meant that each day you would be locked in your cell for a period of twenty-three hours and be granted only one hour out to shower and to stretch your legs. Now, while it was certainly not my intention to make waves or to rub anyone the wrong way, it was virtually impossible to hear anything that was transmitted over the loudspeaker and therefore extremely easy to misinterpret the officers' wishes. The situation became even further exacerbated during recreational hours when all the prisoners were allowed out of their coops, permitted to wander around freely about the confines of the block, and encouraged to engage in raucous behavior. I came to realize very early on in my stay that given autonomy and the ability to interact with others, most of my new associates reverted to their old aggressive tendencies. Peace, quiet, and tolerance were surely lacking within the jailhouse walls.

To be totally honest, it was neither the bizarre antisocial behavior nor the total disregard for common sense that actually plagued me. Rather, it was more the daily noise, high-pitched howling, and hyena-like laughter that almost drove me crazy. That, along with the incessant rantings and nonsensical chatter of the self-proclaimed "leaders of the people" who ejaculated their verbal venom to anyone who would listen, continuously preyed upon my sanity. These learned gentlemen were experts on all aspects of life, the ladies, and the law; and they would spew their words of wisdom and rhetoric day and night through the tiny openings that existed once the motorized cell doors slammed shut.

Often, these rabble-rousers would incite the population by preaching loudly, quoting the scriptures, or just singing aloud. No topic was off-limits for these narcissists, and no vocabulary was spared either. Being a man of some age and experience, I thought I had heard just about everything, but the constant profanity and use of the *N* word became tiresome pretty quickly. Obviously, the conditions were such that a person could let the expletives fly, but listening to every conversation start with either "Yo, my nigga" or "Listen up, niggas" was certainly a bit disconcerting. Thankfully, after about a week, I was able to purchase a small handheld AM/FM radio and headset from the commissary which at least somewhat eased my pain. Incredibly enough, even that at times with the volume on high, it was unable to drown out the incoherent babble that surrounded me.

The announcements continued to come over the PA system, but rather than trying to distinguish what was being said, I decided to observe the other prisoners' reactions to the directives and then to act accordingly. The CO's command center, or "bubble," as it was affectionately called, was located just to the left of the cellblock's entrance and situated perfectly to witness all the activity therein. The spherical shape and tinted bulletproof windows created an Orwellian-like atmosphere where Big Brother could watch and control all. This high-tech information hub and war room was complete with all the latest computerized gadgets and viewing devices. It had an arsenal of cameras, electronic mapping systems, and television screens, along with all the other necessary comforts of home so that the officers could monitor prisoner behavior nonstop around the clock.

Therefore, it was quite surprising that with all the modern technology now available, the messages transmitted from within the bubble were still so distorted and uncharacteristically old school. It seemed almost with purpose and intent that the communiques being conveyed were inaudible in order to cause confusion within the prisoner population. The only other method utilized to restore order and to get the inmates' attention was the carefully orchestrated rhythmic opening and closing of the metallic gates, which not only created a deafening sound but also elicited an earth-shattering vibration. Apparently, most of the cons knew these signals well and were aware of their intrinsic meanings. I assumed that after a few days of this initiation, I too would be hip to all the jailhouse lingo.

It was late morning by now, and as I stood up to peer into the perilous valley below, the cell doors began to rumble. A series of three rapid resounding slams, followed by one last catastrophic crash for good measure, rocked the entire block. The sound system crackled out yet another garbled message, but I could only make out the words *stand* and *count*. Unsure of what to do next, I took a step back from the doorway and gazed out across the canyon. It was the first time that there had been utter stillness since my arrival, and I watched in silence as everyone took their places and stood at attention behind their gates. Then one of the COs went around to each of the fifty-two cubicles and actually verified that there was a live body present in each and every one. I would later learn that the "count" was the single most important procedure enforced at the jail and that noncompliance of any type would be handled harshly.

During the count, which was taken at four specific different times during the day, all prisoners were to stand at their gates facing outward so that their faces could be seen and so that an accurate head count could be produced. In addition, you were neither to speak to another inmate nor engage the officer who was performing the exercise in any manner while the count was in progress. Convicts who participated in any conduct that either prevented or disrupted a CO from completing a proper facility count would face severe disciplinary action. While generally a warning would be issued first, the lazy, repeat, or habitual offender would certainly feel the wrath of the correction staff. Such was life in the county correctional center. The rules and regulations were to be strictly adhered to. All you had to do as an inmate was to abide them.

After the count was completed, it was time for lunch, and even that was served in a particular fashion and under strict scrutiny. The inmates on the work crew were let out of their cells first in order to retrieve the necessary supplies from the kitchen and to set everything up for the rest of the dorm. Then one tier of prisoners at a time would be allowed out so that some semblance of order could be maintained. Speed and accuracy were the real keys to the mealtime process as, often, just when you received your tray and sat down to eat, the signal would come down ordering you to return to your cell. Surprisingly, the rules were somewhat lax regarding taking food back to the rooms; therefore, if you did not finish in the allotted time frame, you could eat the remainder of your meal in the comfort of your own home. In fact, most of the population did just that.

Rather than jockeying for a position at a table or dealing with the constant bickering and bartering for food, the savvy inmates would secure their trays and head immediately back to their suites. There were no explicit rules or regulations on the books regarding the hoarding of food. Accordingly, if you didn't break another rule by stealing someone else's tray or interrupting the food chain supply, you would not be bothered. For me, it was easier to eat whatever I liked quickly and not bring any leftovers back into my cage. Crumbs, unwrapped items, or any other loose edibles could certainly elicit bugs or other unwanted vermin, neither of which I wanted to encounter. My goal in that respect was to keep my limited amount of space as clean and sanitary as possible.

Following the daily lunch break, a period of confined cooldown time was scheduled, and then the bars would be opened for "free time" for all. It was during this hour, after engaging a few of my fellow inmates in conversation, when I once again began to feel that odd and uneasy sensation inside of me that I had experienced earlier. These gentlemen, upon further review, were not your typical everyday convicts. Instead, these were men who possessed much deeper-seated mental and emotional issues, some so severe that they appeared to border on psychotic. As I made more and more inquiries, it finally came to light that once again, just like when I was held in 72, I was currently being housed in the psych ward or "MO" wing of the cellblock. This was a shocking and alarming revelation for me as I had previously met with and been examined by the jailhouse psychiatric team who had cleared me for placement into a regular housing facility. Standard practice was for all new inmates to get reviewed both mentally and physically by the jailhouse staff upon their initial admission into the system. My specific evaluation was conducted while I was in 72, and I was instantly excused from participating in any further treatment plans.

When I approached the sergeant for further answers, I was informed that there was a serious shortage of beds elsewhere and that, unfortunately, I would have to remain in this particular transition or "satellite" stopover until I could be relocated by the housing coordinator. Little did I know at the time that I would be left to languish in the MO dorm for over three weeks, but fortunately, that time spent taught me an early and important lesson: you can endure anything with the right attitude and the proper perspective. I had to realize that nothing in God's world happens by mistake and that I was exactly where I was supposed to be.

Once I obtained a few days under my belt, I started to gain a certain comfort level with my new and unfamiliar surroundings. I had also met a number of very interesting characters along the way: Captain Crunch, OCD Johnnie, and Paranoid Pete, just to name a few. Of these subjects, the Captain was undoubtedly the most colorful and outspoken of the bunch. The extravagant tales of his wartime heroics, coupled by his animated facial expressions, wacky smile, and crazy eyes, truly made for an entertaining afternoon. A man in his early sixties, the Captain claimed to have been wounded in battle numerous times and over the course of many different conflicts. Now, whether those injuries were, in fact, real or were fictitious, he continued to drag his frail decaying body throughout the environs, limping heavily and stopping to converse with anyone who would listen. He spoke frequently about flying bombing missions in every war, including the Civil War, which he professed as being his first tour of duty. Having fought the enemy in Mexico, Hawaii, and Brooklyn and insisting that I was always there with him side by side, he would often ask me if I remembered specific events and happenings.

One such example was when he had his head severed off by a butter-knife-wielding commie who had attacked us from behind. In that case, we were lucky enough to have a supply of Band-Aids nearby so that we could reattach his head, patch him up, and still make the next train back to Texas. Yes, you were never quite sure what Captain Crunch was going to say next; but in the long run, he was just another confused convict trying to do his time in the county lockup.

OCD Johnnie was an altogether different case from the Captain, who spent most of his time by himself in his own dysfunctional universe. In actuality, it was really very sad and disturbing to watch Johnnie try to keep up with the daily routine as it took him considerably longer than anyone else to finish even the simplest of tasks. Just entering and exiting his cell in a timely fashion was problematic for Johnnie as he had to complete his compulsive-obsessive checklist of activities before he could move forward. In addition, he was unmercifully berated by the officers for being late and for keeping the rest of us waiting while he steadfastly acted upon his psychoses. A young, muscular, average-looking fellow, he apparently was somewhat of an athlete in his youth as he was constantly haunted by fantastic illusions of grandeur and would talk incessantly about his playing days as a world-class lacrosse star and track enthusiast.

The accounts of his exploits and his career as a legendary sports figure only brought out further ire and scorn from the guards. Johnnie liked to attract the attention of the staff by wildly cheering and applauding as he relived the glory and triumphs of years gone by. Crassly nicknamed Tom Brady by the COs—Mr. Brady being the star quarterback of the New England Patriots and an actual world-renown sports figure—Johnnie was constantly heckled and verbally abused by the officers. Oddly enough, the other residents showed patience with Johnnie and were outwardly protective of him as well. They realized that he was, in fact, immensely ill and that he needed both their assistance and support. It was amazing to witness how people with similar conditions and maladies could put aside their own prejudices and insecurities and unite around a single individual who was clearly less fortunate than themselves. Helping people to overcome difficulties through empathy, compassion, tolerance, and understanding was a perpetual theme throughout both my prison bid and my recovery as well.

On the other hand, Paranoid Pete was an instigator and trouble-maker who, unfortunately for the rest of us, always found something to gripe about. He was short, wiry, and had an ashen complexion with narrow slits for eyes. In addition, because of his apparent anxiety disorders, frequent panic attacks, and never-ending neurotic tenden-cies, he would constantly flinch, twitch, and look over his shoulder. Pete was viewed as being much more bizarre then he actually was. Yet unlike my good friend OCD Johnnie, it was difficult to have either sympathy for, or patience with, Pete. Due to his unpredictability and his seemingly purposeful antagonistic behavior toward both the offi-cers and other prisoners as well, Pete became a pariah. He was like the proverbial fly in the ointment, the wrench in the works, the square peg trying to fit in the round hole. His persistent and pessimistic prattle got under the skin of everyone around him, and he would often rattle even the coolest of cons.

The bigger problem, however, was that Pete never knew when enough was enough, and this led to both arguments and acrimony among himself and the rest of the rank and file. Physical altercations were commonplace, and full-fledged lock-ins frequently resulted from these fracases. And while Pete was handcuffed and escorted to "medical" every morning in order to receive his necessary and pre-scribed psych meds, sadly, the treatments rarely mitigated his manic episodes, and it was impossible to gauge his tenuous temperament. It was just reality for Pete and the rest of us. The truth is, some really are sicker than others.

CHAPTER 5

Let the Games Begin

Thursday morning, the Tournament begins

I LEFT BETH SLEEPING, KISSED her on the forehead, and headed for the elevators. It was 6:45 a.m. local time, and we had all planned to meet at the Sportsbook at 7:00 a.m. sharp. Breakfast was optional, but I managed to grab a cup of coffee at the Starbucks on the way. My posse had arrived on separate flights last night as some left from Newark and some from JFK. Beth and Karen had taken a real late flight and did not get in until after midnight. While I did not make the trip to the airport to greet them, a limo was waiting upon their arrival to escort them to the hotel. Long days were had by all, and once the girls got to unpack and got settled, we called it a night. I had gotten Karen her own private room as not to infringe on her privacy and also to ensure that Beth and I could have some of our own. As soon as Beth's head hit the pillows, she was asleep, so I just curled up around and thought to myself, *Now I have it all. What else could a person want?*

It was "opening day" for the *Big Dance*, and the next few hours would really set the tone for the entire weekend. Each of us had an unofficial job to perform, and mine of course was to handicap the games and places all the wagers, so my job was already done. By 7:15 a.m., the Sportsbook was already buzzing with excitement, and the boys were all present and accounted for. There were also people from all over the country who had assembled for the opening tip-off. There were Longhorns, Sooners, Fighting Irish, and an especially loud and boisterous group of Cornhuskers. These five specimen were all clad in their school colors, and they would have painted a great picture had they not still been drunk from the night before and undoubtedly slept in the fanfare they were currently wearing. Even so, they were up and raring to go, and Nebraska was scheduled to play in the second game of the day.

It was getting closer to the start of game one of the remaining sixty-three games to be played and the start of the first of sixteen games today. No more polls, no more analysis or opinions, just basketball heaven with the champion to be crowned on the court. Six contests had to be won over the next nineteen days; and one bad game, one slipup, and you would be heading home. That was the beauty of the tournament and made for the love affair that the fans had for this format. On any given day any team could rise up, slay a Goliath and become this year's "Darling" or "Cinderella."

It was rapidly approaching eight thirty and the tiny venue was now packed to the rafters. Unfortunately, for one of the newest and most trendy hotels on the strip, the Sportsbook facility left a lot to be desired. It was a very narrow space which opened up to a small theater-like setting with a restaurant area in between containing several high tables and barstools. Of course, we had procured the perfect vantage point with a large roomy table and six of the most comfortable cushioned stools right in the middle of the action. That was an unofficial job too: getting there early and making sure we got the best position possible, another job well done. The betting windows were situated right behind us, and there were several flat-screen TVs surrounding us on the walls.

Jasmine, our waitress, was already informed to keep the drinks flowing, "early and often," as we liked to say, and the $150 opening tip we gave her seemed to be paying off as she managed to back us up almost as fast as we were making them disappear. I was glad that the most of our bets were placed ahead of time as there were only four betting windows open. The line to wager was already out the door and at least a half-hour wait. In addition, almost all the casinos had strict limitations on the amount you could bet both on the line and the total. For most college BB games, the limits were $1,000/ $500; that is, $1,000 on the spread/line and $500 on the total or over/under. While these amounts might satisfy the average, everyday better, for a gamesman like myself, those numbers were paltry sums. In fact, on the Duke game which was up first, we already had over five figures or 10K wagered on the over, and I was now arranging to bet another 5K on the over in the first half as well. Yes, you can also bet on each half of the game; and since I had a very strong opinion on this contest, I wanted to push the envelope hard right off the bat. The question was, how was I going to get such a large wager down so close to game time?

The answer was simple really: knowing the ropes and having the right connections, in gambling as in life. I knew I still had about fifteen minutes left before tip-off, and I had two plausible options: El Gato or the new mobile offshore gaming app which Jack had recently affixed to my cell phone. This all-inclusive website allowed me to virtually bet on everything from anywhere ranging from NFL games, to the Oscars, to the presidential election, and certainly to college BB. In addition, the limits were much higher than those restricted by the casinos, although the totals were still capped somewhat. Nonetheless, between the two of them, I was able to place the additional 5K on over 67.5 in the first half; and once all was confirmed accordingly, I decided to get up and stretch my legs a bit.

I strolled around surveying the crowd and kept my eyes and ears open to all the action that filled the room. Most of the sports fans appeared to just be wagering a few dollars on the teams that they rooted for, seemingly more out of support and loyalty rather than any actual knowledge of the game. These so-called loyalists usually didn't bet much dollar-wise, but the occasional "fat cat," or "booster" often had a large chunk down on their alma mater. As I walked farther in toward the rear of the complex, I noticed a quieter area with much less fanfare. I ambled over and soon realized that I was approaching the designated "Racebook" part of the facility, and that was why it was desolate. Who cared about horse racing today? There were sixteen college BB games scheduled from 9:00 a.m. and going to 9:00 p.m. Who needed horse racing? Who? Gamblers, of course—real hard-core gamblers like myself.

The break from all the noise was both soothing and enticing, and I decided to walk over to the racks containing the morning line sheets and pull out a few to peruse. The "race book" was the designated area for horse players, and you could virtually bet on any race at any of the major tracks in the country. It was now a few minutes after 9:00 a.m. locally, and I knew that the races back east would be starting shortly. Most post times began between 12:30 and 1:30 p.m. on the East Coast, so I still had time to review the "Sheets" and The Daily Racing Form to see if anything struck my fancy. I located a cubicle so that I could both keep an eye on the CBS BB broadcast, as well as review the current tote board for the odds at Belmont Park. Suddenly I noticed out of the corner of my eye an older man wearing a cowboy hat, faded jeans, and a dark blazer heading my way. As he continued to approach, something familiar about him took over my thoughts. He tipped his hat, sat down at the cubicle next to mine, and began talking to himself under his breath. After a few minutes, he stood up to look at the current odds and then glanced my way. "Hey, partner," he said with a bright smile. "You know anything about these New York tracks?" I looked up at him, grinned, and replied, "You know I do. It's my backyard." "I had a feeling," he responded. "So I guess I'm one for one already today."

Cowboy Roy introduced himself after that, and we began to get acquainted and to share our insights on the ponies. It's truly amazing how one addict can relate to another addict, regardless of the actual addiction, in our case, gambling. I was unable to fully grasp that concept until I surrendered to all of my vices. The camaraderie that exists between people who have experienced similarities in life, its conquests, as well as its failures is a kinship that is built on the bedrock of our existence

Roy was a gambler like myself, and we instantaneously had that bond between us when we met. A displaced New Yorker himself, he had moved out West in the late '70s and never returned. He now hailed from a town outside Albuquerque, New Mexico, where he raised and bred quarter horses for a living. He and his wife were actually in town for an Equine Equipment Expo, which just happened to coincide with the tournament, much to his chagrin. "Where did all these people come from?" he complained. "And why today?" I looked at him, totally astounded. "They're all here for the Big Dance, March Madness." He smiled and responded, "I didn't know that many people still danced." Hysterically, I told him, "They do this week!"

Roy and I continued to chat for a while and we reminisced about the great old days of the East Coast racing circuit and how New York used to be the mecca for the sport of kings, unlike today. Unfortunately, the cold winters, off-site gambling venues including OTB, and the poor conditions and surrounding areas of the tracks had almost left attendance and the "handles" at all-time lows. Except for the weekend of the Belmont Stakes, the parks were virtually deserted. We shared a few more humorous gambling tales, but then we said our goodbyes as my interest in the BB games, as much as his disinterest in them, made us part sooner than expected. I told him I would check back with him later to see how our selections ran as we had collaborated to pick a horse in each of the first four races. "Keep my seat warm," I shouted and then scrambled back through the crowd of screaming BB crazies to find my crew.

When I returned, the boys were already worked up into a frenzy, and their unbridled enthusiasm was enough to get anyone's juices flowing. "We look good already," they bellowed almost simultaneously. "They are just going up and down the court and really scoring in bunches," one continued. I shook my head, took a deep sip of my now watery drink, and thought to myself, *This is going to be a very long four days.* I then reminded them that "it's a marathon rather than sprint." And that they should "stay enthusiastic but also remember that anything could happen." I believe my words fell on deaf ears, but they were all having so much fun that I left it alone and just ordered a couple of more drinks and settled in.

When the smoke cleared two hours later, both literally and figuratively, we found ourselves up over 20K between both the BB and the races. Yes, Roy and I had picked a winner on the second race, the second-place finisher in the third race, and then had pounded a 12–1 shot in the fourth race that paid $25.40, $9.60, $6.20 across the board and netted us over 7K in total. The game obviously went our way as well, but not without some serious drama. After the teams suffered a five-minute scoring drought midway through the opening stanza, our first half over 67.5 play seemed all but lost. With 1:05 remaining on the clock, we were still in need of six more points. As the boys nervously paced around the table, a layup, a banked-in three-pointer high off the glass, and a hard foul left us hanging on the balance with 7.6 seconds left. The score read 35–31 Duke, and one of the worst foul shooters on their team headed to the line. The thought process was that even if he missed, hopefully there would still be time left for someone to score before time ran out. The first shot left his hand, hit the back iron hard, went high up into the air, and then straight down through the hoop. It was a total "brick," but a point was a point. Then the crucial second show was launched and went clean through the hoop, never even teasing the rim. Duke led 37–31; and with 68 total points on the board, we had our first victory. Before we could stop celebrating and rejoicing, the other team raced down the court and hit a jumper at the buzzer, finalizing the halftime score at 37–33 and confirming the win for us.

The rest of the game played out just as we expected, and while it remained close throughout the second half, the "dog" finally wilted down the stretch. However, between the quick pace and the endless supply of foul shots down the stretch, the final score was 86–73 Duke, and we were victorious yet again. Our celebration this time was a bit more tempered as most of the other patrons had bet Duke, laying 22 points as the favorite, and had really taken one on the chin. I calmly just looked over at my posse and nonchalantly exclaimed, "That's why I play totals!" and then excused myself to regroup for a bit and to splash some cool water on my face. When I returned from the Men's room, still giddy with elation, I noticed Cowboy Roy still eyeing the tote board over in the Racebook. He didn't notice me at first, but then when he shot a quick glance my way, he smiled and said, "I guess I hitched my wagon to the right horse today, huh, partner?" I nodded back to him and quipped, "We ain't done yet. There are still races to be run." After exchanging a few more pleasantries and patting each other on the back for a job well done, we agreed to meet back up in an hour to formulate a late daily double on the eighth and ninth races. We shook hands one more time, pointed at our watches as if to synchronize the time for one hour, and then headed away in opposite directions.

The day was off to a remarkable start, but there was still a long way to go. Several games were still being contested, and the second half of the day session, as well as all of the evening activity, were looming. While we did have some small action on the couple of games that were winding down, it was nothing compared to our earlier score. I rejoined the boys over at our table, and even though they looked exhausted, they were still cheering and rooting on our plays. I took the opportunity to grab some alone time back in the room where I was able to renew my notes, log on the final scores, and spark up another joint as I sat back and reflected on the morning. We were having a good day, and besides that and even more importantly to some degree, my thirty-six-hour period of substance prohibition had ended a few hours ago, and I felt the need to take full advantage of that fact. Once fully relaxed and high as a kite, I went through my routine of freshening up, which was comprised of washing my face again, brushing my teeth, utilizing the facilities, and counting and recounting the funds in my pocket even though the amount had not changed from earlier that morning. Finally prepped and ready, I finished off the joint with a few more large tokes and then vigorously took off for the elevators. I was running bit late, and Cowboy Roy was surely to be waiting.

The floor of the casino was still buzzing with excitement as I raced off the elevator and jogged toward the Sportsbook. There was always something about the casino floor that got my juices flowing. Perhaps it was all the flashing lights, bells, and that inexplicable sound of coins falling into the metal baskets below the slot machines. Whatever it was, there was always *action*. And, as one of my cohorts always remarked, "I love the action," and so did I.

It was approaching one thirty now, and with the games in full swing, the crowd had seemed to have doubled in size along with noise level. My boys were still diligently manning our table, but they looked considerably more weathered and out of sync. After a brief strategy session, they decided that they were going to take power naps once the next set of games went final and told me to find them around five o'clock to ensure they were conscious. I confirmed the plan with them and told them to "sell the table to the highest bidder" as it was at least worth a round of drinks. They said that they would take care of the bill, and I told them to be careful as I saluted them goodbye and headed off to find the cowboy.

Unfortunately, by the time I found Roy, the eighth race had already gone to the post, so we could no longer wager on the late daily double. However, there were still twelve minutes left before the ninth race was to be run, and that was the race I found more interesting anyway. I had been following the ponies since I was a young boy and had nothing but fond memories of going to the track as a teenager with my racetrack crannies. Back then, we would take the bus to the local harness oval and bet on the trotters until our money ran out. Later on, we become more sophisticated and started to venture out to the major race pavilions to bet the thoroughbreds and all the big "stakes races." Since then, I always began to take a more active interest in the horses once March rolled around and the Kentucky Derby prep races began to take place. It was also inevitable that somewhere around that time, I would receive a call from my childhood pal Lenny, who was an equine specialist and who must have been to at least twenty derbies in a row by now. I too was fortunate enough to make the trip to Kentucky on three separate occasions, and a better time could not be had. Lenny is one of those absolute characters of the game whose flair for life, hilarious sense of humor, and unique way to tell a story made time spent with him priceless.

In addition, we had a special bond due to the relationship each of us had with the other's father. Both of our dads were old-school throwbacks who enjoyed the simple things in life and who had the ability to control a room with one of their mesmerizing stories, which usually had some type of life message at the end. Many a night, I remember hanging out at Lenny's house well after he went to bed and drinking wine and talking sports, girls, and life with his dad. He was truly a special man. He is missed by all, God rest his soul. Hopefully, he and my pop are having some wine up in heaven, watching a good game, and sharing a good laugh with each other. They were two of the world's finest, both taken way too soon.

The crowd had now spilled into the Racebook, and the noise made it hard to even speak to the person next to you. Two of the games were in the final minutes, and both lines and totals were still in doubt. While neither of those games were one of my "seven selections," I was still curious about the outcomes, but I was much more focused on betting the number 2 horse in the ninth race. Actually, that was my selection of the day regarding the ponies. I had seen her run each of the last three weeks and I was quite certain that due to her strong closer's mentality she would be in prime position turning for home. An extremely fast opening pace was expected as there were several "rabbits" in the field. Accordingly, the expected ensuing speed duel set the race up perfectly for a nice last to first run from my filly. Cowboy Roy was not as optimistic as me and was concerned that in a mile race, my horse would not have the time to catch the leaders if they got too far out in front. I turned to him, grinning sheepishly, saying, "I guess we shall see in a few minutes, my friend, but I have no doubts." With that, I logged into my mobile phone account and placed $600 across the board on the number 2 horse confidently.

The games had gone final and the crowd had dispersed like the parting of the Red Sea. I said farewell to Roy, exchanged cell phone numbers with him and scampered back to the table before the boys had finished downing their last cocktails. They asked where I had been and I told them about my meeting with Roy and the upcoming race. One of my boys asked if he could get in on my "sweet action," and I said sure, knowing that his piece would probably be no more than $2 across the board. With that, he said, "I feel lucky, and you are smoking hot. Give me $4 across the board. You only live once." The rest of the boys chuckled, and I said, "Done!" turning to the monitor behind us which was airing the race.

Just before the gates opened, I explained how I thought the race was going to play out and said not to worry if we fall behind early. The final odds were a surprisingly nice 3–1, and I was quite certain she would be right there at the wire. The pace played out just as I had scripted it, and around the far turn, the early speed horses began to fade. At the top of the stretch, we were poised to take control of the race, and with a Secretariat-like burst of speed, the number 2 horse approached the lone speed horse who remained in front. As the other horse began to flatten out from being used up early, my girl coasted by en route to an easy four-and-a-half-length victory and yet another score for us. I smacked the racing form into my hand several times, turned around to the small crowd that had gathered to see what we were screaming about, and cried out, "That's how it's done, my friends, that how it's done."

As we waited for the race to be "official" and for the prices to be shown, my number 4 across-the-board pal pulled at my shoulder and, in amazement, said, "It was like you knew what was going to happen. That was incredible." He then gave me a hug and continued to stare at me in utter disbelieve. *Bang!* The prices were in: $8.00 to win, $4.40 to place, and $3.60 to show not bad at all. Our $600.00 across the board wager returned us a nice round $4800.00 even, creating a net profit of $3K. For my friend's $12.00 investment, he got back $32.00 for a net profit of $20.00; but from his pure jubilation, you would have thought he had won $20K rather than $20.00. "Did you see that?" he kept repeating. "It was like he had already seen the race and that was a replay—how is that possible?" A retort from the table came back, "Yeah, he does that on occasion. Pretty cool, huh?"

As the boys headed upstairs for their needed naps, I checked my watch and realized that I was overdue for my call with Beth. While I knew that Beth and Karen would sleep in until at least 11:00 a.m., I was sure that by now they had fancied themselves up and were out investigating all the stores and shops that the hotel had to offer. I found a quiet area near the men's room and dialed my cell. Beth's unmistakable "hell-o" in her half-bad-ass, half coy stone that she loved to use with me immediately warmed my heart. Just hearing her sexy, playful voice stirred emotions in me that no other person ever had. I began telling her modestly that we were having "a good day" and continued flirtatiously by saying that if she "behaved," perhaps we could go jewelry shopping later, a hobby of hers. She interrupted me quickly, "You know I always behave unless I'm with you," and then told me about her morning with Karen, which had consisted of coffee and scones at the patisserie, a casual stroll around the hotel and pool area, and a brief stop at the sundry store to pick up a few things. It all sounded good, and I asked what their plans were now. She said that they had reserved lounge chairs at the pool from three to six and that they would be heading over shortly. "Sounds great," I replied. "I will meet you over there by four." We then exchanged a few more playful pleasantries and said our goodbyes.

The thought of seeing Beth soon, no doubt strutting around in her leopard-clad bikini that she knew drove me crazy, made my whole being tingle with delight. It was truly amazing how she affected me. She was my soul mate, my guardian angel, and my lover all rolled into one spectacular bundle of fun and energy. We were like two teenagers out for a night on the town whenever we were together. We held hands, smooched, tickled each other, and just truly loved being together. People would often stop us and ask us how long we had been a couple or if we were newlyweds because we were always smiling and seemed so happy and content with each other. Our love radiated out of us from within, and it was visible to the whole world. We were truly meant for each other.

The sunshine glistened brightly off the water as I made my way through the "aquatic" center entrance. I grabbed a couple of towels from the VIP towel desk and headed off to try and find the girls in the mass of tourists and sunbathers that seemed to stretch forever. It is hard to picture the scene really, but decadence and bling were certainly the words of the day. There were actually four separate pool areas, several outdoor bars manned with bikini beauties for waitresses, and two private VIP lounges swarming with security guards a checkpoint and metal a detector. As I tried to take it all in, I received a text from Beth stating that they were at "pool B" and that she had reserved an extra lounge chair for me.

I found my way toward pool B and after a few minutes I recognized Beth's beautiful silhouette in the distance. She looked great even from afar, and as I approached, she ran toward me and greeted me with a big hug and an even bigger kiss. She took off her sunglasses, and when I looked into her brown sparkling eyes, I felt myself sinking into them. As I continued to stare lovingly at my better half, she said, "What? What are you staring at?" I took her by the arm, drew her close to me, and whispered in her ear, "I'm just looking at my gorgeous baby. The prettiest girl in the pool." As she blushed and wiggled her vivacious curves, I continued, "How's my baby doing today?" She smiled, grabbed my hand, and said, "Great, but even better now that you are here, handsome." And she then led me over to the chairs were she and Karen were camped out. The sunshine was warm and pleasing for a late March afternoon, and as I lay down holding Beth's hand and every now and then stroking her perfect flat midriff, I began to wander off in my head, thinking, *What could be better than this?* I allowed myself to savor the moment and then drifted off to sleep, a big smile plastered on my face.

There were still eight games to be played in the evening session with the first tip scheduled for 4:15 p.m. local time. My final five plays, including the remaining two five-star picks, would be decided tonight, and the paramount games were to start around 6:30 p.m. Accordingly, I knew that I could chill for a while with Beth and Karen, catch the end of the four o'clock games, and still have time to prep for the main events. My plan was to call the guys around five thirty, tell them to get showered and dressed, and to then meet me in my room around seven thirty for cocktails and a predinner smoke out. The girls had planned to hang at the pool until six o'clock, but that still left them plenty of time to freshen up and join us for a drink prior to dinner as well. The limo was scheduled to arrive at 8:45 p.m. to take us all to the restaurant as our reservation was for ten guests at 9:30 p.m. Romeo and Jack were to meet us there after they completed their final accounting of the day's action. All seemed to be moving smoothly as I gripped Beth's hand harder and gave her a soft, passionate kiss on her shoulder. Life was good.

I left the pool around 5:25 and headed back upstairs to make some moves. First up was Romeo as he was still in possession of my package, and I was in need of some "meds." I figured an hour with Romeo doing some "dry goods" and watching some of the action was the perfect Happy Hour scenario. Fortunately, Romeo currently resided in one of the dozen or so apartments that Jack owned in the new condo development which had been conveniently built right next door to the hotel we were staying at. I made my way down-stairs to the casino floor, fought through the crowd, and headed outside into the warm sunshine. As I turned left and headed down the hill toward the strip, I saw the entrance and lobby to the exclusive condominium.

While the building wasn't much to look at from the outside, inside the aroma of elegance and opulence was palpable. The surroundings were immaculate, and the Nuvo decor and crisp architecture almost made it feel like you were entering the future. A guard escorted me to the visitors area and asked me to stand in front of a camera as he called up to Romeo and waited for him to identify me. Once cleared, I was escorted to the elevators and instructed on how to proceed from there. The doors opened on the twenty-second floor, and as I made a series of left turns, I heard Romeo's voice begin to fill the hallway. He stuck his head out of the doorway, a huge ear-to-ear smile on his face, and shouted, "Yo, brother! We are having a very good day, huh!"

Upon entering the apartment, it was far smaller and less impressive than I imagined. There was a very spacious and aesthetic-looking bathroom on the left but after that it was just a large studio with little furniture and less charm. There was no separate kitchen or bedroom. Rather, just an area with a sink where you do your cooking and an alcove where you could place a bed. All the cabinets and drawers were built-ins and were metallic in nature, as was the small stainless steel stovetop and refrigerator. It was truly a bachelor-pad setup and more of a stopping-off place to sleep and to shower than a place to hang out and socialize. However, it was certainly sufficient enough for our needs, and I found a seat on the leather couch while he straightened up a bit.

Romeo gathered the clothes strewn throughout the place and picked up the various newspapers from the floor, all the while continuing to mutter to himself as he glanced back and forth at the sixty-inch flat screen, which totally overwhelmed the room. "Your two games are looking good," he yelled, continuing, "But I'm getting killed on the Cavs game. I played that one hard." Surprised, I replied, "The Cavs game, really? I didn't have much of an opinion on that one...who did you take?" "Cavs-15, and they're only up 3 with eight minutes left." He frowned. A commercial break snapped his attention back toward me, and after he threw the papers and clothes into a pile in the corner, he approached me, saying, "I have a few gifts for you, my friend. Join me over by the sink." He offered me a Diet Coke, and then began unloading a leather toiletry bag packed with all the accoutrements that I had requested. First, two different types of lighters, one mini and one standard Bic. Next, two different pipes, one small water pipe and a larger green ceramic pipe with a deep bowl and some nice in-lay designs. Finally, he removed three small glass vials, two of which were filled and one which was empty. He explained that these were a bonus treat since he had not seen me in a while. I nodded and replied, "What are friends for?"

Next, he made his way over to a far cabinet near the window and pulled out a coffee can, containing several rolled-up plastic bags. "Here is a half-ounce of the smoke I like," he said proudly and continued, "There is another half of the new wave synthetic stuff as well, but you know that I am old school." "Quite the smorgasbord." I grinned and then told him that I would take a quarter of the regular stuff with a sprinkle of the synthetic on top, just for flavor. I asked him to hold on to the rest, and he nodded affirmatively and packed a large bowl into the ceramic vessel. Just as the smoke began to waft throughout the room, the Cavs started to make a run. By the time the next time-out was called, the Cavs had opened up a 12-point lead, and we were sufficiently high. Unfortunately, however, when the bowl burned out, so did Romeo's chances; and after he slammed his fist into the already-dented refrigerator, he grabbed for one of the vials, took a long snort, and said, "Okay, money, what's up next?" The final score was 66–56 Cavs, and while it cost Romeo a pretty penny, he was already ready to rebound and move on.

Romeo poured some bourbon into my Diet Coke and apologized for not having any ginger ale in the house. We then scanned the networks to check for the scores of my two games while continuing to snort, smoke, and chat. As the scores came in, we stared intently at the results trying to compute whether we had won or lost. One win and one very bad loss in overtime in a game where we were getting three points only to have our dog down by two at the time, hit a shot at the buzzer to send the game to overtime, and then lose by 7 in the extra session. If they miss that shot at the horn, we win, but that's the way the ball bounces sometimes. Still at 3–1, I was feeling pretty good, going into my final three games, and was confident in having a winning night.

The phone rang, and I could hear Jack's voice on the other end as he lambasted Romeo about the Cavs pick and reminded him to stick to the game plan. As they continued to talk, I noticed the clock read 6:52 p.m. and rushed to gather all my gifts so I could return to the hotel. One more quick snort, a rub of my gums with the residue, and a swig of bourbon and Coke, and I was good to go. Once I made sure the pipe was out, I rolled it into my pool towel along with bag of weed, grabbed the lighters, and headed for the door. I told Romeo to hold on to the rest of the goods and waved goodbye. He told me to wait a minute, hung up with Jack, and then gave me a big hug as we exchanged some encouraging words and confirmed our 9:30 p.m. reservations. With that, I left Romeo and began the trek back up to the hotel. It wasn't until the brisk dusk air hit my face that I realized how absolutely obliterated I was. I stopped for a minute, gathered myself together, and started back up the hill and back into the lions' den.

After a well-needed shower, which seemed like an eternity but actually was only about fifteen minutes, I strolled back into the living-room area and noticed a note on the table which I had missed earlier. Much as I expected, Beth had showered and then gone over to Karen's room so they could chat while they did their hair and makeup together. She signed the note by writing, "And I hope you like my outfit," which in Beth's language meant that she would be accentuating all of her assets for me to peruse. I loved her fun, carefree, and playful nature as she always had a way to get my juices flowing. A smile came to my face as I began to ponder what she had in store for me. I mumbled, "I can only imagine."

When the girls arrived at my suite, the party was already in full swing. The boys and I had been smoking and drinking for at least a half hour, and the games were just beginning to get interesting. Beth looked absolutely gorgeous in a striped wraparound dress, a dazzling necklace, and leather boots, which were my absolute favorite. She introduced Karen to the guys, said all of her hellos, and proceeded to the bar to make some drinks for the two of them. Just then, my number 2 across-the-board buddy emerged from the bathroom and headed toward the bar area as he was today's bartender du jour. He must have not noticed the girls immediately, but when he saw Beth in all her splendor, he did a triple take and bellowed almost uncontrollably, "Wow," at the top of his lungs. After he picked his tongue up off the floor and closed his mouth, he shook his head again to bring himself back down to our world and said timidly, "Oh, I mean you look nice." Beth, in her inimitable fashion, just smiled, said thank-you, and gave him a kiss on the cheek, whispering, "You look nice too." It was a classic moment that I will never forget and just another reminder of why I loved Beth more than life itself.

We still had three plays remaining during the late session of evening games, two of which were over/unders and also five-star selections, and the third one was a straight-spread play. The totals that I had played were the highest and lowest totals on the board respectively, and I had gone over the highest total and under the lowest total. The over 154 wager pitted one of the top five offensive teams in the nation against a high-paced run and gun lightweight squad from the West Coast conference. The score was 51–41 at the half, and as such, I was quite confident that we would win that one. The under 119.5 game featured two bruising teams from the "power" conferences who both played stellar defense and who were also somewhat limited on the offensive end of the floor. The total had actually plummeted down to 116.5 just prior to tip-off, and I was certain that this was a golden opportunity for Jack to try and middle the game as there was a nice juicy three-point gap to hit. Currently, that contest had fourteen minutes left to play, and the favorite led 38–30 after going on a 15–5 run to start the second half after trailing 25–23 at halftime.

The under wager was by far the most nerve-wracking wager for me as one big run or flurry of points in a few minutes' span could ruin your otherwise pleasant evening. Also, the grueling and unnecessary fouling down the stretch, coupled with the always present possibility of overtime, made an already excruciating tense situation even that much worse. But considering where we were at the present time, I thought we were in good shape. The last and final game of the night was of a hunch play regarding a team that I had followed most of the season. I had always been a big fan of the ACC and found myself watching more of its conference games than any other. By mid-February, after the close of the football season and the Superbowl, my whole agenda turned solely to the hard court. Not only did I document, log, and track all the games played with both the point spreads and the totals, but I literally watched hours and hours of games and highlights as well. East Coast, West Coast, early or late, I was up watching and studying. I truly believed that while statistical data was revealing, viewing the actual ebb and flow of the game, the momentum swings and intangibles, was far more conclusive than any written information could be. The "eye test," as it was affectionately called, was the most integral part of my BB knowledge and was the key to our wagering success.

My team was tremendously skilled offensively, shot the "three" very well, and could play an up-tempo style as well. Their opponent was a midmajor at large selection from the Midwest who prided themselves on defensive efficiency and a methodical style of play. This contrast in styles and difference in philosophies truly gave my ACC squad a decided advantage in my mind, and if they were able to get out to an early lead, I was sure they could put the game away in the first half. The line on the game was a higher line than I usually played, 8 ½ points, but I was confident that the underdog was truly overmatched here. Amazingly, after a 17–2 run to start the game, including 5–5 from three-point range, we were well on our way.

While things did slow down scoring-wise nearing the half, when the buzzer sounded, the score read 35–18, and we were comfortably in front. My heart was racing as I thought about the possibility of winning all three games and turning our "very good" day into a spectacular one. As the games began to go final, my first victory was sealed when the over 154 wager soared way over the total finishing 96–77 or at 173 points. Next, my ACC hunch pick cashed in easily as they won 75–48, dominating throughout and never giving their outclassed opponent a glimmer of hope. So sitting at 5–1 on the day and truly in the cat bird's seat, we eagerly awaited the last of our wagers to go final. The always stressful under contest was still playing out as a power outage in the arena had delayed the game approximately twenty minutes. When the network switched over the coverage, the score was 53–30 with just over three minutes left to play. The tight score almost certainly ensured a foul fest in the closing minute and also brought overtime into the mix as well. As I had mentioned earlier, *overtime counts*! All wagers are based on the final outcome rather than the score at the end of the regulation time. Accordingly, if the game went to overtime tied, 55–55, and then finished with a 65–60 final score, we would lose our under 119.5 bet as 65–60 equals 125.

I began to pace back and forth across the living-room area, as was my custom when I was extremely nervous. I had developed that habit at a young age, and in fact, the carpet in my childhood home had a specific wear mark from my constant pacing over the years. Every gambler has his "thing" or some habit or superstition to calm his tension and relive his nervous energy. Mine was pacing. As a time-out stopped the action momentarily, the atmosphere in the room continued to build into a frantic yet optimistic state. The girls had shifted toward the rear of the room as Beth knew to give me my space at times like these. The rest of the boys kept busy either mixing drinks or puffing on a smoke as they shouted encouragement toward the television screen. One pal came over toward me and whispered, "I don't know how you can do this on a regular basis. I didn't even bet, and my heart is beating out of my chest." I leaned over and replied, "Fun, huh? You gotta love the action." Beth then caught my eye and gave me a playful wink, and after blowing her back a kiss, I retook my spot on the edge of the couch and buckled down for the last minute.

Unimaginably, just as the broadcast came back on, the room phone began to ring. The look of sheer and utter disgust that crossed my face was enough to tell the entire room that someone else better answer it and quickly. "Who could possibly be calling now?" Karen shouted. I thought to myself, *Wow, even the girls got it! Who could be calling now!* The person had to be either insane or so out of touch with reality and the world around them that they were totally oblivious to the situation at hand. It turned out to be the concierge desk, and they were calling to inform us that our limo had arrived and would be waiting near the valet station in order to take us to dinner. A necessary call, but one that still should have waited until after the game. At the next time-out and with fifty seconds remaining, Beth approached me, kissed me on the cheek, wished me luck, and quietly murmured, "Don't have a heart attack. I have plans for you later." I smiled at her lovingly, and then she said that she and Karen were going to head downstairs and sweet-talk the limo driver until we finished. I watched as she sashayed away and then turned back immediately to refocus on the action.

The score was now 57–53, and with fifty seconds still left to play, an eternity, especially when you have the under, the game was teetering in the balance. After a missed layup and a subsequent foul on the next possession by the trailing team, two foul shots were upcoming with twenty-seven seconds remaining. The foul shots were drained and another time-out called as the score reached 59–53. Following some great defense and a steal off an errant pass, I began to think that time was on our side. My mind was racing with different scenarios, and all the numbers began to just jumble together in my head, making things worse. Two more foul shots were made by the favorites, and after a quick layin off a rebound of a missed three-point attempt, the score read 61–55 with 9.7 seconds left.

The final timeout was called by the underdog, and there was complete silence throughout the suite as the boys tried to compute all the mathematical possibilities. I, of course, knew exactly where I stood; and with a quick foul imminent on the next possession, it was really going to come right down to the wire. I was certainly grateful that our number was 119.5 rather than the closing number of 116.5 as the game already sat on 116. After a beautiful inbounds play freed up the point guard to go long, he cradled the pass, backed the ball out and continued to dribble off the clock until getting fouled with 2.3 seconds remaining. As the conference player of the year strutted to the foul line, hands over his head, signifying the anticipated victory, the crowd got to their feet and joined in the celebration as well.

While the contest had all been decided, for all the under/over players in the world, the real moment was still at hand.

The first free throw rolled around the rim and fell harmlessly to the ground, and when the second shot came up short, I was able to exhale, knowing we had it. A last-second three-point heave actually hit the backboard, but that was totally irrelevant for us. Final score 61–55, 116 total points, and *under* for all. I then realized that if that final prayer shot from half-court had somehow gone in, it would have changed the outcome for many, including Jack, who would have hit his middle. However, for me, it was just another hard-fought victory and the perfect close to an almost perfect day. Drinks were raised in celebration, and hugs were exchanged among everyone in the room. I looked up to the sky as if to thank some Higher Power for my good fortune, but I knew that I was alone and just chalked it up to "luck." Smiling, I turned to the boys and pronounced, "It's like a Thermos. Some days it's hot, and some days it's cold. Luckily, today it was hot!"

The celebration continued on, and after a few minutes, we downed our cocktails, finished off one more well-packed bowl of smoke, and then took the party on the road as we made our way downstairs and to our waiting limousine. My cell phone was blowing up at this point, but the only call I took was Jack's. "Well done, my boy, well done," he shouted elatedly into the phone and then continued by saying he was leaving promptly to meet us at the restaurant and to join in on the celebration. 6–1 was quite an accomplishment for any handicapper. As I leaned back and put my head on Beth's shoulder for a minute, I thought about all the hard work and all the hours of preparation that I had put in, and a peaceful feeling of accomplishment came over me. It was like studying for a test and then realizing that you aced it. It felt good, and I was totally relieved. Beth stroked my hair lovingly as I melted into her, both emotionally exhausted and physically wiped out. A nice, relaxing dinner among friends and loved ones sounded like the perfect ending to an almost perfect day.

CHAPTER 6

Groundhog Day

Friday, Day Two of the Tournament

THE MOVIE *GROUNDHOG DAY* STARRED Bill Murray as Pennsylvania weatherman Phil Connors who goes to Punxsutawney, Pennsylvania, to cover the annual Groundhog Day festivities, which as folklore tells us, will determine if there will either be six more weeks of winter or if spring will arrive early. In the movie, Phil experiences his own phenomenon of waking up each morning only to have his previous days' experiences repeat themselves over and over again. This recurring nightmare never ceases, and his day never changes. From the song on his radio alarm clock that wakes him up in the morning, to stepping of the curb into the same puddle, to having the same conversations with the people he encounters—everything stays the same day after day. For me, the first few days of March Madness were analogous to the trials and tribulations of Phil Connors. Just when a new day was dawning, filled with unlimited possibilities and unknown adventures, the script—or in this case, the schedule of games—was exactly the same. Unfortunately, however, the outcome was not guaranteed to be the same as in Phil's case, and I had to endure the identical fears, anxieties, and pressures without prior knowledge of the end result.

Gamblers, by nature, are a very superstitious group, and I myself have several pet peeves and neurotic tendencies which had to be adhered to at all times. Besides a lucky garment or a special spot to sit or even the positioning of the TV guide on the coffee table, the "karma" in the room when watching a sporting event needed to elicit a positive vibration, and no negative thoughts nor actions would be tolerated. There were also many critical don'ts that would, in fact, actually have a guest physically removed from the premises if they dared to do them.

First, and by the far the most heinous of crimes, was for a person to exclaim, "You're a lock to win this one," or "This game is over—you got it," or "No way you can lose this one," or something of the kind, prior to the game actually going final. I have seen patrons thrown out of bars, restaurants, casinos, sport's books, and yes, even my own house, for making such premature and blasphemous remarks. Usually, it is spoken by a nongambler or someone who has no stake in the outcome of the game and is totally oblivious to the "karma rules" that exist in all players' lives. I can actually recount at least a dozen times in my career where the outcome of a contest has changed in an instant after some insensitive novice declared the game to be over. There are certain taboos that all societies and cultures avoid at all costs, and in the gambler's world, the first commandment is—"Thou shall not ever speaketh thy game is over."

My next serious karma nuance was to leave all alone if all was going well, or as some like to say, "don't fix things if they aren't broken." In other words, if we are winning, then the status quo needs to be preserved. That means a number of things, including never changing what you are wearing midgame, never changing the physical positions of either the people or items in the room, and never ever changing the television channel under any circumstance. These were simple rules to follow and ones which guests were made clearly aware of prior to their attendance and involvement in the viewing of an event. If you could not abide by these few easy requirements, you would not be welcomed back. On the other hand, however, if you brought something positive to the table or were just generally viewed as good luck, you would always have an open invitation.

Accordingly and especially after going 6–1 on Thursday, the Friday agenda was to mirror exactly what had occurred the previous day down to the smallest detail. My goal was to create Phil Connor's

Groundhog Day to perfection and thereby recreate the fabulous results we enjoyed yesterday. For me, that meant getting up at the same time, grabbing the same cup of coffee at the same locale, and obtaining the same table in the sportsbook with the same posse being in attendance. Unfortunately, life sometimes throws you a curveball. Today, for some reason, upon our arrival, the Sportsbook was crammed with basketball fans and gamblers alike, and my intricate plan was thwarted as all the tables had already been occupied. We quickly had to call an audible, and our new game plan was to find an alternative quiet bar area that we could take over. If we could generate the casino a ton of instantaneous activity and dollars, we assumed that they would furnish us with necessary accoutrements to carry out our proposal. All we really needed were two mobile flat screens and enough staff to man the bar and the surrounding tables to ensure that the clientele were properly taken care of.

In addition, I also postulated that if we could pull this off, the casino would be indebted to us and hopefully would respond with an accommodation of free food and drinks at a minimum. It seemed like a win-win proposition for all involved. After scoping out the perfect venue, a small deserted cabaret bar located just a hundred yards or so from the entrance to the Sports Book, I sent my most persuasive crony to the concierge desk as I made a few calls myself. Within a matter of minutes, a hotel floor manager appeared and inquired about our plan. He listened attentively, and I could see the proverbial lightbulb going off in his head. He responded by saying that while he could have the screens set up and the necessary staff provided without any difficulty, he would not be able to guarantee any benefits to us as that was not "his call." I explained to him calmly that if he set a two-drink minimum per game for anyone who entered our new establishment, the casino would make huge windfall due to our creativity and ingenuity. In addition, I mentioned both Jack's and Romeo's names and also vowed that we would chum the waters and stir up enough interest to pack the joint before the games even began. He swayed back and forth while rubbing his chin and pondering my latest scenario and then finally responded, "Done, you've got a deal." We shook hands, and he continued by qualifying, "Your first two rounds are on the house, and I will personally buy you and your crew a round of shots prior to each game. That is, of course, if you can deliver."

"Deliver," I barked back assuredly, "you just made the deal of the century."

Within twenty minutes, two sixty-inch plasma screens were installed by the platform stage; and several extra couches, chairs, and stools had been positioned accordingly around the large viewing area to ensure maximum attendance. The commotion itself was enough to cause a minor stir, but when the boys began talking up the new digs on the betting lines, the response was immediate and overwhelming. With still a half hour prior to the start of the opening game, there was already a waiting line to enter the bar, and over one hundred patrons were inside partying and drinking up a storm. As we looked around from our prime location in the heart of all that we had created, we toasted to our success and hoped that we would be as successful with the games to come. As far as the casino was concerned, we were all winners already; and when our first round of shots and drinks made their way over to our table, I received a nod and a look of admiration from the hotel floor manager, my new best friend.

Now that we were all comfortably settled in for the day's events, cocktails in hand, we began to recount yesterday's glory and the lavish celebratory dinner that followed. The limo ride to the restaurant was an experience in and of itself, and we were barely able to make our way through the casino and up to the picturesque venue of the Italian café without causing a major commotion. Romeo and Jack were already waiting at the bar for our arrival, and there was much rejoicing and fanfare when we strolled in. My heart was racing with exuberance, and my whole body was tingling with pride and anticipation as Jack and I greeted each other and hugged and smiled at each other as we basked in the limelight. Romeo handed me a bourbon and ginger ale. We clinked glasses, and he said, "Now that's how it's done, brother." I felt a wave of accomplishment and relief come over me as I poured the bourbon into my booze-drenched body, but I knew that I needed to remain humble as "an early winner can easily become a late loser." After all, it was only Thursday night's dinner, and there was an eternity of action still ahead.

We were seated for dinner at a long rectangular table with four of us on each side and me situated between Romeo and Beth. Jack gave an opening toast: "To good friends and future health and prosperity" and then continued by making several menu suggestions for all the newcomers. The meatball flight appetizer, house salad, and tomato with fresh mozzarella were staples as starters, and we also threw in some shrimp scampi, which turned out to be outstanding. The daily specials and selections of main courses were also fabulous, and Beth and I conferenced together as we always do as we had a habit of sharing whatever we each ordered. It was actually one of our "things" that we did, and I loved the fact that she was so playful and open to trying different dishes. Of course, the beverages continued to flow nonstop, and Jack also selected a couple of bottles of red wine for the table. Romeo countered by ordering two rounds of shots, and by the time the first course was being served, we were all buzzing with delight. In addition, Romeo had also brought a vial of dry goods with him, and I made a number of trips to the men's room, much to the chagrin of Beth, who, while unaware of what was actually transpiring, knew that I was up to no good. However, dinner went off without a hitch, and we all ate and drank to our hearts' context.

Jack topped off the evening by ordering his favorite dessert, bananas foster, and then before he even had time to finish, excused himself by reminding us all that tomorrow was still a big workday and that he needed to turn in early. We saluted him goodbye, finished off our meals and headed to the bar for an after-dinner drink. The joint was jumping, and the sounds and sights of the casino floor were still able to entice my insatiable appetite for more action even after such a lavish feast.

Somehow we all made it back to the hotel's main entrance in one piece. The girls were giddy rather than plastered like the rest of us, and they tried valiantly to keep us focused and moving in the right direction. The boys were stopping and chatting with every group of girls they saw and were also making quite the scene as their volume level and antics were escalating by the minute. I fell back and walked with Beth and Karen, all the while keeping Beth cinched close at my side to both ensure her safety and also my stability. The final escapade, which had us all hurrying for the exit, was when the crew decided to crash a wedding photo shoot and began taking pictures with the bride and her bridesmaids. Not that it wasn't hysterically funny and even had the celebrants laughing and joking as well, but it certainly seemed that a line had been crossed and that some downtime was definitely needed.

When we finally finished chuckling and telling tales from the previous night's chicanery, our attention turned back to the task at hand and the day's "plays". While the schedule was just as intense as Thursday's, today I had set my sights on only four specific selections. None of these games were tipping off until lunchtime, so the morning atmosphere was much more relaxed and composed. I skimmed through some of my research data that I had brought down with me as, unlike yesterday, wagers had not been placed as of yet, and I still wanted to reconfirm a few of my instincts and propositions. Just as I began sipping on my third bourbon of the hour, my cell phone rang; it was Jack. I told him about our busy morning and the accommodations that we had acquired for the day, and he joyfully replied, "That why I never worry about you, my boy. You know how to take care of yourself." I should have responded, "Yeah, because I am a self-absorbed, self-centered, egotistical prick who only cares about himself and his immediate needs." But rather, I just replied, "Comfort is the key as always, my boy," and we shared a good laugh and then got down to business.

It was of the utmost importance for me to watch my tongue and to keep playing my role as my last few days on earth played out in front of me. No one could find out the plan that I had formulated for the end of my stay out west, lest they would be able to prevent its culmination. And while I was sure that the crew's constant state of inebriation would cloud their thoughts and perception, I knew that both Beth and Jack would be able to detect even the slightest changes in my attitude or demeanor. After all, Jack's head was always clear; and since we have been friends for almost thirty years, he truly knew me better than anyone. Beth, on the other hand, while only being in my life for a few years, could sense and feel my pain as if it was her own, and her keen instincts and ability to tune into my psyche made it virtually impossible to fool her. No, I had to keep the charade up for another couple of days; and much to my surprise, I was actually enjoying myself and the company of those around me. Of course, all the booze, ganja, and dry goods helped me to stay in character throughout the day and also to ease my discomfort.

In addition, my responsibility to Jack and all that he had invested in me both financially and personally also kept me focused on my role as his need handicapper and prognosticator. I had to keep up my end of the bargain as far as Jack was concerned; I certainly owed him that much. The tournament was big business for him, much like the Superbowl, and he had put all his trust and faith in me to get him through this weekend, and I could not let him down.

Yet in the long run, I was planning to let all my friends and loved ones down in just a few days, and only my intoxicated and warped state of mind allowed me to rationalize that all away and to continue on my self-deprecating path to destruction. I believed that even deep down, I was no good and that everyone would be better off without me. I hated myself more and more, and I could not differentiate yet between hating myself and hating the acts that I had participated in. Remember, God and a program were still the furthest things from my mind at this point, and spirituality to me meant something about ghosts and the afterlife, not about everyday living. Somehow I knew that if I just continued to spend each hour zoned in on the action, the drugs, and the facade that I had created, nothing else around me would matter.

It was only during a few brief lapses from the insanity that my mind would go blank, my life would flash before my eyes, and the reality of the situation and the pain and suffering I was about to create actually dawned on me. Quickly, however, I was able to extinguish those thoughts in another glass of bourbon or in another trip with puff the magic dragon as I would feel their warm sensations course through my veins and force out all the guilt, shame, and responsibility. Unfortunately, I had already chosen my destiny, and I was way too far removed for any human power to alter my progression. The only hope was some divine intervention, and as far as I was concerned, that only happened on the basketball court when the karma was just right.

It was approaching 9:00 a.m. local time, and since our action was still a few hours off, two of my cohorts decided to go off and play some table games while I and my other friend stayed back and held down the fort. As basketball addicts and also students of the game, we could not pass up the opportunity to watch any of the floor play, and besides, we still had some drinking to do. In addition, as the "royalty" of our makeshift gambling palace, we drew a seemingly never ending crowd of gaming novices who continued to approach us with various questions regarding the odds, totals, and our betting strategies. We helped as many of these lost souls as we could, and if in return they offered to compensate us with yet even more beverages, I would offer them some "inside" tidbits of information in order for them to gain some knowledge and a perceived edge. Most people were more than happy to comply with this arrangement as even that least-experienced bettor knows that any possible advantage that they could obtain was surely coveted.

Also, I was always serious about the facts and opinions which I gave away as I felt that it was a personal achievement to be able to impart my wisdom to those who were in need. As I would learn later during my recovery, it was really my obligation to "give away what was so freely given to me." I pondered for a moment, thinking that maybe I wasn't such a bad guy after all, but unfortunately, that metamorphosis was still a long way down the road.

The other important necessity of the day was to spend more quality time with Beth. While I knew that she and Karen were two peas in a pod, I also knew that she did not make this trip just to go window-shopping and to get her nails done. Rather, she was here because of me, and I needed to show her that I was glad that she was with me and that she was also a major priority. While that would prove difficult with all the other items on my plate, I knew that I had to make the effort. Accordingly, as it approached halftime of the first contest, I decided to take a quick break and head back up to the suite to check in on Beth and also grab a quick smoke. I had the waitress place a "Reserved" placard on my table and asked her to watch my belongings as my other friend had started to doze off, and I could tell that he was on his way to an early nap. She smiled and, of course, acquiesced, and I quickly made my way to the elevators.

Beth was still asleep as I clandestinely entered the suite and made my way over to my bag of goodies. As the smoke filled the room, I saw her stretch, sniff a little, and then ask, "Is that you, my baby?" Rather than answer, I made my way over to the bed, took a deep toke on the pipe, and before exhaling, gave her a long, passionate French kiss, allowing the smoke to fill her mouth and enter her body. After exhaling and without opening her eyes, she whispered, "You know, my boyfriend does that to me all the time, but he usually puts his hands between my legs first." After almost choking from laughter and recognizing her playful mood, I responded, "Well, here at Chez Beth, we do things a little bit differently." "Oh really?" she replied. "How's that?" Instantly and with no further enticing needed, I flung the covers off the bed, revealing her already glistering and gyrating lower region and began to envelop her with my mouth and tongue. Her moans of delight cascaded throughout the entire suite, and as she held my head firmly between her thighs, I could feel her tensing and relaxing as she exploded over and over. Her impulsive nature, unmatched libido, and sheer sex appeal drove me absolutely wild and made her totally irresistible. The chemistry between us was palpable, and I had never felt so comfortable, so relaxed, and so in sync with anyone in my entire life. We had the kind of love that you dream about, and it was truly a blessing to have her in my life. She was my partner, my guardian angel, and my soul mate. We were *one*.

Several minutes later, and with both of us gasping for air, I climbed to the head of the bed, kissed her cheek, and whispered, "Good morning." "Good morning," she murmured. "You should probably leave soon as my boyfriend should be stopping by any minute." That was the last straw. I began to tickle her in all of her most sensitive spots, bellowing, "You think you're so smart, don't you, little Ms. Wise Ass, all coy and cool." As she squirmed and begged me to stop, our eyes met in a moment of absolute bliss; and as we stared at each other, I knew that I was destined to be hers forever. We kissed and held each other for what seemed like an eternity until the alarm clock sounded and snapped us both back into consciousness. While I got up to shut off the alarm, she couldn't resist one last joke, cackling, "I like the continental breakfast here—short, sweet, and very satisfying. Remind me to put that on my comment card when I check out." I just shook my head, threw a pillow at her, and headed to the fridge for a needed beverage.

Our unexpected but extremely enjoyable interlude ended with Beth energetically bounding around the room and asking me a million and one questions about the day's schedule. I assured her that today would be much more relaxed and that we could spend most of it together. She loved hearing that and danced around in delight, grabbing me and kissing me periodically as I tried to explain my proposed itinerary. We decided that we would meet for a private lunch alone at 2:00 p.m. and then reconvene with the rest of the group poolside around 3:00 p.m. for some fun in the sun. I told her that I would have the boys reserve some prime pool real estate and also pick up Karen before they made their way over. That way, we wouldn't have to rush and could join them all when we were ready. "Sounds like a perfect plan," she said appreciatively. "And perhaps we can stop the pool shop and pick out a sexy bikini for me to wear. You know how you like me to look good for you!" I nodded approvingly as she reached around me from behind and began nibbling on my neck. I knew what that meant, and as eager as I was, I whispered, "We'll have plenty of time for that later, baby, I promise." She licked my earlobe, gave me one more squeeze for good measure, and sheepishly remarked, "I guess I can wait awhile, but remember, a promise is a promise." With that, she skipped into the bathroom, flashed her beautiful top shelf at me, and then closed the door behind her. I shook my head again, straightened up the place a bit, and then headed back downstairs, still smiling ear to ear like the cat who just swallowed the canary. Life at that moment was actually worth living.

The crew were all back in their assigned positions when I returned. "How was the halftime show?" one of them blurted out as the others smirked. "Best damn entertainment I've ever seen, extremely gifted," I responded. "Any other questions?" "Yeah, I got one," said my two-dollars-across-the-board pal. "Where's our action today, and what should I be doing?" "Memphis-6," I told him. "And you should be getting us another round." With that, several more cocktails were ordered and delivered, and we all sat back and watched as the Tigers dismantled their opponents to the tune of 68–43. Yet another good start to an already fabulous morning, and I began to fantasize that the day would continue to play out just like yesterday. I thought to myself, "Groundhog Day could actually be a wonderful proposition, especially if it's your best day ever that keeps playing over and over again!" I guess it was all based on your perception.

Unfortunately, however, my perception these days was somewhat off-kilter, and I had begun to think and act like Phil Connors does in the movie. Phil has a life-altering revelation after a few days pass, and he begins to grasp his circumstances. He realizes that if each day was going to be a replica of his previous day, then all of his actions, as well as the consequences of those actions, would be irrelevant as time would be suspended and the future halted. He could eat whatever he wanted and as much as he desired because tomorrow would start all over again as today, and he would be right back to his old skinny self. There could be no punishment or ramifications for his vices. If he was thrown in jail or humiliated or even injured in some way, tomorrow he would wake up again right back where he was the day before—no harm, no foul. It was amazing to watch Phil's character, morals, and self-respect all go flying out the window once he became fully aware that there would literally be no reprisals for any of his behavior.

Most of us have fantasies and dreams that we do not act upon, usually because of the possible ramifications that these antics could illicit. However, if you remove the fear, the anxiety, and most importantly, the guilt and remorse from the possible equation, the end result, more likely than not, will change. I began to feed off this same attitude of nonchalance as I knew that in a few days' time, I wouldn't be around to answer to anyone; and therefore, it really didn't matter how I conducted myself or what harm I created either. They key once again was not to let anyone else around me become aware of my indifference as any 180-degree modification would certainly raise some eyebrows. Accordingly, I was very subtle in my descent into oblivion and never caused any unnecessary conversation or concerns regarding my demeanor. But just in case, I began to formulate a list of excuses and divergencies in my head in case I was called out on any of my behavior. I also knew that Beth was the most likely candidate to notice any initial attitude adjustments, so I needed to try and be my usual cordial self whenever we were together. I had truly become an actor upon the stage, and the curtain was to fall very shortly.

The Michigan/VCU game was up next, and it was the centerpiece of our early day's action. I had placed my largest and most confident wager of the morning/afternoon session on the over and had secured the number at over 141. Unfortunately, much to my dismay, the number began to tumble as the game approached, and at tip-off, it sat at 138. This unanticipated movement against "my side" created a sinking feeling in my stomach, but as I frantically reviewed my notes, scoring charts, and statistical ratios, my mind began to ease somewhat as I truly believed that the game would still go over. I told the boys and the nearby crowd as well not to worry, yet I felt a wave of doubting and depressed eyes crash down upon me like I was the Poseidon just before the tidal wave hit. While my crew nodded and confirmed that they were with me no matter what, I felt the need to expand upon my viewpoint in order to calm their nerves.

I explained that VCU played a pressing full-court style of defense which not only led to turnovers and easy baskets for them but also, if the press was properly broken, would certainly create layup opportunities for their opposition. Michigan had both strong guard play and excellent ball handles throughout its lineup, so even if the pace was frenetic, they should be able to handle themselves accordingly. That being said, we settled in to watch the scenario play out. Thankfully, just before the whistle blew to start the action, a round of shots arrived, compliments of the house, and we all reared back and fired then down. We were as ready as we could be.

The first half was one of the most exciting and intriguing halves of the tournament. Initially, Michigan looked unfazed by the VCU pressure, and they had built a 41–21 lead at the under four-minute time-out. However, the Rams turned the final minutes into a chaotic helter-skelter contest, closing on a 15–2 run and finishing the half down only 43–36. The 79 total points certainly was better than I had even imagined, and as long as the second half wasn't a total fiasco, we should be fine. After all, all we needed was 63 more points to be victorious, and usually the second stanza generated a higher point total than the first. There was an eerie hush throughout the room during the entire halftime break as no one wanted to say anything that might jinx us or our chances for victory. I made a quick pit stop on the nearby powder room and dampened my face and neck with cold water in order to keep myself cool. *Never let them see you sweat*, I thought to myself, and then I closed my eyes, took a deep breath of the heavily scented air, and trudged my way back out to the ring.

The game methodically moved along in the second half with each team cautiously looking for an advantage. While the slower pace kept the score down to some degree, Michigan was in front 54–45 with 11:50 left to play. Then, within the span of only twelve seconds, VCU's point guard and their most aggressive defender picked up his third and fourth fouls and had to be delegated to the bench to prevent him from fouling out. You are allowed four fouls in college basketball but are disqualified from playing once you receive your fifth, so the VCU coaching staff needed to protect their star player and rightfully removed him immediately from the action. Michigan, sensing an opportunity to expand their lead against a now more vulnerable VCU squad, intensified their own defensive pressure and gave the Rams a taste of their own medicine. Seemingly unprepared for this surprise tactic, VCU didn't know what hit them; and before they could regroup, the Wolverines had gone on a 12–1 blitzkrieg, capped off by a long three-pointer and a resounding dunk, which sent the crowd into hysterics.

The quick scoring burst left the score at 66–46 with just over nine minutes remaining and allowed me to crack a small smile and breathe an optimistic sigh of relief. Yet the game was far from over, and my main concern now was that Michigan might start playing it safe by trying to kill as much time off the clock as possible with each possession. While the thirty-five-second shot clock all but made extinct Dean Smith's four corners' stall offense, many teams would work the shot clock under ten seconds before they would even begin to run their offensive set. VCU, however, was desperate at this point; and after reinserting their all-American guard back into the lineup, they ramped up their defensive fury in an attempt to speed Michigan up and force them to make mistakes.

The tempo of the game returned to a much faster pace, but VCU was unable to significantly cut into the lead, and they still trailed 76–58 as the clock reached the four-minute mark. At the next time-out, everyone in the room got up to stretch, smoke, or run to the bathroom before the final few minutes played out. I, of course, located a nearby path of carpet where I could pace back and forth until the commercials ended, imagining the entire time how we would achieve yet another victory. We only needed eight more points to put us over the top, yet my insides were still a bit queasy. Not only was there a ton of money at risk, but this one was more personal as I wanted to prove to all the doubting Thomases that my knowledge and instincts were on the money.

As the clock wound down, Michigan hit an open three-pointer with 1:07 left stretching their lead to 83-60 and making us winners again. The crowd in the bar erupted when the shot pierced the net, and a huge weight was lifted from the shoulders of the collective group. The final score was posted, revealing an 85–65 Wolverine blowout, and the smile on my face told the whole story. It's a major feeling of accomplishment when you work hard for something, and it pays off. Unfortunately, those moments are usually fleeting, and humility was a word that I was still unable comprehend.

CHAPTER 7

Shakedown Street

Tuesday, April 21, 2015

THE DAY BEGAN IN THE usual manner with the cell doors crashing rhythmically open and close, and the announcements from the bubble blaring out through the dorm. I washed up quickly and gathered myself together to be ready for the count which would be following shortly. Once the morning drills had been completed, the gates parted for breakfast, and I made my way down the catwalk and over to the food cart. The workers were extremely quiet even for the morning service, and there was an uneasy feeling in the air. I also noticed that there were several more COs present today than usual and that they seemed visibly annoyed about something. "Move it along," one officer commanded. "We don't have all day." I tried to hear their conversation as I passed by them, but I could only make out a few faint words: *sheriff* and *lockdown*. Several of the other inmates were speaking in small groups near the water fountain, and one of them said the word *shakedown*, which for some reason immediately gave me a sinking feeling inside. I knew that I heard this word somewhere before, but I could not remember where or in what context. However, as everyone slowly and solemnly made their way back to their cells, it became crystal clear that something unpleasant was about to unfold.

As the day progressed, there was a lot more whispering and hushed conversation throughout the cellblock. In addition, it became apparent that we were all going to be locked in until the "shakedown" was to occur. I wracked my brain trying to restore my knowledge of this unknown slang term until it finally hit me. *Shakedown!* I remembered, that's when they turn the whole dorm upside down and search each and every cell from top to bottom for weapons, drugs, paraphernalia, and any other illegal substances which are not be possessed by the inmate population. I also recalled that I was warned of this military-style operation by both an ex-con on the outside and in 72 by Junior when he and I were jawing one day.

Apparently, it only takes place when a severe situation has occurred within the jail, and then the entire facility comes to a grinding halt and locks down. In this instance, I would later find out, there had been an altercation in one of the more violent dorms between two rival gang members where one sliced the other with some kind of homemade "shiv." The weapon contained a razor blade, which was clearly a prohibited item; and consequently, the sheriff had ordered the shakedown in order to quash any further violent outbreaks. While I was aware that there was no contraband of that sort in my cage, I still quickly did an inventory of my belongings and began to organize all of my property. The heightened awareness continued to build, and the tension was so thick that you could cut it with a knife, but all we could do was sit tight and wait for the hammer to fall.

Several hours passed by, and after being served our lunch trays in bed, rumors began to spread that the troops would be arriving around 1:00 p.m. I was still unable to fully comprehend exactly what was going to follow, but never in my wildest dreams did I ever imagine the physical nature or severity of the actual inspection. Then just past one o'clock, the announcement came over the PA: "On the shakedown, on the shakedown." The place went dead silent, and I turned my attention to the dorm entranceway, which I could clearly see through the double-paned plexiglass window of my gate. Initially, several high-ranking officials made their appearance. You could tell immediately that they were officers of stature from both their decorated uniforms and casual demeanor.

Once inside, they cleared a pathway and stood aside as one of the sergeants bellowed, "Send in the turtles." Immediately, from out of nowhere, seven heavy-armed SWAT team members in full riot gear made their way into the block and stood at attention. They were covered from head to toe in protective armor, including helmets with tinted facial visors, full metal jackets, and thick plastic shields which protected their entire torsos. At first glance, it certainly seemed like an excessive show of force, but I assumed that it was standard protocol for this type of exercise. The "turtle" description was quite apropos as these gentlemen much more closely resembled the famous fighting Ninja Turtles of cartoon and movie fame than anything human. The sergeant then nodded his head and directed the operation to commence, and all in unison, the turtles made their way up the stairs and toward my end of the cellblock. It was truly the first time since my incarceration that I was overwhelmed with fear, and as I felt my body freeze and become numb with horror, I began to fully understand the gravity of the situation.

I continued to watch the turtles approach intently, and as they came closer and closer, I shut my eyes and began to pray. Fortunately, they come to a halt right before they reached my gate, and as the cell door to my left opened, orders were barked out, telling the inmate inside to lie facedown on his bed and not to move. Then three of the officers rushed into the cell and restrained my neighbor by cuffing his hands behind his back and shackling his feet together with a metal bar to limit his movement. When they all surfaced, they were escorted downstairs by the rest of the turtles and then continued through the block and departed through the open entranceway. This process resented itself several more times on the lower tier, and then the turtles made one last run back up toward my location.

My heart was pounding fiercely, and I held my breath as they passed my door. Although I could see them positioned right outside my gate, this time they grabbed and subdued the gentleman just to my right, and they led him away bound in similar restraints as I had seen earlier. Unfortunately, this convict was not as accommodating as the previous ones; and therefore, a greater degree of force was utilized by the officers in order to make him comply. I released a huge sigh of relief when they all passed by me again, but I was quite curious to know why those inmates were singled out and also what their fate was once they were removed. Later on, I did learn that the two specific neighbors of mine were alleged gang kingpins; and since the earlier altercation was supposedly gang-related, they were going to be "questioned" regarding the incident. Finally, once the turtles exited for good with their last detainee in hand, a calm yet eerie moment permeated the block. However, much like the serene instances prior to a major weather event, it was just the calm before the storm.

The next several minutes saw a flood of prison personnel come pouring through the entrance until at least two hundred COs were crammed into the lower level. The scene was frantic and chaotic, to say the least, and I wondered where all the officers had come from. Apparently, many off-duty police were called in to man the shakedown, and other officers were pulled from various locations within the jail in order to conduct the necessary inspection of each individual dorm. In addition to the large and overwhelming police presence, many large and diverse metal-detecting devices were also brought in, including the "Boss" chair, which looked like an archaic electrocution machine. This contraption was utilized to detect any hidden metal upon an inmate's body, including your internal under canties, as well as your ears, nose, and mouth. Two enormous portable metal-detecting stations were also set up on each end of the block, and I was told that they would be employed to scan our mattresses for weapons and other concealed contraband which could be easily hidden within the plastic and foam filling.

Then when the drug-sniffing dogs made their appearance, it became evident that this was definitely more than a drill. In fact, if you were trying to hide something, whatever it was going to be detected. Accordingly, the torrent of noise which arose from the persistent flushing of toilets became deafening as any and all illegal substances were literally sent down the drain. The water was supposed to have been shut off prior to the shakedown to prevent the population from discording any incriminating evidence, but for some reason, it was still up and running. As I watched all that was taking place around me, the only question remaining was, what was going to happen next?

The COs broke into groups of three and proceeded in teams to move in front of each of the fifty-two units. Upon the command, the metal pass through compartment in the middle of my cell door, the one where meals where placed during lock-ins, was opened, and I was instructed to place my hands through the opening palms up. At that point, my hands were cuffed, and I was told to step back away from the door and stand at attention. When the door was then opened, the officers rushed in, took hold and control of me, and began to ransack my cell and search all of my belongings. They tore through everything like a summer tornado out on the plains and left a pile of destruction in their wake. My clothes were strewn throughout the room, my papers scattered across the floor, and my bed and linens ripped apart and then hurled out my gate and over the railing into the valley below. Afterwards, I was led away from the cell and taken to the personal body-search area downstairs where my person was to be examined. Desperately, I tried to turn back and view the action still transpiring in my room; however, I was ordered to "face front and keeping moving." And as I had no intention of bringing myself any extra undue hardship, I willingly complied and continued down the catwalk.

The ground floor was absolutely mobbed with people and activity, and we were all packed in tightly like a can of sardines. I waited patiently on line with my chaperone close beside me and watched as inmate after inmate took their turn in the boss chair. The procedure actually lasted only a few seconds and consisted merely of sitting on the device momentarily and then standing up and placing each side of your face on a thin flat aluminum slab for testing. If no bells or whistles went off, you were released without incident and were escorted back to your box. However, if the Boss detected any type of foreign substance, you were removed expeditiously from the dorm and were not to be seen or heard from again.

After I made my way through the process and was cleared by the inquisitioner, I was ushered back to my room for one last questioning session. When I arrived there, the two other COs were still surveying the mess they had created and were rummaging through some papers that I had filed away in a legal envelope. One of them also had a small plastic bag with several small items that they had confiscated from my property. The bag contained a spoon, several old pens and pencils, and a small wire twist which had come from my radio headset and which I used on occasion to try and floss my teeth. "Nothing much here," one of them remarked. "Just a few loose odds and ends and some graffiti on the walls." "What are you, an artist?" said the other one. "You got some nice work here." I chuckled quietly a bit to myself sarcastically, but it must have been loud enough for them to hear as I was asked, "What's so funny, convict?" "Can I speak frankly, CO?" I inquired. "Sure," he replied cockily. "I am a middle-aged white man who knows more Shakespeare than gangland lingo. Do you really believe that I am responsible for writing any of this?" I continued, "I don't even know what half of it means!" He paused, glanced around the cell again, and then responded, "Perhaps not, convict, but it's your house now, so you better get to cleaning these walls sometime soon." And with that, he unlocked my cuffs, signaled to the others, and the three of them walked out, leaving me to clean up the huge mess they had left behind.

The noise and the chaos began to subside somewhat as they passed the last of the mattresses through the mobile metal detectors, and normalcy started to return to the block. I gathered my clothes off the floor and folded then the best that I could as I was still trembling with fear about all that had just occurred. It was a totally helpless feeling having someone have absolute dominion and control of your life, a sinking feeling, one that left you feeling worthless and insecure on all levels. One where fairness, justice, and honestly didn't reside, but rather where the "man" ruled your world with an iron fist; and if you didn't abide by the rules, you would be dealt the consequences. The one thought that kept popping into my mind was, what if the officers had actually found something questionable in my affairs? Or even worse, what if they had chosen to plant something in my cell in order to justify the search? How would I have combated either of those dilemmas, especially if I was innocent of the charges? It would obviously be my word against theirs, and even though I liked to gamble, the odds of me beating the house in this instance would be slim to none.

Thankfully, by this time, I had already experienced my spiritual awakening and had a Higher Power in my life, so I turned my thought toward my program and the guidelines and tools contained therein. I began to ease my mind and body by praying quietly and thanking God for all His care and help not only today but over the past year. I reflected back on the medallion given to me by Francis and repeated the inscription over and over again in my head: "Do not be afraid, I am with you always." I knew that my Higher Power was watching over and protecting me from harm and that He would continue to do so as long as I conducted myself in a prudent manner and strived to do the next right thing. I had faith in my life, a powerful faith; and as I sat there in my box praying for comfort and guidance, I knew that all would be fine.

By the time I finished reorganizing my digs, the clock had struck 4:00 p.m., and it was time for dinner. The COs came around and opened our door flaps so that the food crew could deliver our savory meals and juice. Apparently, we were going to remain locked in for the remainder of the day; and unfortunately, it was difficult to get comfortable since we were all still without our mattresses and linens. In fact, the mattresses had been placed into two large stacks in the middle of the dorm, and all the sheets and blankets had been removed with none of them being replaced as of yet. While the meal service was being delivered, I questioned the inmate worker who was disseminating the trays and asked if he had heard anything regarding either of our confinement or the return of our bedding. "Nothing yet," he answered back, "but it looks we can expect a long night ahead."

The dinner du jour was not really dinner at all but rather the standard lunchtime staple of bologna, lettuce, and two pieces of bread served with half pint of milk to wash it all down. Due to the shakedown and the prison-wide lockdown, the inmates who worked on the kitchen staff were unable to fulfill their work obligations as they also were subject to the restrictions of the detainment and could not get to the kitchen to prepare the normal grub. The day continually became more stressful even though the inspection had ceased, and when I went to wash up before eating my gourmet plate and realized that the water had finally been shut off, I became exasperated yet again. Having no running water, no water to flush the toilet, and no idea what to expect next was truly not a good combination.

Time was passing very slowly, so I decided to just close my eyes and try to mediate for a while. I rolled a towel up so that I could cushion my head and neck and lay down on the hard, inflexible metallic slab where my mattress had been situated. My aching back immediately twinged in pain, and I tried shifting around in order to alleviate my discomfort. Luckily, I was finally able to doze off, if only due to my sheer mental exhaustion, and only awoke due to the clamoring of the cell gates for an unscheduled count which was going to take place. I was startled and a bit disoriented, but I knew not to talk to nor to engage the CO performing the count even though I was extremely curious to find out what I could expect next. There was no information being emitted over the PA system nor any news coming from the other inmates. Perhaps most of them had previously experienced a shakedown in the past, but being a newbie myself and only two weeks into my prison career, I was nervous, uninformed, and remained quite irritated.

After the count, I decided to open the one and only book I had in my possession, hoping that it would distract me from all the negative thoughts racing in my head. I had received the novel just the day before from a neighboring convict and had yet to delve into the story. Reading completely diverted my attention, and while I did have a moment or two where I zoned out a bit, the narrative was very entertaining, and I began to immerse myself more and more into the tale. As the day came to a close and the shakedown nightmare drifted off into the past, I realized that I had successfully survived the ordeal and felt more confident and self-assured than ever. After all, I could tackle any obstacle as long as I faced it one day at a time.

CHAPTER 8

The Sun and the Stars

Friday, later that day

My OVERALL RECORD NOW STOOD at 8–1, and as I left the mayhem at the "cabaret bar" and sauntered over to the restaurant to meet Beth for lunch, I certainly was flying on a pink cloud. Further along in my recovery, I would learn the true meaning of that expression, but for now I was just high as a kite, and seeing Beth's smile and shapely figure in the distance only magnified that feeling. As I approached from across the casino floor, she teasingly rocked back and forth, swaying her hips from side to side, and gestured for me to come toward her. My eyes soaked up every inch of her feminine wiles; she was truly the most beautiful woman that I had ever seen. We kissed, and then she grabbed my hand and led me into the mouth of the Golden Dragon, the overly authentic-looking Chinese eatery where I had made a reservation. The choice of venues was easy as I knew that Beth loved Chinese food, and it was one of my favorites as well. The Dragon had recently received a "five chopstick" rating in one of the local restaurant guides, and I also heard good things about it from both Jack and Romeo. It was just slightly after 2:00 p.m. by the time we were seated, and I was aching with anticipation to have some real alone time with my Beth.

After ordering several different appetizers and a delicious-sounding chicken and shrimp dish for our main course, all of which we were of course going to share, we raised our glasses and toasted to the day ahead. I couldn't take my eyes off her, and she began to blush a bit as I continued to stare at her radiant face. She smiled back at me and said, "What? Is there something wrong with me?" Rather than ruining the moment by answering that totally open-ended question with a sarcastic wise-ass response, as usual, I took her hand and whispered back, "No, baby, you are my perfect angel, and I love you more and more every day that we are together." She squeezed my hand, and we shared a truly wonderful and intimate moment that only two people madly in love could experience. I didn't want the moment to end or the feeling in my heart to dissipate. Times like this in life are far too seldom, I thought to myself, and I wondered how many more of them I would actually have to enjoy.

As the food began to arrive, we made some small talk about the boys, Karen, and the rest of the day's plans. Beth was already dressed for the pool as she was wearing a fancy white lace coverup over her bathing suit, which much to my delight wasn't covering up much of her assets. I was wearing my typical morning sweat suit outfit but had asked the crew to stop by my room and grab my swimming attire before they made their way poolside. We ate, chatted, and flirted during the entire meal, and it felt so nice to get back to some normality and some of the simple pleasures of life, good food, and great company. When the bill arrived along with a plate of fortune cookies, I motioned for her to come sit next to me so that we could cuddle a little and share our fortunes. We kissed again, and I stroked her long magnificent legs under the table as she opened up the first cookie. She chuckled a bit as she read it out loud, "We all have dreams and fantasies but they rarely come true." Then she placed the tiny piece of paper on the table, looked up and continued, "All my dreams and fantasies have come true Honey, thank you." And as I melted into her arms and hugged her for dear life, I simply replied, "Ditto."

We finished our drinks, gave our compliments to the staff, and then headed upstairs to join the others for an afternoon of fun in the sun. Prior to entering the lavish lagoon setting, we made a quick pit stop at the pool pavilion so Beth could peruse a few of the newest bikini fashions. She selected and modeled several striking and skimpy two-piece ensembles, and as I watched her change in and out of the glamorous gear, I felt myself getting extremely excited. As she ducked into the dressing room to try on her last selection, the saleswoman asked me if I would like a soft drink while I was waiting. I told her that I was fine and then continued on by explaining to her that I was having the time of my life watching Beth posing and strutting around the store barely clothed. In fact, I suggested that she might want to charge all significant others an hourly viewing fee and serve cocktails as well because I was certain that any red-blooded gentleman would pay handsomely to watch what I had just witnessed the past few minutes. She laughed hysterically and replied, "You know what, that's actually not a bad idea," and we both continued to laugh it up as Beth shimmied her way out of the back room. "I can't leave you alone for one minute," she scolded. "What do you think of this?" The white string and tassel top together with the hip-hugger bottoms clashed exquisitely with her smooth tan skin and made her look like a mythical goddess.

Before I could even get a word out, the saleswoman cried out, "You look…absolutely…gorgeous," pausing between each breath as if she was even shocked how incredibly sexy and magnificent Beth looked. "And you," Beth quipped at me, "what's your opinion?" "Take one in every color," I replied. "I'm buying." She giggled approvingly as she turned and shook her cute little caboose back into the dressing room, and I yelled, "You can leave that one on if you like. I know I would like it." Since neither of us could decide which suits to buy, I told her to grab her three favorites, stating emphatically, "Don't worry, they won't go to waste." She strutted over to the register, suits in hand and still donning the white stunner. After I popped my eyes back into their sockets, we thanked our personal peddler and made our way out to the desert oasis.

While it was a surprising warm day for March, the pool decks were relatively quiet and serene. There were mostly groups of young women scattered about, and I surmised that most of the men were still glued to their TVs and the ongoing game action. Karen had sent Beth a text alerting us to their location, and we spotted them almost immediately. The boys looked both relaxed and comfortable and were sprawled across several lounge chairs in a cozy, shady, and secluded tree-lined alcove. Out in the sun next to Karen were two strategically placed chaises which were positioned so that Beth and I could sit together and still engage the crew in conversation. We settled in without much commotion, and while Beth showed Karen all of her new purchases, I conversed with one of my pals. He asked what I was drinking and if Beth cared for anything, and then handed me a small piece of tissue paper with something inside. "Try this when you get a minute," he said softly. "I recently got a bunch from an old friend of mine from Colorado." I carefully unwrapped the gift, not knowing what it was, and saw a gummy-bear-like candy which was shaped like a dragon and was about an inch long. Puzzled somewhat but without responding, I quickly popped it into my mouth and began to chew with vigor. He had been distracted talking to Beth about her drink order, and by the time he turned back toward me, I had already consumed the entire treat. He whispered quietly, "Only take half. They are very strong." Unfortunately, that information was a bit late. I opened my mouth to show him that it was already gone, and he just sat back, smiled, and calmly responded, "Well, this should be interesting."

It turned out that the item was a THC-infused gummy dragon, which was one of the many new and creative products being sold in Colorado since the recent legalization of marijuana there. That news actually made me feel more at ease since I was somewhat used to the effects of THC in its various forms, and at least it wasn't some type of experimental narcotic or other psychedelic hallucinogen. However, the next two hours were certainly a trip as I was totally energized and could not refrain from either talking or laughing the entire time. While it was actually quite amusing initially, after some time, I could see that Beth was getting more nervous than entertained, and I sensed mentally that I was out of control even though I felt great physically. As I looked at her in all her sexual splendor, I began to imagine what it would be like to have sex with her with all of this adrenaline and THC racing through my body. However I knew from the look on her face that she wanted no part of me at the moment.

Eventually, the effects began to wind down, and I started to regain control of my senses little by little. Beth, looking quite annoyed, said that she was hot and was going to take a dip in the pool and asked me if I would walk with her over to the water. A cool plunge sounded great, but I also accurately surmised that she was not only looking to cool off physically, but rather, she was also looking to discuss what had just occurred and to cool off mentally as well. I followed close behind her as she made her way into the shimmering water and then flung her around and pulled her toward me. As we drifted toward a shady deserted area covered by palm trees, she looked disgustedly into my eyes and barked, "Really? Was that necessary?" I tried to explain that I had unwittingly taken too much of the product and also that I had never tried it before. I continued by saying, "Hey, I feel fine, and it was just a little harmless fun, no big deal." Unfortunately, those were not the right words nor at the right time, and she tried to wrestle herself free from my arms. "What? I'm fine," I reiterated. She just shook her head and looked at me in total horror, and I knew then that there was more to this than met the eye.

The next hour or so was one of the most difficult and painful time of our entire relationship. It became very apparent that Beth had witnessed several significant changes in my behavior of late and was wondering what the causes were for these dramatic diversions. Of course, I tried to play dumb and told her that I had no idea what she was talking about, but being the incredibly intuitive and shrewd woman that she was, she wasn't buying it. Then as the conversation intensified, she pushed several of my internal buttons, and my anxiety and fear came pouring out as anger and rage, and I totally lost my composure. I stormed off away from her like a petulant child, all the while spewing my venom carelessly and without regard. When I returned to the chairs, I quickly snatched up my belongings and shouted to the crew to be in the lobby at 7:15 p.m. for dinner. Before they even knew what had happened, I was gone; and obviously my cover was blown, at least with Beth.

It is truly remarkable how the course of any given day and even our lives can change so rapidly if something is either said or not said. How could I possibly communicate to Beth the way I was feeling when, in most instances, I couldn't even admit to myself that something was wrong? No, I had to continue to conceal my troubles and my pain even if it meant avoiding her at times, or even worse, blatantly lying to her face. While this deceit and ambivalence only perpetuated the difficulties between us, I could never admit what my true intention was nor the fact that even she could no longer help me. I had already become a slave to both fear and guilt, and unfortunately, there was only one way out for me, or so I thought.

As I exited the pool area, my cell phone rang numerous times, and I saw Beth's number appear on the display. I chose not to answer it as I didn't want to make matters worse, but this tactic backfired, as the message she left clearly indicated. I listened intently to her words as I made my way through the hotel and over to the elevators. Her tone and demeanor were calm and direct, but I could tell that she was not only peeved but also concerned. I was still in a pissy mood as I entered the elevator, but I quickly altered my thoughts to the relief I would find once I was securely in the bosom of my room and my substances.

Upon returning to my suite, I found several gift baskets of various shapes and sizes located on the kitchen counter. Fortunately, one of them was an assortment of gourmet and finely aged bourbon products, including several bottles of whiskey and some fancy infused cheeses and dried meats. Hurriedly, I tore apart the plastic wrapping and grabbed the pint-sized bottle of Gentleman Jack, which I knew would be quite tasty and which I also knew would clear my head. I put the bottle to my lips, took a long swig of that sweet nectar and welcomed the burn in my throat and the simultaneous shiver throughout my entire body. After another large gulp, I reached for the thank-you card which was still attached to a piece of the plastic wrap. It read, "Nice job, my boy! Just a little something to whet your appetite. See you at dinner. Jack."

The other baskets contained cards with similar thoughts and sentiments and the best one after Jack's bourbon melange was sent by Don Palermo. "Arrivederci, my friend. Thanks to you I am off to Italy for a month's vacation. Salud! All my best, Guiseppe." There was also one from El Gato and one from the Chicago boys, who both congratulated me in their own personal styles and with their own personal flair, mostly garbled gambler's humor with gothic undertones. Another splash of bourbon hit the back of my throat as I walked into the bedroom to grab my small water pipe. It was already packed and loaded and with my good friend Gentleman Jack at my side. I returned to the living room and crashed into one of the oversized chairs. I lit the pipe and cannonballed the intense hit of smoke, sending my brain into delirium and the bourbon cascading down my face. As I leaned back in the chair and felt the warm sensation of the pot and alcohol consume me, I knew there was only one thing to do: call Romeo.

Before I could even begin to gather my thoughts, my cell phone began to chime; and as I jumped up to answer it, I saw that my prayers had been answered; it was Romeo. "Nice two for two today so far, my man. You're on fire." "It's all part of my master plan," I answered and then asked if I could make a pit stop at his place prior to dinner as I had done the previous night. He said he had some "errands" to run before dinner but that he had some time now if I wanted to cruise over. Since I was already half in the bag, I replied, "I'll be there in fifteen. Ready the troops," and that was that. I threw on a pair of shorts and a clean polo shirt, placed all the gift baskets on the dining-room table, had one more encounter with my friend Gentleman Jack, who was nearly dead already, and headed out the door.

It had been my modus operandi the past few years to run away from my problems rather than to face them. I sought relief in every imaginable fashion from drinking to drugging to gambling to stealing and even to hurting myself when I became really desperate. Now, however, severe bouts of depression were clearly the greatest obstacle which I had to battle. So rather than being alone with myself, I usually preferred partaking in these worldly pleasures with a friend who would allow me to remain outside of my head and create yet another helpful distraction. Romeo would neither judge me nor lecture me on the attributes of abstention, and I always felt at ease in his company. Throughout our brief meeting of the minds, we talked basketball, odds, and action while we continually engaged heavily in both dry goods and ganja. By the time I stumbled my way out of his apartment, I could barely remember any of the day's earlier events, let alone the fact that I still had to reconcile with Beth. No, my only care in the world at moment was trying to make it back up the hill to the hotel without passing out or creating a scene. I stopped briefly to finish the last drop of soda in my can of Diet Coke, and while I noticed that the sky had begun to darken and that the moon had risen in the distance, I realized that I was alone once again, and it frightened me tremendously.

In my haste to get to Romeo's, I had left my cell phone behind, and there were five messages blinking when I returned to my abode. The first one was from Ann, who was just checking in to see if I was alive. Then there was one from Jack, one from the front desk, and two hang-ups which I imagined were from Beth. I really was in no state of mind to respond to any of them, but I thought that I had better at least call down to the front desk and see what was up. My call was quickly diverted to a hotel manager, who calmly explained that while our rooms were all reserved for tonight, a problem existed for tomorrow and that I should make it a point to stop at the VIP reservations area next time I was down in the lobby. It was 5:45 p.m., and I knew we had dinner around seven to seven thirty, so I said that I would be down in about an hour. "That will be fine," she replied. "Have a lucky day." I thanked her for calling and then said a fair goodbye to my friend Gentleman Jack as I raced into the shower.

Beth was nowhere to be found, but I knew that she had the evening's itinerary and that she knew where to be and when. I called the boys to remind them to be in the lobby around 7:00 p.m., but could hear from the noise in the background that they were already on the casino floor. My head was spinning not from all the goods I had ingested but rather from all the issues that were swimming through my mind—Beth, dinner, the boys, the rooms, Jack, Romeo, and of course, the games which were already in full swing again. I dressed quickly, gathered a few necessities together, and then sat for a moment at the dining-room table. It looked more like a funeral parlor or a wake than a casino suite as the oversized baskets dominated the scene. I closed my eyes in order to quiet my thoughts and the pounding of my heart, but it was to no avail. Instead, I reached for my goodie bag and packed yet another oversized bowl, thinking that was the only way to soothe my frayed nerves. My heart and body were still fluttering with anxiety, but as soon as the smoke entered my pores, I felt a rush of serenity pass through me. The pipe was my only path to sanity, or so I thought; and after one final hit, I was ready to join the others to face the music.

I approached the front lobby and made my way over to the rip station in order to discuss the room accommodations with the reservation manager. An attractive young woman with a perky little body and her hair pulled back tight in a bun came toward me and introduced herself as Ms. Foster. Apparently, there has been a crush of reservation for Saturday night, and we were all going to be bumped from our current digs. She continued by saying that while there was a good chance that something might open up, nothing could be guaranteed. She then went on to inquire if I would still need fair rooms, and it was then that I remembered that the boys were all leaving at some point tomorrow night and that I would only require lodging for Karen, Beth, and myself. "Actually," I replied, "let me get back to you on that as I may only need two." She instructed me to contact her tomorrow afternoon, and I thanked her for her candor and for giving me the heads-up and then headed for the exit.

The boys were all gathered by the revolving doors, and as we said our hellos, we made our way outside and toward the restaurant next door. Karen and Beth were already standing out by the concierge desk, and I noticed that Beth was all smiles. She high-fived the crew as they approached her, and as I got closer, I noticed that she was wearing my favorite multicolored striped dress along with her "fuck me" pumps, which accentuated her luscious legs. She looked absolutely gorgeous and she shot me an alluring glance as I reached out for her hand. We kissed and hugged, and I told her how sorry I was for my earlier behavior and that I was looking forward to the evening and talking about everything. "Me too," she whispered and then gave me another long emotional embrace. I could feel her trembling a bit, and I knew that she was holding back some tears, but she pulled it together and took my hand and led the group to the adjacent steak house.

When we arrived, Romeo was right out front smoking a butt and holding court with a few of the female employees. He saw us approaching, stomped out his cigarette, and welcomed us with open arms. I asked him privately not to mention our earlier rendezvous, especially to Beth, and he nodded in understanding. He then led us to the small outdoor terrace location, which was vacant and actually appeared to be closed. After reaching over the low perimeter gate and unlocking the entrance way, he showed us where to sit and then disappeared inside for a moment.

The patio was covered with palm trees and decorative lighting, and our area consisted of a large couch with two adjoining love seats and a crystallized firepit in the center, which also acted as a table. This was obviously not the venue where dinner was to be served, but it was perfect for our premeal drinks and nosh. A few seconds later, Romeo returned with the restaurant manager, a cute waitress, and a large imposing security officer who reminded me of Oddjob from the classic 007 James Bond flicks. As I inquired how business was with the manager Rick, he snapped his fingers and exclaimed, "Oh shit, I forgot," and excused himself immediately. Both Romeo and I looked at each other, rather puzzled, but our query was answered when Oddjob and another gigantic security guard wheeled out two sixty-inch plasma TVs and began to set them up on each side of the love seats. The warm glow from the crystal embers reflecting off the screens cast a magnificent aura against the bright stars and full moon above us. I glanced upward to the heavens to try and appreciate the truly magical view, and I got a chill up my spine. It was like we had found nirvana.

The drinks arrived just as the satellite feed came on the TVs, and just as we were raising our glasses for the first toast of the evening, Jack strolled in. "Hello, hello," he bellowed, then turned toward Romeo and continued, "I see you have things under control already." Apparently, Jack and Romeo had previously arranged our private party; and the intimate setting, firepit, and first-class service all added to the ambiance of this special night. While the others browsed through the menu and soaked up their cocktails, Romeo, Jack, and I slipped away for a minute to discuss business. There were still four games being played, two of which we had considerable action on and one in particular that Jack seemed quite antsy about. He explained that he had his largest play of the tournament on the final game of the night and that he was anxiously awaiting the tip-off. I didn't ask him the amount of the wager, even though I was dying to know, but I wished him luck and told him to do a shot to relax.

"A fine idea, my boy," he answered, "I'll even buy." "Even better," I replied. "But make sure you pay the tab before that last game goes final, just in case," I told him laughingly. He chuckled and then, with a real serious expression, remarked, "Let's hope we don't have to worry about that." As we made our way back to rejoin the others, I noticed that Beth was absent. Immediately, I scoured the area to find her and then realized that she was smoking a cigar with one of my crew just outside the iron gates of our secluded enclosure. Apparently, the lone rule that the restaurant strictly enforced was their no-smoking policy, and even Jack and Romeo had to abide by that one. I watched Beth intently as she swayed back and forth smoking, talking, and joking. Occasionally, she would glance my way and give me a wink or a slight wave to acknowledge that she was fine. Whenever I viewed her from afar, the world seemed to stand still, and suddenly it became very clear to me. I was so crazy in love with her, all of her; and witnessing her fun, lively, and carefree manner filled my heart with inexplicable joy and happiness. Tonight, however, I was experiencing something different; and as I began to feel warm and flushed all over, my emotions turned from love and hope to darkness and despair. It was as if all the seven deadly sins suddenly invaded my soul all at once, and I became paralyzed by fear. I became angry, envious, and my pride was taking a severe blow just because Beth was interacting with someone else and was not with me. Jealousy was raging throughout my body, and then the lust kicked in. I wanted her so, so badly that my loins began to tingle, and I was truly excited and overwhelmed by her presence.

But rather than make a scene, I retreated back to the booze, the food, and the games in order to get some comfort. I fell into the realm of greed, gluttony, and sloth as I positioned myself in the large oversized couch and chugged some shots while grabbing mouthfuls of shrimp and calamari. I had run the entire gamut of emotions in just a few short minutes, and I was totally confused by it all. Unfortunately, I had yet to acquire the knowledge that all these feelings and emotions stemmed from some form of doubt of the future, of the unknown, and even of the present, and it would be quite some time before I gained the skills necessary to cope with these issues. Learning that and, even more importantly, how to live my life in a state of love rather than a state of fear would eventually end up being my one true goal in life.

The games were now heating up, and rather than continue to think about things, I immersed myself further into the action and our current wagers. During one of the time-outs and before Beth had returned from her smoke, Romeo grabbed me for a quick snort in the upstairs office that we had visited the other night; only this time, we were joined by two of the lovely waitstaff, who also partook in the nefarious activity. Destiny and Joy were both young and extremely attractive, and I wondered where the night would have progressed to if I was twenty years younger and unattached. But being that Ann and I were still married and that Beth was lurking just downstairs, I shook off this brief fantasy quickly and returned to the issue at hand. I still needed to talk to Beth about our earlier spat, as well as comfort Jack as the games began winding down. I pulled Romeo aside briefly and told him that I needed to return to the festivities outside and to Beth. "Oh, sorry, kid," he replied. "I didn't realize how long that we've been gone. You know me, once I get started…" "No problem, brother," I assured him. "And thanks for the pick-me-up." He kissed the girls goodbye, whispered something in Destiny's ear, and then led me back down to the party.

I was significantly buzzed yet again, and for some reason, probably my intense guilt and remorse, I felt the need to address Beth immediately and discuss our day. Unfortunately, this was an ongoing problem for me as I always seemed to try and resolve my difficulties when I was totally inebriated rather than when I was sober and coherent. Beth had returned from her smoke and was seated next to Karen and chatting away with a couple of the boys. Luckily, I got distracted by Jack, who was standing by one of the TVs and loudly lambasting the lackluster effort of one of our teams. As he turned away, disgusted, I saw that the score read 44–21 at the half, and I knew that was not good. I stopped dead in my tracks and reflected for a minute, trying to comprehend why smart, rational people create situations in our lives that can lead us into serious peril and possibly damage our lives forever. I tried to analogize this with my relationship with Beth, but then rationalized that thought away because my situation with Beth was obviously different. We were in *love*, and after all, all's fair in love and war. As I glanced back over in her direction, she caught my eye and called me over by patting the seat next to her and tilting her head toward an open spot on the couch. I pointed to myself, looked around casually, and mimed to her, *Me?* And as she nodded back in approval, I negotiated my way over, never losing eye contact for a minute.

The remainder of the night with Beth was pure bliss. We held hands, snuggled up together on the couch, and playfully fondled each other when no one was looking. It was if a gray cloud had been lifted from above my head, and the sky had become both lighter and brighter. You could almost hear the static energy between us humming in the evening wind as we returned to *our* world that only the two of us inhabited. We were like two sixteen-year-olds out on their first date where nothing else in the world seemed to matter except what was happening between the two of us. I had been living in my own black hole of darkness and sadness for far too long, and Beth proved to me that with the right person by my side, I could escape into the light. She held my hand and pulled me out of the abyss, showing me love, compassion, and understanding that I never knew existed. She helped me to find myself again and to recreate the warm, passionate, and caring man that I once was. And as we made our way over to the far end of the patio where our table had been set for dinner, I was actually thinking that life was worth living, at least for the moment.

The games had all gone final by now, and for me, the last two games ended in a split, which left my record standing at an impressive 9–2 for the first two days of action. Unfortunately for Jack, however, the lone loss came in the contest where he had placed his greatest wager, but in all, I still knew that he was way ahead. I also knew that he now owed me a considerable amount of change as compensation for my consulting work and winning prognostications. We had earlier made a tacit agreement that was partially performance-based, and as long as I finished at least a game over 500, I stood to make money. Of course, neither Jack nor I expected that I would go 9–2 and be seven games over the magic 50/50 plateau, but neither of us was complaining. The way it actually washed out, I was due $65,000: $5,000 for the first game over 500, the example being 3–2; and then another $10,000 per game for each game winner after that number, which amounted to another $60,000 for the other six winning games leading to the 9–2 total. This $65,000 from Jack, coupled with Thursday's huge winnings and the profits I had today, put my two-day total well into the six-figure range. It had truly been a two-day bonanza that was the pinnacle of my handicapping career, but of course, the timing was quite ironic. While I would get to savor the kudos for a couple of days, I knew that I would never actually get to enjoy the fruits of my labor as the clock was ticking and my time was dwindling.

Dinner was comprised of the best salads, steaks, and side dishes that one could imagine. The beverages flowed continuously throughout the courses as well, as did the jovial conversation and laughter that echoed against the surrounding building. Beth sat next to me so that we could chat, hold hands, and eat off each other's plates. The evening was moving along better than I could have ever anticipated, and I knew that there was still much more fun and excitement ahead. The after-dinner plan was to spend some time in the casino playing the various table games and enjoying the sights and sounds of the action. This was to be the crew's last full night of activities as the last of them was scheduled to leave on the red-eye flight just before midnight tomorrow. With this in mind, I wanted to show them a really good time, and I even coaxed Jack into joining us for a while. Romeo had disappeared right after dinner, stating that he had some late-night plans, and I assumed from the wink he gave me as he departed that he was meeting back up with either Destiny or Joy, or perhaps both of them. The boys and I decided to pick up the tab for dinner as we wanted to show our appreciation to both Jack and Romeo for all they had done for us, and then we all made the short trip back to the hotel for the grand finale.

Friday and Saturday nights at the casinos on the strip were like Mardi Gras each and every weekend. The hotels were packed with players from all over the world, and there was an ever-increasing Asian invasion which seemed to permeate the gaming sites. Perhaps it was due to the higher table limits and minimums on the weekend than during the week, or perhaps it was just convenience of traveling to the gambling mecca from the West Coast. But either way, they came with tons of cash, and they obviously loved the action. I mention this because our first pit stop of the evening was at a $25 per hand minimum blackjack table which had just opened up and which was immediately converged upon by a group of older Japanese woman. We welcomed them to join us as there were still several open slots at the table. I sat in my customer anchor position at the far end of the action as my gambling IQ always prevented me from sitting anywhere else. My rationale for this predetermined placement was that regardless of the other players' decisions prior to my turn to play, I would get to make the last move before the hand was decided. In fact, my choice would affect the final outcome for the entire table; for if I either drew a card or stoodpat on my current hand, that action would decide the fate for all the players. It was truly the critical and most important seat on the felt, and I cherished the responsibility.

Beth and Karen stood idly by my side as we began to play as they were a bit squeamish to wager such a large amount on each hand. Two members of my posse were seated in places 1 and 4 respectively, and two of the Asian women grabbed spots 2 and 3. Seat 5 next to me on my right remained open, and the dealer allowed Beth and Karen to occupy that area until someone else came along to claim that position. The atmosphere was electric, and as the cards were shuffled and dealt, I felt my insides tingle as my level of intensity began to rise. The karma and vibe surrounding us seemed both positive and right, and within a few minutes, I was already hundreds of dollars ahead.

Our Asian counterparts were confident and skillful players who knew the intricacies of the game, continually made the correct decisions and were also consistently winning. Only one person at the table was actually struggling and appeared quite nervous in both his appearance and demeanor; that was my $2 across the board friend who was obviously over the head. Also to add insult to injury, he began making several bad mistakes that even a novice gambler would not dare make. As the atmosphere began to shift more negatively due to his ineptitude, even the two older ladies began to grumble, make comments, and look in his direction. Finally, at one point after he actually picked up his cards and repositioned them, thereby creating an immediate misdeal and killing the hand for the entire table, one of the women glared of him and shouted in a thick Asian accent, "WHAT'S A-MATTER, YOU DON'T KNOW HOW TO PLAY?" adding after a few seconds of silent disbelief, "GO, GO—YOU LEARN HOW TO PLAY, THEN COME BACK!"

Being both shocked and embarrassed by this unprecedented attack, my boy looked at me for some guidance but there was nothing for me to do except to try and hold back and contain my laughter. He tried in vain to respond to the woman, but he was so flustered that ultimately he just stood up and staggered away from the table, mumbling to himself as he left. Feeling terrible for him, Beth and Karen tried to comfort and console him as he aimlessly walked away from table, still seemingly in shock. It was then when I looked into the woman's eyes and saw her wink at me that I broke down into hysterics. To this day, it was one of the most bizarre and hilarious moments that I have ever witnessed.

That was the beginning of a strange but wonderfully enjoyable evening that saw us bounce from blackjack to roulette to craps and finally back to blackjack as we approached the wee hours of the morning. Beth and Karen decide to turn in around 1:00 a.m. but the rest of the crew stayed behind still embracing all the activities. Finally, about 3:00 a.m., we all had enough; and after cashing in our chips at the redemption window, we headed for the elevators.

It was then, however, that I noticed some stirring over by the Sportsbook and told the boys that I was going to walk over and check it out for a minute. Two of them said good night and continued to go upstairs while the other said he would join me to see what was up. Upon our arrival at the entrance to the betting parlor, we realized that they had begun to post the odds for the action that was taking place later that day. We commandeered two comfortable armchairs, settled in quietly, and eagerly watched as the numbers illuminated on the Big Board. The place was dead silent except for a few faint and far-off voices, and as I turned to consult with my buddy to get his take on the first few lines, I heard some low gambling snores and saw that he was fast asleep. I sat back pensively, reflected on all that had occurred the past few days, and tried to comprehend where I was and where I was going. For some unknown reason, I actually felt comfortable, and I figured I was truly in the place where I was supposed to be. So I took a sip from my drink, glanced back at the board, and turned my focus and attention back to the March Madness.

CHAPTER 9

Southern Hospitality

Saturday

IT WAS ANOTHER BRIGHT AND sparkling spring morning across the desert. Thankfully, we were all able to sleep in today as the games were not getting into full swing until around noon local time. The clock read 10:03 a.m. as I made my way into the dining room to peruse the room service menu and to order breakfast for Beth and me. Coffee was a necessity as well as an ample supply of sweetener. In addition, I knew that Beth would require something substantial to eat as she always had a hearty appetite in the morning. Come to think of it, she had a hearty appetite all the time, and that was just another nuance of her being that intrigued me and made me love her even more.

The selection of breakfast goodies was quite voluminous, and I decided to order a number of things so that we could share them all and also so that Beth would have a nice variety to choose from. I pushed the button on the phone marked "Room Service" and placed the order as I knew that it would take a while for the food to be delivered and that I would have plenty of time to rouse Beth. With the first task of the day already completed, I headed back toward the bedroom and heard Beth stirring. As I approached, she contorted her body in a huge stretching motion and mumbled, "Hey, baby, what are you doing over there?" "Breakfast," I answered. "It will be about forty-five minutes, so you still have time to rest." "Excellent," she replied groggily. "Wake me when it gets here." And then she rolled over and continued to doze.

I smiled at her amorously and then decided that since I had some time to kill, I would review the game-day schedule and the odds while enjoying a morning "wake and bake" to get the juices flowing. For me, there was nothing better than starting my day with a relaxing smoke, and if coupled with a strong cup of joe or large iced coffee, the yin and yang effects of the THC mixing with caffeine really created a breakfast of champions. However, since I knew it would be a few minutes before the coffee arrived, I settled for a short bourbon with a splash of ginger ale just to have something to sip on. The cool vapor rose from the water pipe and infiltrated my lungs as I inhaled slowly and steadily. Then when the bourbon cascaded down the back of my throat, refreshing and burning my insides all at once, I was ready to tackle the day.

The great carmaker, entrepreneur, and well-known bigot Henry Ford was quoted as saying, "Business and booze are enemies." He would later profess that "brains and initiative are dulled by even the casual use of alcohol...sloth and impropriety are a drinker's best friends." While I hated to disagree with Mr. Ford, I had to on this occasion because without my morning indulgences, my brain would remain stagnant and would not allow me to function on a coherent working level. But once my body either received the nectar of the gods or felt the billows of smoke wafting through my head, then and only then was I able to awaken from my dormancy.

After a few more tokes on the pipe and another splash of Maker's Mark over ice, I began to make some notations and to jot down my initial thoughts regarding the day's options. Luckily, there were only eight games to be played today rather than the sixteen games that were contested on both Thursday and Friday so my focus could be somewhat more concentrated. I first eliminated the games that were "nonpayable" for various reasons, which left me only five remaining possible waging opportunities. Then I reexamined my previous data which eliminated a couple of more teams from the mix; and there-fore, when the smoke cleared, both literally and figuratively, I was left with three possible scenarios. Not bad for a few minutes' work.

It was just then that I was distracted by some noises in the bedroom, and when I got up and peered inside, I saw that Beth was awake and that she had already made her way to the bathroom. A loud knock on the door refocused my attention, and a voice from the outside hallway bellowed, "Room service." I quickly answered the door, showed the waiter in, and cleared my papers off the table so he could set the lavish feast down appropriately. As he began to unload the trays from the pushcart, the smells filled the room, and I heard my stomach growl in anticipation. He uncovered each plate one at a time and announced its contents, "Bagel with lop and all the fixings, well-done mozzarella cheese omelet with well-done home fries and well-done sausage links. French toast with warm maple syrup, assorted muffins and pastries, coffee with cream and extra sweeteners, and finally one large orange juice. It was truly a real smorgasbord, and as I quickly surveyed the contents on the table, I knew that Beth would be happy. "Anything else today, sir?" the waiter queried. I glanced over the items again and answered, "Nope. I think you've got it all. Job well done. Thank you." And with that, breakfast was served.

Just as I started pouring myself a cup of hot, steamy coffee, the bedroom door swung open, and there was Beth standing stark naked, looking as gorgeous as ever. "See anything you like?" she asked, but before I could even answer, she shot back, "I do—breakfast!" She bounded over toward the table, kissed me hard on the lips, jumped onto an empty chair, and placed a napkin daintily on her lap. "Feed me," she whimpered, all helpless and needy. "Aren't you going to put something on first? This is a respectable place," I asked, puzzled. "Nah, this way, whatever I spill on myself, you can just lick off after." That one was a tough to argue with. So what also could I do but pour the coffee, take my seat, and commence to feed the attentive, hungry, and stunning bare goddess sitting before me. It was by far the best breakfast in my entire life, and the food wasn't bad either.

Once we were finished, and since Beth was already naked, I asked her to join me in the spacious steam shower so that we could get cleaned up. When I explained to her that my intentions were purely wholesome, she pouted, exclaimed, "Forget it then," and then darted away from the table and into the bedroom. I disrobed immediately, hurried past her into the marble-and-gold-encrusted glass enclosure—which was big enough for me, Beth, Karen, and the entire crew combined—and waited for her to join me. We shared a very private, tender, and intimate time together that morning. It was a moment that I will never forget. I stroked her hair, washed her silky, smooth tan skin, kissed her passionately, and caressed her with all my heart in an expression of sheer, unadulterated love that had previously seemed unfathomable to me. We didn't make love in the shower that morning, but I have never felt closer to another person in my entire life than I did that day with Beth. We were two kindred souls, and our strong attachment and warm affection for each other was truly undeniable.

If the rest of the day played out anything like this morning, I was surely in for the ride of my life. After toweling off and getting dressed, Beth called Karen to check in on her, and I went to make my daily morning call to Jack, which was late, but better late than never. Jack informed me that he was fortunate enough, with some help from his pal Ernie whom I mentioned earlier ran the Sportsbook at our next destination, to obtain a two-bedroom suite for Beth and me as well as a separate single room for Karen just down the hall from us. That was a perfect scenario as the boys could utilize the extra bedroom in our suite for all their necessities without disturbing Beth and me, nor intruding on our privacy in any way. The plan was set and already in motion, and I had an exhilarating yet internal calmness come over me that had been alluding me in recent days. I could sense Beth's excitement as well as I knew she loved staying at this particular venue as it was our usual stomping grounds whenever we traveled out West together, and it held a special place in our hearts. We glanced at each other amorously yet again as we packed our belongings into our bags and contemplated the next chapter in our adventure.

The new hotel we were departing to was not located on the strip but rather was five miles due south on the interstate. I knew the trip would not take long; however, with the traffic on a busy Saturday afternoon, you never knew what to expect. I arranged for a limo to pick us up at 2:30 as check-in time was generally around 3:00 p.m.

After packing basically all that we could for the time being, Beth said that she was going to go help Karen get organized and that she would be back no later than 1:30 p.m. I checked the clock. which read 12:18 p.m. and blew her a kiss as she strutted out the door. I had a little over an hour to kill before her return. which was just enough time to recreate my buzz, review my game notes again, and place a few wagers with Jack.

As I began to load a monstrous bowl of weed into the pipe, I remembered that I still had to retrieve and listen to the messages on the room phone in case there was something urgent. Upon review, there were three messages left: Karen's, the front desk's, and Romeo's. Naturally, I skipped over both Karen's and the front desk's and went directly to Romeo's. "Good morning, brother," It began. "I know that you are heading south today, so since you won't be right next door any longer I will stop by before you leave to give you some parting gifts and to square up all of our accounts. Let me know if that doesn't work for you. Otherwise, I will be at your place at 1:00 p.m. sharp. Ciao." Thanks goodness for Romeo, I thought. I had totally forgotten about the other products he was still holding for me and also to allot a few minutes for the checkout process, but I knew that we would still have plenty of time to account for everything. Some he would be here shortly. I quickly listened to the other messages and then went back into the dining room, pipe in hand, to contemplate my final wagering selections for the day.

The first two games had already tipped off and were approaching the half, so I turned on the TV to view the halftime show with the hope of catching some late breaking news or necessary information. My attention was directed toward two of the later games in particular where I noticed that the totals seemed somewhat awry. I calculated what my wagers should be on each of these contests and then made a few calls to see where the numbers currently stood. While I knew that Jack would already be swamped by now, I texted him my thoughts and waited for a response. His answer came back faster that I had anticipated and was positive on all accounts. Accordingly, I asked him to place $5K on the first game and $10K on the second so that I could get in at the present figures and lock up my position.

Several texts came back stating, "Got it," and then "You're in, my boy," followed by, "Good luck," and finally, "Call me around 3:00 p.m." I responded, "10–4," and thanked him appreciatively for all his help. With yet another task completed, I had nothing left to do except wait for Romeo to arrive, so I sauntered over the bar and prepared cocktails for us both in anticipation of his arrival.

Romeo arrived a few minutes later, goodie bag in hand, and I greeted him with the pipe and a rum-based cocktail which I knew he preferred more than bourbon. We toasted, toked on the pipe, and then discussed the day's action as we intently watched the ongoing game activity. As he peered around the room during a time-out, he noticed all the gift baskets and sarcastically asked, "What, did you get engaged last night and forget to tell me?" I laughed and replied, "Not to my knowledge," and then continued, "They are just gifts from my admirers." "Admirers!" he screamed. "To the victor go the spoils," I replied. "And 9–2 certainly deserves at least some booze and cheese, no?" He smiled, raised his glass in salute, and proclaimed, "Absolutely. Hail to the chief!" I told him to pick out a few things that he could use as I wasn't planning on shipping all the presents over the new hotel. He thanked me, and we both rummaged through the baskets and selected an item or two to our liking and then just stacked the rest of the stuff neatly on the far end of the table. I thought that I would offer the remaining assortment to Beth, Karen, or the crew, and then whatever was left over I would just leave for the hotel staff, along with a nice, hefty gratuity. After a few more minutes of smoking and drinking, Romeo said that he had to run and that, unfortunately, he probably would not be able to see me later as it was Saturday night, and he had other plans. "I'll catch up with you tomorrow at some point," he said as he departed and wished me luck as he scrambled out the door.

"You too," I bellowed back. "And what about squaring the bill?" "Tomorrow, no worries," I heard faintly, and then he was gone.

Soon after, Beth returned with Karen; and as I appeared from the bedroom, I noticed Karen's luggage in the doorway, which I took as a sign that they were ready to roll. I walked over and gave Beth a big smooch, greeted Karen, and asked if I could get either of them anything. They both responded that they were good, and as I turned back toward the bedroom, I told them that I was almost finished packing and that the car would be downstairs shortly to drive us over. I called down to the concierge desk and asked them to send up a bellhop for our baggage and also to ensure that our side would be waiting. With that, I completed one last final inspection of both the bathroom and the boudoir to make sure no evidence was left behind and that I had removed all of our necessities. All seemed to be accounted for and in order, so I wheeled the suitcases out into the main room and over to the entranceway. The girls had crashed on the couches and seemed a bit melancholy. "Who died?" I asked as I went to pour myself yet another beverage.

Neither of them reacted immediately, but then Karen replied, "It's nothing really… I just had a fight with Jeffrey, that's all." "He's an asshole," Beth chimed in as she stood up and came toward me. I had only met Jeffrey on a couple of occasions, and while I did not know him that well, he didn't seem to be much of a husband or part- ner to Karen. When Beth reached me, she threw her arms around me and gave me a big hug as she whispered in my ear, "Not all men are as handsome and charming as you are, my love." I smiled at her and then turned to Karen and proclaimed, "Well, I hope the day of pam- pering and pleasure that I have planned for you guys will ease your pain somewhat." "Oh yeah," she said. "Do tell." "Yeah, do tell," Beth added enthusiastically. "What? And spoil the surprise," I remarked coyly. "My lips are sealed for now." And as they conferenced together trying to imagine what I had planned for them, I saw that both their moods had changed and begun to lighten. I realized then that I had better come up with something fabulous, and quickly, or my prover- bial goose would be cooked.

The checkout box process was a breeze, and I was barely away from the group for five minutes as they conjugated and chatted out front by the vehicle-pickup station. I sent a text to Jack letting him know that we were departing momentarily, and he wrote back, "Great. Remember to call me at 3:00 p.m.… I will be awaiting your call…TTYL." I took a couple of deep breaths just to steady myself. I was still a bit tight from my meeting with Romeo and then joined the others outside. As the stretch limo pulled in and the group began to file inside, I reflected back on the past four days and all the fun and excitement that I had experienced. However, as I ducked my head and entered the chariot, an eerie and foreboding feeling encompassed me, and I wondered if I would be able to accomplish all the goals that I planned for the next few days to come. Would I have the courage to go through with it all? That was really the only question still remaining.

I chose neither to disclose Romeo's earlier visit to Beth nor his delivery of my care package as I thought that she would not approve of these antics. While she rarely lectured me or even confronted me regarding my drinking and other incendiary activities, I did not believe that full disclosure was necessary. After all, it was one thing to enjoy a cocktail or a smoke in a cordial setting among friends, but it was something else entirely scheduling clandestine rendezvous in order to get plastered or to get my fix on. No, Beth needed to be spared some of the gory details of my ongoing alcohol and drug abuse until the penultimate hammer had fallen. Besides, it was much easier not to tell than to continue to try and explain away certain events through the use of guile or blatant untruths. There was no reason to start sending up flares now to alert her to my impending doom; she would know all about it soon enough.

You could easily spot the glittering destination as we made our approach from the highway. The casino stood majestically against the backdrop of the surrounding desert and the far-off mountains. The recently completed southwestern-style motif hotel catered to both local residents and, even more so, to the rich and fortunate clientele which it drew from the neighboring states. The down-to-earth and comfortable atmosphere was the perfect setting for Beth and me as the stress and nonsense of the East Coast mentality was scarce at this venue. While it may have lacked some of the decadence and extravagance of the megahotels on the strip, its quaint and homey charm and allure was quite intoxicating. Not only did it possess an arcade and bowling alley for some wholesome fun, it also contained a multiplex cinema and a five-star spa and salon right on the premises. The outdoor pool area and facilities were small in comparison to many other locations, but what they lacked in size, they made up for in both appearance and ambiance.

In addition, and perhaps most importantly to me, the Sports Book arena was easily one of the best facilities in the entire world. The large amphitheater setting and numerous wagering stations made it a true gambler's paradise. Furthermore, since the Sports Book and Race Book were separate entities, yet next to each other in the great hall, the crowds were never overwhelming, and traffic was able to flow freely. There were also several restaurants and watering holes scattered throughout the general vicinity and even an old-world hot-dog vending cart where you could purchase a dog with all the trimmings for just seventy-five cents. It was an old-school joint with old-school charm and values where serious gaming enthusiasts could kick back and enjoy the day without feeling like they were imposing upon anyone. And besides all that, I was treated like a royalty due to Jack's involvement and contacts therein, and I never got tired of hearing, "Any friend of Jack's is a friend of ours. What can we do for you?" Some things never get old.

After we arrived and disembarked from the limo, I hurried quickly inside and headed directly over to the VIP check-in desk. I stood calmly trying to decide how I would handle the initial dialogue at the counter and whose name I would drop first, Jack's or Ernie's. However, once I gave my name to the young teenage-looking girl who came over to assist me, she immediately excused herself, and the more matronly-looking guest relations manager took over. "Ah yes, good afternoon. We have been expecting you," she espoused professionally. "Wonderful," I replied. "I hope that all is in order." "It is now," she remarked. "But Mr. Ernie had to pull some last-minute strings in order to accommodate your requests." "Really? Well then, I guess I will have to make sure that I thank him for his efforts later when we are reminiscing about old times," I answered flippantly. She glanced up at me at that point, and I smiled confidently back at her. I knew from that moment on that we understood each other. Bashfully, she reviewed all the arrangements one by one, which of course were all complimentary; and when she finished, she asked if there was anything else that she could assist with me. Seizing the moment and sensing her discomfort, I said, "Well, since you asked, I could use some help scheduling some salon and spa treatments for my companions. I hope you can find some availability sometime this afternoon." As her complexion began to whiten and a lump the size of a man's Adam's apple formed in her throat, she dialed the phone and asked for someone named Stephanie. After conversing for a few minutes, she redirected her attention toward me and pronounced, "It won't be a problem, sir. Just stop by the spa and ask for Stephanie, and she will satisfy your needs." It sounded a bit provocative, but I got the message. I thanked her for her diligent work and told her to have a good day and to keep smiling and then left to find the others.

Upon returning to the lobby, neither the girls nor the crew could be located. Rather than getting jumpy or pissed off, I decide to call Jack but then quickly realized that it was only 2:30 p.m. I certainly knew better than to try and reach him earlier than requested and with four games tipping off between 2:15 p.m. and 2:50 p.m. he was sure to be preoccupied. Instead, I decided to strike while the iron was still hot and make my way over to the spa to find Stephanie.

The fragrant aromas, atonal music, and peaceful aura stimulated my senses immediately as I entered the meticulous salon. There were beautiful people everywhere, and I was greeted by two stunning young gals who welcomed me and handed me a bottle of pure mineral water. "Thank you," I remarked. "I'm looking for Stephanie. I believe she is expecting me." "Let me see if she is available," one of the girls replied. "Just give me a moment." As she departed behind a large etched glass door, I browsed around the shop, eyeing all the "scenery" while pretending to be focused on the various products that they had scattered about the display shelves. An older, more sophisticated woman then approached me and announced, "Good afternoon, sir. I am Stephanie. How may I assist you?" I was initially startled by her grace and beauty, but once I regained composure, I was able to elicit my manners and charm and explain to her my predicament. Once she heard my tale of woe, she nodded and replied, "You must be Ernie's friend from New York. I was told to accommodate you in any way possible. So your problem is solved. Please join me over at the desk." "Stephanie," I answered, "I think I've fallen in love with you already." "Really?" She smirked back. "That's wonderful, but I guess that I will have to wait in line behind… I'm sorry, what were their names again, Beth and Karen?" *Wait!* I thought to myself. *Brains, beauty, and a quick wit too—perhaps I should consider this?* Thankfully, that fleeting thought evaporated from my mind quickly and all I could do was laugh at her response and reply, "Touché!"

Stephanie led me over to the private booking area to schedule the appointments, and she had already blocked out a three-hour time slot for each of the girls so that they could receive massages, facials, and waxing. She also said that they would experience all the perks and extras that any noteworthy guest would be entitled to. "That sounds great," I replied. "Thanks so much for all of your help." "The pleasure is all mine," she responded flirtatiously. "Please put all the charges and fees on my room account," I added, "as well as a generous gratuity." "That's quite gracious of you. Give me a second to total everything up, and then I'll be right back," she answered. As she sashayed away, it was impossible not to be struck by her incredibly erotic manner and feminine duplicity. It was obvious that I had some questions for Ernie at this point, not necessarily to act upon but at least to satisfy my manly nature.

When she returned a few minutes later, she handed me a receipt for my signature and informed me that the hotel had picked up the tab for Beth's services and that she had added a 30 percent gratuity to the bill based on the full costs. "Very good," I said overly enthusiastically, and then when our hands touched momentarily, we looked up at each other and shared an awkward moment of poignant silence. There certainly was some chemistry between us, and she was undeniably attractive, but this was clearly neither the place nor the time for any diversions. Thankfully, one of the other employees called out her name, and the tension was broken. I quickly signed the chit, snatched my water bottle, and hurried off to the exit. I heard a faint voice behind me call out, "It was really a pleasure meeting you. And don't worry, I will take good care of them." And with that, the door closed shut behind me.

My heart was still racing as I made my way back to the casino floor. My cell phone then began to vibrate, and of course, it was

Beth, and not a second too early. "Hey," I exclaimed, "where are you at, baby?" "Having a cocktail at the piano bar with Karen. Where are you?" "On my way over now," came my reply. "I just need to talk to Ernie for a minute first." "Okay, baby," she said with anticipation. "But don't keep me waiting too long. You know how jealous I get." I swallowed harshly, almost choking on my words, but did managed to say, "Just give me ten minutes, promise."

I hastened over to the gaming parlor to find Ernie and spotted my crew assembled under the large incandescent odds boards that loomed above the betting windows. As I approached farther, I noticed Ernie just outside of the large back office talking to one of his flunkies. He observed me coming toward him and stealthy moved behind the betting clerks to greet me at the vacant far end of the counter. It was great seeing Ernie again, and we shook hands and patted each other on the back like old friends do. I thanked him for his assistance in making all the necessary arrangements and asked him if I could treat him to dinner in order to show my appreciation. "Let's see how the day plays out," he said heartily, and then he reached into a drawer and pulled out what appeared to be an oversized deck of cards. "These are for you and your buddies," he announced. "Go have some fun and touch base with me later." I looked closer at the stack of cards and realized that they were not, in fact, playing cards but rather dozens of free-drinks coupons for the in-house bars and lounges located throughout the casino. "Be careful with those," he instructed and then raised his hand in a farewell salute and headed back to the office.

It was imminently approaching 3:00 p.m. as I started for the piano bar to locate Beth and Karen. I stopped momentarily to try and text Jack but received no reply, so I continued my trek across the busy hotel lobby. Beth's laugh could be heard resonating from inside the bar, and I snuck up behind her and embraced her fondly. "Hey, handsome, I thought you got lost," she said cheerfully. "Just taking care of some business," I casually replied. "What have you been up to?" "What you see is what you got—oh, and I ordered you a bourbon and a tequila shot since I know you love them," she teased back. "Perfect, just what I always wanted," I remarked. She pouted and responded somberly, "But I thought I was what you always wanted, darling." We chuckled together, kissed passionately, and then joined with Karen in downing the shots. "You two are really too cute," Karen chimed in, and then she began asking questions about the hotel and what our plans were for the rest of the day and evening.

I gave her a brief synopsis of the hotel's history, including both Jack's and Ernie's involvement therein, but then interjected that they had better get going if they were going to be able to keep their 4:00 p.m. engagements. Simultaneously, they turned, dumbfounded, and I followed by bellowing, "You don't want to keep Stephanie waiting. She is expecting you at the spa at 3:45 p.m. sharp." "Stephanie? The spa?" Beth muttered inquisitively. "Of course," I boasted proudly. "And I suggest you finish up here and head upstairs expeditiously so that you can get changed and properly prepared. I will have the luggage brought up instantly. I hope you enjoy yourselves." "I know you were up to something," Beth shouted, continuing, "You never cease to amaze me, my love." And with that, I received a long, affectionate kiss from Beth, as well as a thank-you and a peck on the cheek from Karen and then watched as they giggled and pranced off like two schoolgirls. I felt a sense of inner pride and elation for a good deed well done but then realized that perhaps my motives and intentions were not entirely pure. Either way, I rationalized, I had still done a virtuous act regardless of my objective, and it was time to reward myself.

After I proceeded to finish the drinks on the bar, including the ones the girls had left behind, the butterflies began to flutter in my stomach as I projected about the hours ahead. Armed with the countless amount of free-drink tickets in my pocket and still possessing an air of conceit, I stepped outside briefly to check my phone for any important messages and also to find a bellhop who could ensure that our bags would be speedily delivered upstairs and without any delay. I discovered a very professional-looking chap, handed him the luggage receipts, along with a hefty tip, and he confirmed that he could personally handle my request. "Certainly, sir, right away. I'm on it," he professed confidently. "Very good," I replied. "And please remind the ladies in the suite to move their cute little asses. They have an engagement to keep." "*Sir?*" he implored hesitantly. "Just tell them to try and be on time," I reiterated and passed him another large bill as I ducked back inside.

Now, finally, it was time to reap the benefits for all of my kindness and generosity. The boys were easy to spot as they had secured some prime real estate at the main sports bar and were already whooping it up. "Gentlemen," I proclaimed as I joined the commotion, "let the games and the antics begin." "You're too late," came back they reply. "We've started without you, and we are already on our way." "Well then, I better catch up. Perhaps these will help," I uttered as I tossed the drink cards out onto the table. They roared with delight as they collected them up, and calls for more drinks crescendoed throughout the barroom. "More anything?" one of them asked rhetorically, pausing and then continuing, "More everything!" It was obvious that the boys were pumped up and raring to go, and since I shared their zest and enthusiasm, it was clear that we were all in for a long day of tomfoolery.

As the drinking intensified, I felt my mind and body altering and morphing into my alter ego: the life of the party, the go-to guy, the man. Moreover, I was the leader of our little posse and the one with all the contacts and gaming knowledge, so I was entitled to the praise and kudos. So as my ego and sense of importance swelled, so did the amount that I drank, and once again I was off to the races. This was a pattern I knew far too well, and as the vicious cycle progressed and the hours flew by, I was lonesome once again to battle my inner demons. I was portraying my ongoing role in the production of life and continually perpetuating the adverse behavior that would elicit my downfall. As the great bard William Shakespeare penned in his classic play *As You Like It*, "All the world's a stage, and all the men and women merely players. They have their exits and entrances, and one man in his time plays many parts."

I was tired of playing my part, tired of the daily self-inflicted abuse, and most importantly, tired of the weak, empty, malevolent coward that I had become. I sensed that my ultimate exit was approaching rapidly, that the show needed to be cancelled. And I owed all of this to my vices and addictions, or so I thought. I had no concept that these were just the symptoms of my underlying malaise and therefore had no inkling that there could be either a cure or solution to my despair. Accordingly, I surrounded myself with those colleagues of mine, the action, the booze, and the drugs since they were the only friends that I could actually count on during my times of need. They were the things that were keeping me alive. So when I finally did realize that these comrades of mine were betraying me and were, in fact, the Brutus to my Caesar, that truly was "the unkindest cut of all." Henry Ford was correct when he stated, "Alcohol is the greatest enemy of self-control… Liquor channels energy in all the wrong directions and tempts the imbiber into improper behavior that they would otherwise not do… It is the greatest destroyer of character." Thus, as I stood there dousing my soul with drink after drink, trying to contemplate my next move, I understood that both my hand and role had already played out and that it was time to fold.

CHAPTER 10

The Buck Stops Here

May 2014

IT IS TRULY AMAZING THE education that you can receive while in jail. Unfortunately, however, the practical usage for this knowledge is strictly limited, and often you actually learn more than you need to know. The county correctional center where I was detained is located within one of the wealthiest counties in the nation. Yet if you ever spent any time incarcerated therein, you would think it was situated in a third-world country. The magnitude of the human rights violations which occurred on a daily basis was absolutely mind-boggling, and once they became more and more dire, I had to take certain actions. Of course, prior to initiating any sort of rebellion, I always referred to the jailhouse-issued "inmate handbook," circa 2010, in order to familiarize myself with the proper procedures. While at first I found the handbook somewhat informative, later on, it clearly proved to be a work of fiction and just a smoke screen for the masses.

Each new incoming prisoner was to receive a copy of the inmate standards of conduct upon his admittance and processing into the county prison system. The first dozen or so pages contained the sections relating to "rights" and "services" that would be provided to the inmate population at large. The remainder of the booklet focused entirely on the disciplinary consequences convicts would incur if they violated one of the ninety-two rules and regulations listed therein. The rules ranged from attempted arson to possession of contraband, to littering, to weapon making. Now, while it is evident that certain strict guidelines need to be in place in order to govern the prison setting, it should also be evident that the enforcement of such guidelines should be uniform in nature rather than arbitrary or capricious. This patent distinction was truly the most imposing obstacle in maintaining order and decorum within the stone walls.

As it turned out, most of the lies, deceptions, and common everyday abuses stemmed from the same issue: the almighty dollar, or more correctly speaking, the lack of it. Apparently, the correctional center was equipped with a yearly budget which was derived primarily from taxes, subsidies, and other so-called programs. It was the task of the county's appointed sheriff and his Sheriff's Department to handle the day-to-day operation of the jail and also to manage the annual budget. And while I am quite sure that it is an arduous job to run such a large enterprise, perhaps it would be easier if the system was not fraught with sheer incompetence, blatant racism, and an overall insolent atmosphere. The abhorrent and inhumane behavior that the population was subjected to by the COs and other staff members amounted to no less than extortion and extreme misuse of power. Of course, there were exceptions, and many of the senior and properly trained officers did, in fact, conduct themselves in an appropriate manner. These, however, were the select few; and for every one of the "good cops," there were at least a handful of others who just "didn't get it."

Lack of funds or financial cuts were the excuses that you would hear from the officers whenever they actually engaged you in conversation. They were bitter and jaded concerning the governing and control of the complex, and unfortunately, they displaced their anger on the convicts rather than dealing with it constructively. The COs' labor union, the Correction Officers Benevolent Association, or COBA, had lost much its strength and vigor over the years; and therefore, the COs were left without proper representation themselves on many occasions. Contracts, raises, and benefit packages were at a standstill in their negotiations, and the constant impasses led to much of the discord within the rank and file. Naturally, a toxic state of affairs arose between the unhappy and unappreciated captors and their unruly and often uncooperative captives, who already had taken issue with a legal system that had undoubtedly failed them. This commingling of adversarial factions created a whirlwind of intolerance as well as a totally impractical system of operation.

Thus, the question became not whether or not I was going to take action but how and by what means available I was going to proceed. As a newcomer to the prison lifestyle, I certainly was not looking to cause any problems for myself; however, several injustices required immediate attention and had to be addressed. First and foremost were the passages in the handbook relating to personal clothing, uniforms, bedding, and the hygiene of those items, which were all listed under inmate "necessities." The subdivisions described what each inmate shall be issued upon either admittance to the jail or upon request by the individual. The basic list was comprised of two sheets, two pairs of underwear, two T-shirts, two prison uniforms, one pillow, one pillowcase, one blanket, and one air mattress. Initially, however, all that I actually received from the above roster was one uniform, one blanket, and one air mattress, that's it. None of the other promised clothing or basic essentials were afforded to me, and when I asked my fellow cons if this was the norm, the standard reply was, "Welcome to county."

Furthermore, yet another issue which sprung up was the opportunity to wash your prison uniform or "oranges." Since you were required to wear your oranges at all times, except when you were in your cell, it was impossible to get them cleaned because you did not have an available backup pair to wear in the interim. Accordingly, the proper etiquette and decorum outlines in the hygiene section of the handbook could not be adhered to due to this virtual predicament. These ongoing and universal hypocrisies infiltrated my daily routine until I found the proper format to combat them: "the inmate grievance process," which I was hopeful could yield some productive results.

The grievance program was created to provide the populace with a mechanism to voice their complaints in a meaningful fashion. The ultimate goal was to resolve any and all gripes in a timely manner. Basically, the first step was to accurately complete an official grievance form, and then forward it onto the Grievance Unit via internal jailhouse mail. However, any request which was either too vague or failed to clearly set forth the required supporting evidence or information would be returned as insufficient. If, on the other hand, your form was accepted, then within five business days, a grievance coordinator would issue his findings, including the specific facts and circumstances underlying his determination. While this decision was viewed as being fair and unbiased, after reviewing several of these so-called impartial rulings, it was quite obvious that they were discriminatory in nature.

My first personal grievance experience occurred approximately two weeks into my bid and dealt specifically with the uniform and laundry issues that I mentioned earlier. Not only had I yet to be issued an extra set of oranges, but the washing machine in the cellblock was broken as well so you could not successfully launder your clothes even if you had the availability. Accordingly, I asked for and received the necessary grievance paperwork from the bubble, filled it out correctly, signed and dated it on the bottom, and sent it onward for examination. Within three days, I received a response in the mail acknowledging both the receipt of my grievance and also informing me that an appointed grievance investigator would be contacting me in the near future. I was shocked that the system seemingly worked, but my initial enthusiasm would begin to wane not too long thereafter.

After about a week, I was awakened one morning by a gentleman in plainclothes who appeared outside my gate and introduced himself as one of the grievance officers. While he appreciated my concerns and expressed a legitimate desire to remedy the situations, he apprised me that my grievance had been denied due to fiscal restrictions and budgeting cuts throughout the system. In spite of that, he did further explain that even though the jail was issuing only one uniform per inmate at the present time, he would follow up with regard to the laundry issue as that was a bona fide health and hygiene matter that needed to be rectified. Feeling somewhat discouraged but at least not ignored, I thanked him for his efforts and asked when he thought that I would hear from him again. He replied, "Hopefully sooner than later," and then he disappeared as quickly as he had emerged.

Astonishingly, a few days later, I was startled by the cry of "LAUNDRY CALL—bring out your laundry!" I jumped up and witnessed two officers wheeling in two large bins and carrying mesh laundry bags which were to be distributed to each prisoner in order for them to store their laundry pending collection. The bags were individually numbered to ensure the proper items were returned to the proper recipients, and when your cell was called, you were to bring your satchel down to the appropriate receptacle and then return to your cage. I quickly gathered up the few undergarments and socks which I needed to wash, but my uniform was still an obstacle. When my number was finally announced, I proceeded down the catwalk, deposited my clothes accordingly, and then addressed the officers. I rationally conveyed my dilemma regarding my lack of backup pair of oranges, but unfortunately I did not find a sympathetic ear. "Not my problem," was the response, followed by, "Put in a grievance if you have a problem." "I already did," I replied emphatically. "That's why you are here now!" And as soon as the words came out of my mouth, I knew that I had erred. "Oh… so it was because of you that I got my ass chewed out this morning. Thanks a lot, pal. I'll have to remember that." I timidly took a step back and kept the rest of my thoughts and displeasures to myself, but I learned a valuable lesson: restraint of pen and tongue goes a long way sometimes, especially in jail.

Eventually, I was able to obtain another shirt and then, later on, a second pair of pants which enabled me to rotate my daily attire and disinfect them when necessary. In addition, I learned how to utilize my sink and toilet in to wash my garments periodically and, in the evening, would hang them on a line so that they could dry overnight. Slowly, little by little, I began to gain some jailhouse knowledge and to think in survival mode. By asking questions and taking advice from my follow cons, my assimilation became easier and easier. While it certainly was a vast deviation from the comforts at home, I knew that the quicker I accepted things as they were, the sooner I would achieve some peace and serenity. It was time to start remembering and utilizing my recovery program even more as I had all the tools that I required right inside my head.

The next major injustice that had to be addressed was the inmate visitation allowance and the procedures which regulated the process. Pursuant to the pages listed in the handbook, all inmates were entitled to two one-hour visits each calendar week. The days and times of these sessions were also limited, and there were no visits allowed on either the weekends or any official county holidays. Of course, that in and of itself was prejudicial against those incarcerated as most of their friends and family members worked during the week and could only get to the jail on their days off or on the weekends. Furthermore, the actual feat of gaining access to the jail on the appointed days and the scheduled hours was so onerous and demeaning that many outsiders became disheartened by the whole treacherous ordeal.

About a month into my bid, I finally decided that enough was enough and penned my second formal grievance regarding the oppressive treatment being inflicted upon my innocent loved ones. At that time, I should have been granted a minimum of eight visits in total, yet only three of my visitors had gained access to the facility. In addition, often when Ann and The Prince made the trek over at the proper time, they were forced to wait hours on end only to be later informed that they would be unable to enter the jailhouse. The same fate was met by several of my friends and close associates, some of whom would arrive at 10:00 a.m. and stay until 3:00 p.m. in the designated "waiting area," which was actually just a large trailer possessing neither air-conditioning nor heat, and then be advised in a demeaning fashion that they would have to leave. This mistreatment and verbal abuse of innocent victims ran rampant throughout the visitation proceedings. These unfounded, unwarranted, and heinous activities inflicted by the COs were an utter and total disgrace. To treat blameless, ingenious citizens as criminals rather than the honest, hardworking, and law-abiding people that they were was truly an abomination. The jail staff, officers, sheriff, and even the county's elected officials should all be ashamed of themselves and also should be held accountable for their conduct.

On one specific occasion, after being held at bay for over three hours and completely overwhelmed and exhausted by the experience, Ann and The Prince were finally permitted entry. When I enthusiastically arrived from the housing area to great them, I could see the noticeable pain and displeasure on their faces. Even worse was the fact that less than ten of the possible seventy-five visiting stations were occupied, and yet the persecution and harassing behavior still persisted. Once again, I was rudely awakened to the harsh reality of how truly inhumane and callous the entire prison system was.

Ultimately, my complaints were summarily dismissed, and the only response that I received was a sealed correspondence containing the pertinent handbook pages regarding visitation and a one-sentence reply stating that I was still entitled to my requisite two weekly visits. With regard to the treatment of my family members, my pleas were ignored, and the only artificial handwritten comment was, and I quote, "Your family may contact the Sheriff's Department directly if they feel that they were mistreated." No apology, no empathy, nor any possible justification for their actions, nothing. Thus was the county correctional department's handling of problematic and dubious matters. It was just another display of the severe flaws that pervaded through the "big-house" dictatorship. Afterward, it was revealed to me that all this material law was a result of a lack of overtime being provided to the officers manning the visitation area and that their attitude and posture was a linear result of this deficiency in compensation. Avarice and the mighty dollar continued to rear its ugly head.

While these first two instances contained some indirect financial ramifications, the next few illustrations possess more inherent fiscal dimensions. In fact, all three of the next "inmate services" were such moneymakers that annual concealed bids were sought out from private independent outside vendors and carriers. The commissary outlet, the phone network, and the medical care contracts were all large for-profit operations which brought in significant revenue for the correction center. Agreements were negotiated generally on a yearly basis, and whichever contractor came in with the most beneficial package customarily won out. This was clearly apparent from the poor selections of items available from missionary, the subpar telephone service, and the ineptitude of the medical staff on a continuous basis.

The inmate exchange, better known as the commissary, was a storehouse of varying products which could be purchased by the inmate population. Commissary sheets were delivered to the convicts once a week, and they could pick and choose whichever items they desired as long as they had sufficient funds in their individual accounts to cover the expense. Once the sheets were completed and recollected, the goods would then be delivered by the commissary staff on a selected day later that week. The available purchase options ranged from candies, cakes, and snacks to stationery, to toiletry articles, to clothing, and finally to miscellaneous supplies. Unfortunately, the markup on just about every one of these selections was so highly exaggerated that many of the choices became prohibitive to buy. That, coupled with the meager generic quality of most of the offerings, made the possibilities seemingly unjustifiable. When the price of a ballpoint pen, which in actuality was just a three-inch flexible plastic implement that could barely write, was $1.00, and a ten-pack of Bic pens on the outside costs approximately $1.99 retail, then you can easily notice the disparity in pricing. These inequities dominated the entire list of provisions, but when your hands are tied and the commissary is the only store in town, what choice do you have?

Furthermore, the nutritional value of the food selections was far from desirable. The roster was basically comprised of sugary sweets and prepackaged pastries which were nothing more than wasted calories and excess glucose. Not a protein-based product was to be found, not even a can of tuna fish nor an assortment of nuts. The closest thing to a healthy treat was a small bag of wheat pretzels, but even those were coated with honey. While I assumed this was the norm for all the county jails in the neighboring areas, I was informed by some of the well-known recidivists that most of the other nearby detention centers not only had a better variety of goods available but also had much better values and even weekly sales in particular items. So apparently, yet again our caveat, the guidelines and regulations as listed on the commissary sheet also made it perfectly clear that "all prices were subject to change without notice…they reserved the right to limit quantities…and no refunds or exchanges would be permitted at anytime." I guess the old proverb of let the buyer beware prevailed at all times within the county lockup.

The archaic bank of pay phones, coupled with the antiquated calling methods that needed to be utilized, were the next bones of contention existing in the cellblock. There were five old-fashioned stall phones connected to one another, and they reminded me of the types that you would find a city street corner or an airport terminal during the 1980s. In fact, I hadn't even seen phones of this nature in at least a decade since they were finally removed from several of the local town and village parks near my home. The main problem, of course, was that both the internal hardware and technology were considerably outdated, and this created several hardships for the unaware users. Between the awful reception, daily mechanical mal-functions, and unexplained dropped calls, the process of making an outgoing connection was truly frustration.

Now if that wasn't bad enough, the Corrections Department made a bad situation even worse by devising calling system that both minimized the length of each communication while maximizing the profits for themselves. In order to initiate an outward transmission, a prepaid phone account needed to be established by the person accepting the call, and a series of numbers had to be punched into the keypad by the sender in order to validate the origination to said call. After all was confirmed and verified and the recipient had agreed to answer, not unlike the manner utilized for placing a collect call, you had five minutes to converse with a friend, lawyer, or loved one. Of course, any and all conversations were subject to scrutiny, recording, and further review by the powers that be, so you certainly needed to watch your p's and q's while conducting your dialogue.

The proverbial icing on the cake, however, were the outlandish charges that accumulated just of his five-minute interplay. In fact, a local intercountry telecommunication for the maximum amount of five minutes commonly cost about $5 or approximately a dollar per minute. This ludicrous price in today's day and age of phone negotiations and bargain contracts was not only exorbitant but was also bias toward those inmates who were indigent, had little, or no funds available to them. In addition, the licensed carrier and purveyor of the phone exchange also charged a hefty service fee at the inception of the account, thereby putting yet more funds into the greedy pockets of all involved and taking still more away from the interned. These monopolies and the control they wielded over the service commodities turned an unsettled situation into one of hatred and rebellion and only intensified the already stained atmosphere that existed.

The correctional center did, however, excel on one level: that was the employment of gross incompetents. This was no more apparent than by viewing the doctors, nurses, technicians, and other professional staffers who were cast to manage the prison's medical center. When I arrived at the jail, the sheriff was already on his third team of care providers in the last four years, and my understanding was that each one had been more inept and unprofessional than its predecessor. Not only had people perished due to the substandard treatment and overall indifferent and lackadaisical attitudes of the medics, but once again the sheriff was prostituting himself by peddling the prisoners' personal safety on the open market and seeking the sweetest deal possible rather than the proper quality of care. When the fiscal needs of an institution come ahead of the patients' health concerns, there are bound to be horrific results.

Unfortunately, due to my advancing age, my chronic type 2 diabetes, and a recent surgical procedure, I had the direct misfortune of dealing with the medical staff on a daily basis. Initially, I went passively through the motions and just followed the instructions that I was given; but after a few weeks' time, I began to notice that something had gone amiss. Furthermore, once I commenced to make inquiries regarding the medication that I was being prescribed, as well as the dosages, my chart was marked accordingly, and I was branded as an agitator. Then when I continued to ask to see the checklist of drugs that they were pumping me full of, the nurse not only refused to supply me with the pertinent information but instead informed me that I would have to put in a "sick call" request and speak to one of the doctors directly. I tried to think of this as progress and perhaps a step in the right direction—that was until I had the unfortunate pleasure of meeting Dr. Jumbabwe.

If I hadn't been in jail and could have displayed my crass, sarcastic nature, I would have asked the good doctor which prestigious third-world university he had procured his degree from. However, under the present circumstances, I chose to extract a certain degree of respect and to placate matters rather than exacerbating them. In spite of my amicable demeanor, our conversation began with "Dr. J" asking me if I was some kind of troublemaker who was looking for problems rather than his warm bedside manner. I sensed immediately that a confrontation was evident, yet I tried to keep myself in check and not to be baited by his adversarial remarks. In addition, his thick foreign accent and total butchery of the English language made his nonsensical rantings more humorous than threatening. This gentleman was clearly underqualified, undereducated, and understandably clueless when it came to the Hippocratic oath, yet he would be the one making the necessary health decisions for my life.

As time progressed, I realized that it was both difficult and debilitating to fight everyone and everything, and I learned to acquiesce to the pessimistic prison lifestyle. While it was true that prior to my incarceration my regular intake of prescription medication was two pills a day and now in jail I was consuming close to a dozen daily, it was easier to just accept my situation than to constantly rock the boat. The deck was stacked against me, and as I said earlier, the house—or in this case, the *big house*—always wins. Some days, however, were tougher than others; and when the malfeasance reared its ugly head with fervor, it was excruciatingly hard to stop, wait, and not react.

When a trained nurse examines a patient yet is still unable to provide even the most nominal of treatments—a Band-Aid, an aspirin, or even an ice pack—without first obtaining authorization, then the system is clearly flawed. Prisoners who are obviously either sick or injured should not have to wait days on end in order to gain some form of comfort or relief. Fortunately, I personally never experienced a severe medical condition which required immediate attention; for if I had, you might not be reading this now. And while some may consider this to be a grim accounting of the events that transpired, I can assure you that it was real then and that it still exists today. Actually it's quite ironic, for if the prison ever lost an inmate due to illness, they would only be hurting themselves by reducing their future profit margin and eliminating their chance for further remuneration.

The present recidivism rate at my particular correctional center is an astonishing 81 percent. That basically means that four out of every five inmates will be back in this facility at some time in the future, usually the near future. Evidently, not much "correcting" was going on behind these walls. In fact, just the opposite was occurring, and the system was perpetuating rather than alleviating the behaviors that put us here to begin with. After all, when the facility is operating at full capacity and all the beds are occupied, then profits rise, salaries get paid, and all involved can justify their existence. It's the same rationale that airlines and hotels utilize when they offer half-price fares to entice patrons to either fly or stay with them when they ordinarily might not. Perhaps the county should install websites such as "Jailocity" like Travelocity, or "Prisonline" like Priceline, or even "Incarcerations to Go" like Vacations to Go in order drum up more business and facilitate further criminal activity. This merry-go-round mentality that regurgitates convicts rather than rehabilitating them, along with the attitude of riches rather than recovery which only further promotes the need for more jails, prisons and detention centers, can no longer be tolerated.

Thankfully, my journey into repentance commenced long before my incarceration. Accordingly, I had more of an opportunity to utilize my knowledge and experience correctly than most of my comrades in arms who never had that chance for salvation. It is truly pathetic when the course of action employed is only influenced by the priced placed upon another person's head. We are all human beings, created in God's image and supposedly forgiven for our sins, so why then are we shunned and left as failures? Why? Because money talks and is the ultimate equalizer, and it has been that way ever since man was created.

CHAPTER 11

Back to the Future

Saturday evening

I HADN'T NOTICED THAT THE sun had begun to set behind the distant horizon until I ventured outside to get a breath of fresh air. For obvious tactical reasons, there are neither windows to view the sunlight nor clocks to keep track of time on the casino floors. This had been the case since the early days of Lansky and Siegel and the pioneers of the great desert haven who realized from the beginning that they needed to create the proper atmosphere in order to generate the greatest profits. It was the same logic which initiated the wage of chips rather than cash at the gaming tables, as well as the complimentary beverage service provided to those who were playing. Everything, and I mean everything, that exists in the realm of the casino exists for only one reason: specifically creating an advantage for the house. Perhaps it may be only the slightest of edges, but over the long run, even that miniscule benefit will reap extreme rewards. After all, as the saying goes, "The house always wins."

I bummed a cigarette off a cab driver who was out front waiting for a fare, and as we chatted about the lovely weather, he informed me that is was approximately 6:30 p.m. There were still two games being contested on the hardwood, but most of the action had already been decided. Our wagers for the day were a profitable 1–1 as we won our $10K bet but lost our $5K stake in the final seconds. The boys had been utterly enjoying their last few hours of debauchery and had no reason to slow down the pace as they all planned to collapse on their red-eye flights back to the East Coast. I, however, wasn't going anywhere and, in fact, had a wonderful evening planned for Karen, Beth, and myself. It just so happened that the '80s tribute band that Beth and I saw perform the previous year and totally loved was playing at 11:00 p.m. in the disco club, and I knew that we had to attend. The only issue was that the show was already sold out, and I would need to pull a few strings in order to achieve my goal. However, with Jack and Ernie as my allies, I knew that nothing was impossible and that they would work their magic and find a way to get us in.

My cell phone rang as I stomped out my cigarette butt, and when I scanned the number on the display, I realized that it was not one that I readily recognized. Therefore, rather than answering the call, I let it go directly to voice mail in case it was some interloper or other unwanted distraction. However, when the same number appeared again seconds later, I decided to tempt fate and pushed the call button. "Hey, baby, it's me," the enthusiastic voice cried out, and I immediately knew that it was my Beth. "The salon is marvelous," she continued and then went on to explain that she and Karen had just finished their treatments and that they were going to shower and wind down at the spa before heading back to the room. "Sounds like a plan," I answered. "Let's say in an hour upstairs then?" "Perfect," she replied. "I can't wait to see you and thank you for the awesome afternoon." "In that case, I will make sure that I am properly prepared," I quipped back and then blew her a kiss goodbye before hanging up.

With an hour at my disposal to get organized, I realized that there were several loose ends that still needed to be secured, including dinner reservations, transportation for the crew to the airport and of course Jack. The boys and I had nibbled throughout the day on various bar snacks, so I was far from hungry. However, I knew that the girls would be famished and that I had to account for their needs as well. Accordingly, I strolled back inside and made my way over to the guest service station. I was cheerfully greeted by a very helpful staff member who informed me about all of the new possible dinner options as they had recently added a number of new bistros. Once I got the skinny on the food, I also was able to arrange a ride for the boys, thereby killing two birds with one stone.

Feeling a sense of accomplishment, I decided to call Jack immediately thereafter in order to finalize the last of the evening's details. This time, he answered with a harried, "Hello, my boy," exhaled rapidly, and then professed, "I am still putting out a few fires over here, but I should be over there later on, say, around 9:30 p.m. I have to meet with Ernie too and review a few things. I'll call you from the car when I'm on my way. Is all well on your end?" "Just fine," I responded. "Take care of your business, and I will see you later, no worries." Calmer, he replied, "Thanks, my boy. See you then—oh, and eat without me," and then he was gone.

After contemplating all of my current options, I chose to reconnect with the crew for one last celebratory drink and farewell toast. I was showered with cheers, applause, and high fives as I made my return to the venue. The gratis drink coupons were all but gone, as were the boys themselves. As I surveyed the situation and recounted the day's events, I was really quite pleased how it all had played out. The trip was a great success. Everyone certainly enjoyed themselves, and my ultimate objective had yet to be derailed. So as we endured one more round of beverages, absorbing all the alcohol and toxins with fervor and all seemed right in the world, it dawned on me that this would be my final encounter with them all.

I departed the lounge area and began my trek up to the suite when I passed by the hotel's souvenir shop and found my way inside. I purchased a few supplies and sundries and also perused the aisles for a possible treat for Beth. Unfortunately, nothing struck my fancy; but knowing that Beth and Karen weren't scheduled to leave until midday tomorrow, I still had time to procure a parting gift for my betrothed. Not that the trip, the spa day, and all the other extra intangibles were not enough, I still felt the need to indulge myself one more time and find her that special something. However, the knickknacks available at the store were far too inadequate for such a grand gesture, so I needed to find another alternative.

With that thought still lurking in my mind, I approached the security checkpoint, revealed my credentials, and entered the platinum residential tower. I chatted briefly with the elevator guard as we soared upward to the twenty-second floor, and he held the door open for me as I exited the lift. "Have a wonderful night and an even better tomorrow," he suggested eagerly, and as I walked down the long corridor alone with my notions, I knew that I needed to heed his advice. The next twenty-four hours or so were going to be my last here on earth. After that, it was all a crapshoot.

Not surprisingly, I arrived back at the room prior to Beth, which allowed me to unpack my bags and also to prepare cocktails while I awaited her entrance. As soon as I heard her fumbling at the door, I rushed over to greet her and to shower her with affection. She dropped the package she was carrying, and we embraced and kissed tenderly for several minutes. Afterward, I led her over to the bar area where I had situated the drinks and laid out an assortment of chips and nuts. Beaming, she said, "I could get used to days like this." Apparently, Stephanie had gone all out to provide them with a truly unique encounter while extoling all of the kudos and praise upon me. "Whatever you said to or promised that woman," she smugly expounded, "I'm totally on board with if she is going to pamper me like!" "Really! I'll have to make a note of that," I gibed back at her, more playfully than antagonistically, and then I stuck my tongue out at her. "Hey, don't stick it out unless you intend to use it," she chided as she lifted herself up onto the counter. Sensing her arousal and always being the opportunist when dealing in carnal matters, I positioned myself between her legs and whispered, "You mean like this?" As I lowered myself to engulf her, she situated herself more securely, arched her back, and guided my head downward in unadulterated anticipation. I felt a stirring in my loins as she slowly gyrated around my tongue and mouth. She moaned in ecstasy as she reached her plateau over and over again until she wilted in exhausted delight.

I stood up, took a long swig of bourbon and then grasped a large ice cube between my teeth. As I swirled the ice around my mouth, completely numbing my tongue, I crouched back down to her still pulsating lips and began to flick my frigid tongue against her. She convulsed wildly and once again firmly grasped the back of my head, pulling me in toward her and suffocating me in her womanhood.

The intensity of her next climax was so erotically charged that I could no longer contain myself as all of my nerve endings were sent into high alert, and the rush of magnifying energy was uncontainable. I allowed myself to elicit the necessary release and gasped momentarily in excitement as my body quivered. I then refocused my attention back on Beth by kissing her luscious thighs and torso delicately and then finally resting my weary head onto her lap. She soothingly caressed my cheeks and face as I tried to stop trembling, and we remained there together, ever so close, basking in the moment.

Once I regained my strength, I cautiously scooped her up and carried her into the bedroom. Her eyes remained shut as I carefully placed her onto the bed, and she sighed peacefully and curled up among the pillows. While I fixated on her from above, I realized how pure and absolute our romance was. She saw me as no one else ever had. She unconditionally loved me; we were soul mates. I had been existing in a small chamber in my mind for far too long without ever understanding how to free myself. Beth not only set me free; she emancipated and liberated my body and spirit and allowed me to live and breathe again. She held my hand and directed me through to other side, and I cherished her for it. I had been empty and alone for as long as I could remember, but the sacred bond that now existed between us reincarnated me. She was my angel from above, my universe.

Understandably then, this itself was the crux of my dilemma. An inner struggle between right and wrong, good and evil, my Beth and my demons. It was impossible for me to fathom a true resolution for my difficulties as the hole had been dug far too deep. I had been living a lifestyle fraught with lies and misconceptions, which, if accurately revealed, would collapse my entire world around me. The schism between light and darkness was too profound. So while Beth's resolve was both powerful and enlightening, my self-deprecating and destructive nature had desecrated my essence beyond repair. I worshipped Beth with all my constitution, but even that could not offset the guilt, shame, and remorse that plagued me on a daily basis. The torment was crudely overwhelming. I could only perceive one way out: my way.

As Beth rested quietly on the bed, I stealthy hurried into the shower to remove all the evidence of our prior encounter. I felt invigorated and vibrant and couldn't wait to spend the rest of the night rejoicing in her splendor. Upon exiting the bathroom, I noticed Beth stirring a bit and imagined that she was having a good dream as a cute smile ran across her face. She aroused suddenly and, when she saw me looking at her, inquired vehemently, "Why am I going home tomorrow if you are staying until Monday?" She followed it up with, "Are you trying to get rid of me or something?" Startled, I stammered back, "What…me…no, why would I?" "Okay then, it's settled," she replied. "I'm changing my flight right now, and we will fly home together on Monday." "What about Karen?" I balked. "That's why you were leaving tomorrow, so you could fly back with her." "She'll be fine. She travels all the time for work, and she's used to traveling alone. Besides, she will probably sleep the whole flight anyway. Nope, I've made up my mind, baby. Case closed."

And with that, with Beth's sudden revelation, all of my meticulously laid plans and intentions were thwarted. I stood there in shock and disbelief as she called the airline to switch her itinerary. All the while, I was praying within that somehow her directive would fail. I had not accounted for this unprecedented deviation, and I felt my body temperature rising in severe angst. My solution, of course, was to retreat into the parlor room and locate my bottle of bourbon. As I began to pour myself a double, my level of panic escalated, and I knew that the liquor alone was not going to suffice. Accordingly, I strolled nonchalantly back into the bathroom and found my bottle of "relaxation pills," pulling out a couple before Beth could notice. "How's it going?" I asked calmly. "So far, so good, but I'm on hold at the moment," she responded. "Okay, I'll be inside relaxing if you need me," I said, seemingly unruffled, and then blew her a kiss and returned to my task at hand.

I tried restoring my breathing and heart rate back to some sense of normalcy by closing my eyes and putting my feet up on the ottoman, but the images flashing through my mind wouldn't allow it. All my scheming and cajoling these past few months was about to fly out the window in a matter of minutes due to this highly unpredictable last-second turn of events. My only hope was that the flight would be booked solid and that the airline would not be able to accommodate her. While I heard her chatting on the phone, I was unable to detect what was being said. However, when she entered the room all smiles, I knew that my fate had been irretrievably altered.

I immediately tried to lighten my mood and jovially asked, "So?" "All set, my dear," she answered magnanimously, and I could see that she was quite pleased and proud of herself. "Great," I replied. "I guess you better go tell Karen." "On my way to do that now," she boasted, continuing, "Oh, and then I need something to eat. I'm starving. Please pick a place for dinner. I'll be back soon." She then gave me a kiss on the forehead, ruffled my hair, and glided out the door.

Still in a state of bewilderment, I sat mystified, trying to recount how I could have allowed this calamity to occur. I had been so vigilant and precise regarding this most paramount of matters that it was inconceivable to me that it was now beyond my grasp. I obviously could not think of carrying out my goal with Beth present as that would be too traumatizing for everyone involved, especially her. No, I had been trapped in my own web of lies and deceit, and I would now have to wait before I could take any further action. I would have to grin and bear my failure and put on a "happy" face. I proceeded to the bedroom, washed my face with cold water, and dressed for the evening, thinking all the while, thank goodness Romeo brought me over the remainder of the "products" as I was undeniably going to need them now.

After finishing all my nightly preparations, I still had ample time to partake in some of the more potent dry goods that were at my disposal. If I couldn't get myself in the right frame of mind, then my narcotic friends would. "Better life through chemistry" had always been my motto, and it was time to take my own advice. By the time Beth returned, I was seated pensively in one of the oversized chairs, drink in hand, reading over my game notes for tomorrow. I appeared no worse for the wear, which was clearly my goal, and I was ready both mentally and physically for our night out on the town. I looked up at her and asked, "How'd she take it? Is all okay?" "Yeah, she took it better than I thought," she replied. "Although she did give me some grief and Italian guilt as I was leaving just for good measure." Beth continued by telling me that Karen seemed almost relieved by the news as she, Karen, could now just crash for the night and then catch up with her work on the plane ride back tomorrow. "So," Beth continued, "it's just you and me tonight cowboy, so you better strap on your…whatever and get ready for the ride." I wasn't sure how to process all of that information at once, but I did know this: we were both in for a night that neither of us would forget.

It was just before 9:00 p.m. when we found an intimate table in one of the bistros that had been recommended to me earlier. The menu possessed a nice variety of appetizers and small plates, which I knew was right up Beth's alley and also coincidentally had a vast selection of whiskeys, including several bourbons. The atmosphere was electric as the Saturday-night crowd was full of energy and optimism. Beth looked incredibly sexy in her leather miniskirt and matching boots, and when she got up and sauntered over to the bar to examine the tequila selections, I felt the eyes of every man in the room upon her. She asked the bartender if she could taste one particular brand, which she seemed to really enjoy, and then came back with a tray of shots in hand. "Try this," she insisted. "I think you might actually like this one!" "Can I chase it with some bourbon first?" I asked curtly, but then remembered my manners and that this was supposed to be our special night. So I followed up with, "Sorry, baby…tonight I will try whatever you like." Not realizing I had left the door wide open for her suggestive wit, I was smacked in the face with, "Great, I'll remember that later when we're in bed." Even she couldn't hold back her demeanor after that one, and we shared a contagious laugh with each other as we partook in the ritual of the shots.

The remainder of dinner was fun and carefree, and I mainly just watched Beth consume the elaborate dishes that were served while I focused on the flight of fine specialty Kentucky bourbons which I had smartly ordered. I checked my cell phone, which read 9:47 p.m. and also revealed that I missed several calls in the interim. Beth loathes it when I check my phone constantly during meals, so I had set it on mute and left it in my pants pocket. Three messages were retrieved, informing me respectively that our dinner and drinks had been paid for, compliments of Mr. Goodrich. I mumbled to myself, "Mr. Goodrich," trying to recall the name, but nothing registered in my mind. Beth shot me a disparaging look as I fiddled with the phone and asked apathetically if everything was all right. I filled her in on all the news and said that we should find Jack after we were finished eating. She nodded, fluttered her eyes at me, and then went back to her meal.

I supposed that we would find Jack with Ernie over by the Sports Book, so after dinner, we made our way across the casino and toward the grand theater. The tables were beginning to fill up as it was now after 10:00 p.m., and I also noticed that the table minimums had risen considerably as well. Saturday night was obviously the premier casino night of the week, and it was clear that the patrons were out in large numbers and were craving some action. I held Beth tightly around her waist as we maneuvered through the crowd, making sure that she was close by my side at all times. As we entered the Sports Palace, the scene thinned out considerably, and I saw Ernie out in front of the betting windows being interviewed by a well-dressed newsman.

We approached tactfully as not to disturb them, and when Ernie noticed us getting closer, he gave me a quick glance and held his hand and pointer finger to indicate that he needed a minute. I steered Beth sideways and directed her over to the "sheet" station which contained all the morning odds for tomorrow's action all mapped out on long eleven-by-fourteen-inch sheets of paper. We studied the games for a while and discussed whom we liked and didn't like and then heard a voice from behind us call out, "Well, well, well, what do we have here? The great prognosticator and his gorgeous partner in crime. Thank goodness the windows are closed for the night." It was Ernie, of course, and he and Beth embraced, exchanged a few pleasantries, and then began mocking me together mercilessly. As they joked and laughed it up at my expense, Jack arrived; and when they paused momentarily to greet him, he chimed in, "Please don't stop on my account. No one deserves a good taunting more than my boy here, regardless of his current winning streak." The three of them continued their antics for a few minutes until finally I responded sarcastically, "I didn't need to travel three thousand miles for this. I can get plenty of abuse back home." "Aw, poor baby," Beth consoled me and then held my cheeks in her hands and placed a long, wet kiss right on my lips. "Well, I guess that helps." I sighed. "But don't either of you two clowns try that," I directed at Ernie and Jack. "Pucker up," Ernie bellowed. "Tonight is your night, bro."

We continued to amuse ourselves by sharing a few more witty barbs, but then Ernie got called away for an instant, so the decision turned to the evening's events. "So what's on top for you guys tonight?" Jack inquired. "Our favorite '80s dance party at eleven," Beth replied. "And who knows what else after that?" She winked at me. I joined in quickly, "Yeah, we may need your assistance with the show, my boy, as it appears to be sold out." Jack chuckled. "Sold out…let's see what we can do about that. Give me a second." So with both Jack and Ernie off taking care of business, I seized the moment, pulling Beth close to me, staring into her sultry eyes, and telling her that I loved her more than life itself. It was a hungering, insatiable love that was impossible to express in words, mightily overwhelming yet pure and ingenious. The moment was eerily foreshadowing of me, and as I felt a tear well up in my eye, I hugged her with all my force, hanging on for dear life.

Jack reappeared and said that he had spoken with the night casino manager, who in the hierarchy of the gaming kingdom is second to no one but the actual hotel owner, and he told Jack to stop back and see him around 10:45 p.m. with regard to our admittance to tonight's performance. I glanced at Jack's watch and noticed that it was almost 10:30 p.m. So we didn't have long to wait. However, since Beth was getting a bit antsy, I suggested that we find a blackjack table and play a few hands to kill the time. We managed to find a $10 minimum table, which for a Saturday night was quite rare, and I pulled out $600 in order to purchase $200 worth of chips for each of us. Jack balked momentarily but acquiesced when I said, "Just a few hands…for fun." "Yeah," Beth joined in. "Loosen up a bit, Jack. After all, aren't you supposed to be like Mr. Vegas?" Jack smiled back at Beth and finally replied, "Sure, but only because it's with you two. Your wise-ass friend over there knows that I don't play table games anymore." "It's only a couple of hands," I remarked. "And besides, I staked you anyway!" "Not the point, my boy," he reminded me. "As you are well aware, but… I'm in, only on one condition." "What's that?" I said nervously. "All the winnings go to Beth," he demanded. "Where else would they go?" I responded flippantly, and with that, we all sat and began to conquer the felt.

After just a few hands, one of the pit bosses approached Jack and handed him a message. Jack read the piece of paper, nodded back in acknowledgement, and then informed us that we were being summoned. Beth turned to me, looking somewhat concerned, but I told her not to worry and to just go with the flow as Jack was a master of his craft. "Why doesn't he play table games any longer?" she whispered to me as we got up to leave. "It's a very long story," I answered back. "Remind me later."

I gathered up the chips, gave a nice tip to the dealer, and took Beth's hand as we followed Jack to our undisclosed destination. Between the main security center and the nightclub venue where the show was to take place stood a large, hulking older gentleman surrounded by a cluster of younger security officers, all of whom had feeds connected to their ears. "Jack," the man bellowed, "a pleasure as always." "No, no, the pleasure is all mine, Charlie," Jack answered respectfully. "Please meet my good friends from back East." Charlie clasped Beth's hands and welcomed her and then turned my way, saying, "Ahh, and this must be our resident bracketologist who is taking our town to the cleaners." We shook hands, and he continued, "Your reputation certainly precedes you, my friend. According to Ernie, you really put a dent in a few places this week, huh?" Trying to stay somewhat humble in front of this rather imposing figure of a man, I thanked him for his kind words and replied, "I learned everything I know from my friend and mentor right here," directing my attention toward Jack. "Data, discipline, and determination," I continued, "are the three Ds to success." "I like that." He nodded back. "You mind if I use it?" "It's all yours," I said, and with that, he gestured toward the club entrance.

It was quite the scene as the house security team led the four of us over the grand entranceway and cleared a path for us to proceed inside and over to the main ticket area. "This is where I say goodbye for the night," Jack exclaimed. "I have one more real busy day ahead of me tomorrow, and I need to get my rest. Charlie will take good care of you guys. Call me in the morning, my boy, and try to stay upright," he concluded. For Beth's sake, I let that last comment slide so as not to embarrass her in anyway and then gave Jack a big manly hug and thanked him for everything. Beth did the same in a more feminine style, adding a kiss, and then we followed Charlie into the dimly lit lounge.

The staff all came to attention when they saw Charlie tread closer, and he was greeted by a mature, matronly woman named Sarah, who seemed very eager to please him. "These are two friends of mine, and more importantly, two friends of Mr. Goodrich's," he clarified, "who should be accommodated with every generosity possible regarding tonight's concert." He then handed her two complimentary admission passes for the show and waited for her to stamp them and log them into the computer. "All set," she replied. "And where would they like to be seated, sir?" "Please call over Mr. Bruno for a moment so I can discuss that matter with him in more detail," he commanded. "I must return to the 'point' as soon as possible." While Charlie seemed a little impatient at this stage of the proceedings, he managed to keep a smile on his face and made some small talk as we awaited Mr. Bruno's arrival.

Beth then cautiously asked, "What's the point?" in response to Charlie's earlier comment, and while I chuckled inside to the double entendre, Charlie explained that the point was the nickname for the central surveillance office located above the casino floor. From that vantage point, the entire casino and surrounding areas could be viewed at once with just the push of a button. Just then, a slender dapper man with sharply defined features appeared and was introduced to us as the hotel's entertainment director, Mr. Bruno. He and Charlie talked together with great intent, all the while keeping their voices just low enough so that I was unable decipher the conversation. Beth turned to me in fascination and remarked, "All this nonsense for us?" She followed it up with, "Oh, and by the way, who is Mr. Goodrich?" I shrugged back bashfully as if to say, *Your guess is as good as mine*, but she wasn't buying my naiveté. She gave an antagonistic face in return, to which I responded, "Behave," which only added to her annoyance. Once finished with his conversation with Mr. Bruno, Charlie told us that he needed to return to his busy schedule, verified that all was in order, and explained that we were in good hands with Mr. Bruno. We thanked him for his benevolence and then watched as he left with his entourage. It was truly quite impressive.

The dance hall itself reminded me of an old 80s comedy club with long rows of narrow tables positioned perpendicularly to the stage, which was situated on the floor level below. There were also a few VIP tables located on the ground floor, as well as several secluded booths which were on a raised platform that encircled the outskirts of the large venue. Between the floor tables and the stage was an enormous dance area, as well as two tremendous bars which were located on each side of the stage respectively. While the stage and dance floor were well lit, it was rather dark throughout the rest of the theater. The crowd was young, loud, and enthusiastic; and although I was but surprised by the group dynamic for an '80s tribute band, figuring that there would be more people in attendance who actually lived through the decade, the vibe in the room was quite intoxicating. Beth shifted her position closer to me and tucked one of her hands into my rear pants pocket, which quickly got my attention. "Sorry," I said distractedly. "I was just checking out the scenery." "Scenery, huh? That's what you are calling them these days…scenery." "Baby," I replied apologetically, "you know I only have eyes for you. Besides, they are little girls, and you know that I prefer older and more experienced women." "Watch that older crap," she barked as she pinched my buttocks continuing, "And I prefer sophisticated or mature rather than older, make a note of that." "Yes, dear," I replied as we chuckled and embraced each other.

Right then, one of the security officers motioned to Mr. Bruno, who in turn guided us through the crowd and down to floor level. As we neared the final walkway accessing the ground floor, we could see members of the hotel staff carrying a table and chairs in the direction to where we were headed. Upon our arrival Mr. Bruno inquired, "I hope this will be satisfactory?" and he then pulled out a chair for Beth so that she could be seated. After securing Beth, he nodded at me suggestively and then motioned for me to join him off to the side for a brief conference out of Beth's earshot. I casually positioned myself with my back to Beth, and he extended his hand, saying, "Here is my card with my cell number. Should you require anything, anything at all, please feel free to contact me. Mr. Goodrich told me to be at your disposal for the evening and also sends his regards and hopes that you both have a wonderful experience." He then finished by stating, "Alexandra will be over shortly to serve you. Have fun, and remember, the tab is on us, so feel free to indulge yourselves." We shook hands, and after he sized Beth up one more time before he left, assumingly to try and get a better idea of exactly who he was dealing with and why we were getting the royal treatment, he just smiled, waved goodbye and disappeared into the night.

Beth looked somewhat discombobulated by all the attention we were receivng, and when I sat down beside her, she just stared at me with bewilderment. "What's that blank look about?" I asked. Still obviously distracted, she muttered back, "Who are you? And what is going here? This is not normal." She continued with, "I feel like we are in *GoodFellas* or something and that we might get whacked any second." I got a good laugh from that one and replied, "We are just guests of the house, distinguished guests, and believe me, no one is getting whacked." Alexandra then arrived with a bottle of champagne, a bottle of Wild Turkey, several assorted mixers, and four shots of Cuervo Gold with all the trimmings. "I hope I got this right," she began. "I wasn't sure about the soda, so I brought you a couple of bottles of each. How's it looks?" "It looks perfect," I replied then thanked her for her diligence and slipped a C-note onto her tray. I figured Beth would have killed me right then and there if I placed it anywhere on her body, so I took the more conservative route. I still felt Beth's eyes staring at me, so I cut it short with Alex and turned my attention back toward her, "Baby, this is all for you… and for us," I assured her. "Let's have a toast and enjoy the fanfare." She skeptically agreed, passed me a shot, and shouted, "To us," and then gulped down the drink. "One more thing," she interjected. "I want to know who this Mr. Goodrich guy is!" I thought to myself, *Yeah, me too*, but replied instead, "You'll find out later, promise."

The band come on stage, and as the music began to engulf the building, the crowd began to work itself into a frenzy. The sights and sounds of the '80s filled atmosphere with nostalgia, and I found myself drifting back to simpler, happier times. Beth's mood lightened dramatically, and I marveled at her genuinely cheerful and amusing disposition. In fact, every time I availed myself of her natural affection for life, it made me smile and realize how ingenious she truly was. I was so fortunate to have her by my side, and I was also quite sure that I would have been lifeless long ago if not her presence to my world.

As the beverages began to flow more rapidly, I felt myself begin loosen up a bit both mentally and physically. Beth and I stood and held on to each other as we swayed to the tunes and viewed the throngs of partygoers moving to the '80s classics. Then from out of nowhere, a geriatric woman grabbed my hand and led me out into the maze of bodies. Beth was hysterical with laughter as she watched the elderly lady elbow her way through the crowd and begin to shake her body with me still in tow. Having no other choice, I reciprocated her gestures until she stumbled over to Beth, grasped her hands, and pulled her out onto the dance floor as well. The three of us danced and cheered our hearts out until our new acquaintance summoned us closer and then scolded me as she patted my face, saying, "Now you finish this dance with her and never leave this beautiful woman on the sidelines again." With that, the mysterious grand dame disappeared as quickly as she had appeared, never to be seen or heard from once more. Beth's exuberance could not be contained at this point, so I let myself go as well, and we sang and danced our way into the wee hours of the morning, never once straying from each other. It was a magical night and one which I would never forget. For a change, I allowed myself to live in the now and for the moment. And the now was certainly spectacular.

CHAPTER 12

The Calm After the Storm

Sunday morning

I DO NOT REMEMBER EXACTLY when I crossed the imaginary point of no return, that line drawn in the sand you either step across to the forbidden side or back down from and turn around, but I knew that I was well past it now. The rising sun poured through the curtains like shimmering diamonds as it danced off the gold and glass reflective towers. I truly enjoyed the tranquility of this glittering haven more than the chaos and action of the main drag. It was early Sunday morning, and perhaps even the most loyal of heathens took a respite on occasion.

Beth was sleeping angelically like the savior whom God had sent to rescue me, and for the moment, she had done just that. My OCD, obsessive-compulsive disorder, was in full force this morning, and I utilized this nervous energy to tidy up a bit and organize all that I could. I heard a faint cooing noise and saw Beth stretching and peering over at me bleary-eyed. Her freshly awakened face was so cute and innocent, and she patted the bed next to her, asking me to come and join her. I couldn't help but smile, and since I knew that it was far too early for Beth to actually arise, I climbed back into the bed, wrapped myself around her, and we spooned and snuggled until we fell back asleep in each other's arms.

The ringing of the house phone woke us a few hours later, and I heard Karen's voice cheerfully greeting me good morning as

I answered the receiver. Karen was quite the thunderbolt, and she needed to know immediately what the plan was. She was showered, dressed, and ready to go and was quite curious to know where we stood. I let Beth handle the initial discussion and morning salutations, but then reacquired the phone in order to instruct Karen on the details of the day. Beth leaped up and headed toward the bathroom to wash her face, and as she did, I got a glimpse of her perfect hourglass figure and her magnificent legs, which were my downfall from the very beginning. I had always been a leg, thigh, and butt man, and Beth possessed all three in immaculate fashion. In fact, it was her legs above all of her other voluptuous attributes that first caught my eye four years ago on that hot August afternoon. Little did I know then that this chance occurrence would alter my life from that day forward.

We met on an average, bland Tuesday in the heat of summer, when I arrived at my favorite watering hole somewhat earlier than usual. The joint was empty as the lunch crowd had previously departed, and happy hour was still to come. I was meeting a friend and another associate for a drink, a few laughs, and to discuss a bit of business. As I made my way over to the bar to set up my station and claim my bar space, a voice from beyond shouted, "Noodles, great to see you, my friend. I'll be right over." "Take your time. I'm not going anywhere," I yelled back. Tim MacGregor was the bar manager, head bartender, and a good friend of mine whom I had known for several years. We had a close and personal relationship and spoke frankly to each other about life, love, and all of our other daily misfortunes. On this particular day, he was leaving abruptly to attend one of his son's soccer games, but he cordially addressed me and placed my standard four coasters on the bar to accommodate my selection of beverages. There was always a bottle of beer, a bourbon, and ginger ale, and lately, more often than not, a chilled canister of Southern Comfort with a splash of lime juice coupled with a large rocks glass in which to pour the chilled nectar. He informed me that Allen, another of the usual barkeeps, would be along shortly and asked if I needed anything else before he left. "I'm good," I assured him and then went on to tell him that I would keep an eye on things until Allan showed.

We hugged briefly, and with that, he was off to the parking lot, and I was off to oblivion, or so I thought.

Allan arrived a few minutes later, as did my other guests, and we began a spirited dialogue as we toasted and drank. And then it happened: she walked into the lounge and directly into my life. She was the most gorgeous woman that I had ever laid eyes on. A stunning tan beauty in short shorts, a cutoff shirt, and legs that seemed to go from the floor to the ceiling. It was Beth. I took a long swig of beer and tried to act casual, but I could not cast my gaze away from her striking presence. I was totally captivated. The rest, as they say, is history; and once I finally got up the nerve to approach her and our eyes met, it was kismet from the start.

Today's plans, however, had changed quite dramatically. Originally, the day was to have consisted of a lavish brunch, some tender and heartfelt goodbye wishes, and a trip to the airport to see the girls off. Afterward, I was to proceed back to the hotel and set all in motion in order to culminate my objective: the deliberate termination of my existence. I had counted and sorted out all the necessary pills and narcotics to do the job, and I was completely certain that with the right amount of alcohol thrown into the mix, the potion would yield the desired results. Unfortunately, I had never contemplated that Beth's action could deter my goal. Yet there she was, in all her splendor, a carefree smile on her face and thoughts of the next few days together likely dancing in her head.

Beth strutted out of the bathroom with an air of jauntiness, and as she turned to look into the large full-length mirror, stretching her arms over her head, her T-shirt lifted up, revealing her firm thighs and delightful derriere. I could no longer resist her unadulterated femininity and carefully sidled up behind her. I wrapped my arms around her tiny waist and drew her toward me so that she could feel my excitement against her. I then kissed her neck ever so gently and enticed her earlobes until she sighed with delight. As I moved my hands close to her ample breasts, her body quivered in anticipation. Her nipples were rock hard, and she purred when I brushed against them and then smoldered when I licked the first one and then the other. She guided my head upward, and when I saw that irresistible expression of desire on her face, I knew that I had activated the launch sequence.

As she reached down and began to message me slowly, she pulled me closer and whispered longingly, "I want him inside me." I knelt down, lifted up her shirt, and began to kiss her magnificently toned stomach. Her legs danced with each flick of my tongue, and as I stood and spun her onto the bed, she slid off her top in one simultaneous motion. Our eyes locked, and I drove her backward so that I could feel the heat against my body as she parted her thighs. Her perfectly manicured flower glistened with moisture, and as I maneuvered myself to meet her and began moving my mouth across her sweet spot, I could feel her begin to tense up and latch on to the bedding. The screams echoed throughout the suite, and as she got louder and louder, I got harder and harder. She came until she was out of breath, and I could feel her body begin to ease as I cradled her in my arms. The pheromones flowed from her open pores, and I was covered with her scent and her juices. After a brief interval of rest, she turned to me willingly and declared, "Now it's your turn, handsome."

Beth tossed her head, lurched her body upward, and stared wantonly at my naked body. She lowered herself until our bodies met and then began to engulf every inch of me with her mouth, sending waves of passion into all of my nerves and pathways. The physical sensation was so intense, but the mental ecstasy was even greater. I shot up almost unconsciously, repositioned her on the bed, and carefully slid myself inside her as she wiggled and tensed up with desire. Our lovemaking was an emotional, mental, and loving experience that brought us together in complete wholeness; it was totally indescribable. We moved harmoniously like two well-oiled machines whose pieces fit perfectly with each other. As we continued full throttle and she climaxed again and again, I too became ready to explode. She implored me, "Take him out...cum all over...please...now." I cautiously eased myself out and began to move my hips across her exquisite abdomen. My face began to flush as my level of pleasure and excitement ascended, and I leaned back, grabbed hold, and emptied myself onto her as she teased my nipples and encouraged me to persist. We collapsed, united and stuck jointly together like two wet noodles, basking in the adoration between us. I had never been with anyone before who made me feel so confident, so desired, or so loved. Lovemaking with Beth was just that, making love, and a more wonderful discovery was never to be found.

As we lay there still intertwined and shivering with pleasure, I wondered how this woman could turn me from a strong, virile man into a whimpering and helpless teenager in a manner of seconds. A simple passive gesture, casual smile, or insignificant brush sent my pistons firing into high alert, and I would lust for her uncontrollably. I was so infatuated with her, all of her, and I could only imagine that this was what true love and happiness really felt like. And while I wanted these emotions to endure forever, realistically, I knew that I still had a job to complete, even if it had been put on hold momentarily.

Tucked away in a far corner of the casino was a favorite old-school joint of mine which served the best breakfast west of Mississippi. Famous for its 1950s fair and decor, the ambiance was only surpassed by the homestyle flavors and aromas that emanated from the large open kitchen. While only able to seat about forty patrons at a time, I was aware that midday crowd would be sparse, so I strategically planned our arrival just past noon. Most of the locals and regulars dined much earlier, and the rest of the "touristas" usually cleared out by later morning so as not to miss any of the day's action. We arrived to find the place only half occupied and were seated immediately in a perfectly situated booth. I positioned myself next to Beth on one side of the table, with Karen on the other to allow Karen to be the focal point of the conversation. She would be departing shortly, and I wanted to ensure that she didn't feel left out or like the third wheel, along with Beth and me just for the ride. The girls dominated the dialogue, and I only chimed in occasionally between devouring each of the rich and savory dishes that were presented. I attributed my voracious appetite to my earlier interlude with Beth, and once the meal had concluded, I sat back, brimming in total satisfaction.

Upon exiting the dinette, we made our way over to the front lobby to locate our ride over to the airport. I asked a passerby for the time and then assured the ladies that we had ample time to reach our destination as scheduled. Accordingly, they decided to make a brief pit stop in the women's lounge to powder their noses and to do whatever else was necessary. I waited patiently, daydreaming of the hours ahead and how Beth and I would spend the rest of the day. Knowing that she would want to do some shopping, I formulated a plan whereby we could go sightseeing, shopping, and people watching and still return to the hotel to join Jack for dinner. Pleasing her today was my ultimate goal, and I was going to spare no expense to achieve that outcome. After all, this was to be one of the last days that we would ever share, and I wanted it to be the one that she would always remember.

As we reminisced about the past few days and chuckled over all the outrageous antics that had occurred, the driver pulled into the terminal and approached the curbside check-in area. Beth and Karen kissed and hugged for quite a while, and then Karen walked toward me. "I had a truly spectacular time," she admitted and then confessed, "I really needed this." "We all did," I replied and then let her know that I was glad that she had decided to join us. She gave me a quick thank-you peck on the check and a brief embrace, and then turned and headed into the terminal. As I glanced back around at Beth, who was leaning voluptuously against the sedan with devilish look in her eyes, she inquired, "Now what, handsome?" "Don't worry," I explained, "I've got a few ideas." She grinned amusingly and said, "I bet you do."

It was a sunny and warm spring afternoon, and it appeared as if the whole city was out gallivanting about. The traffic on the wide boulevard was sparse, but the pedestrians and voyeurs made the streets barely passable. I asked the chauffeur to stop at one of the less-populated intersections, and Beth and I exited the car hand in hand and made our way out into the sunlight. My idea was to stroll along the expansive concourse, take in several of the most animated sights, and then culminate our journey at the large shopping mecca located in the grand rotunda. "Where are we off to?" Beth asked enthusiastically. "Don't you worry your pretty little head," I responded and then shifted gears and let her know how truly ecstatic

I was that we had the whole day together at our disposal. She nestled against me held me tight and mumbled, "That's all I've ever wanted."

As Beth and I commenced our tour, we managed to maneuver our way through the throngs of onlookers and position ourselves perfectly just in time for the start of one of the more lavish outdoor spectacles. The fountain, laser, and water extravaganza was situated in front of the most stately gambling hall in town, and it drew vast crowds hourly to witness the impressive attractions. Beth stood in front of me, and I rested my chin on top of her head as I wrapped my arms around her waist and held her in anticipation. The display was mesmerizing and quite romantic as well, and we kissed and curled up with each other throughout the entire performance. The experience fully embodied our relationship, and the love and admiration we showed for each other was easily discernible. In fact, it was times like those where our intimacy was so overwhelming that I knew for sure that Beth was my true and only soul mate. We totally completed each other.

Afterward, we continued down the thoroughfare until we found ourselves smack in the midst of a walking carnival where scores of performers were showing off their unique skills. There were mimes, jugglers, magicians, and even a few animal acts with exotic creatures and even more eccentric handlers. We laughed and frolicked about like two school kids taking in as much of the entertainment as possible. Then as we approached the massive shopping mall and promenade, I realized that it was time for an extreme and meaningful gesture on my part.

One of Beth's favorite activities was browsing through exclusive retail shops and viewing all the wares available for purchase. One of my favorite activities was observing Beth as she glided around the stores, while also noticing particular items that seemed to strike her fancy. She had impeccable taste, especially when it came to jewelry, and I had learned her preferences and propensities over the years. We strolled together hand in hand through the dimly lit pathways of the mall until we came upon a bright and dazzling storefront. As I peered upward to read the facade, I recognized the name immediately and knew in an instant that this was the place to find Beth a worthy gift.

As we excitedly entered the impressive emporium, we were greeted almost simultaneously by an excessively clad hostess who was both overly gracious and quite complimentary. "Good afternoon and welcome." She beamed and then continued, "What a striking couple the two of you make." Seizing the moment and never lacking a smooth reply, I nodded and shrugged. "It's easy to look good when you have someone this alluring on your arm. I only hope that you can find something as exquisite to adorn her with." "We shall certainly do our best," she answered. "Let me find someone to help your right way." Beth poked me sharply on my side, caught my eye, and murmured, "Behave yourself—and stop being so damned charming." "I will try, but you know that it's difficult for me not to be enchanting," I reminded her. "Blah, blah, blah," she jabbered back and then commanded, "Well, try—and stop ogling all of the salesgirls!" I turned toward her in curiosity. "Me? Ogle? You must have me confused with someone else." "No, I've got your number," she informed me, continuing, "And that answer may cost you a few extra diamonds just for being such a smart-ass!" I glared back at her, biting my lip. "Yes dear, the floor is yours. Knock yourself out."

We casually began to peruse the various showcases and then were approached by another effervescent young lady who introduced herself and asked Beth what her preferences were. While the ladies chatted, I drifted off a bit and decided to make my own way around the numerous aisles of gems. Clearly, this was a highfalutin establishment, and I tried to keep an air of decorum in both my manner and appearance. Since I had previously bestowed upon Beth several bracelets, earrings, and necklaces, my thoughts focused on a ring of some kind, but I knew that it would have to be something conspicuous rather than unassuming. A display of rings then caught my attention, and I asked a nearby staffer if he could aid me in getting a closer look. I purposely chose a gentleman to assist me as I knew that Beth was keeping a close watch on me, and I didn't want to elicit her ire any further. This was to be a cheerful and heartfelt endeavor that I wanted to be a memorable occasion, and I could not allow anything to deter us from that.

Gregory was a pleasant fellow, and he meticulously secured several of my selections and placed them gingerly on the counter for me to view. As I considered each one intently, I tried to imagine which one Beth would cull, and I was therefore able to narrow it down to two vastly different choices. The first was sleek, elegant, and classic looking, and its intrinsic glint took my breath away. The second was far more elaborate and ostentatious, and yet it had that pizazz which I knew she was fond of. Rather than making the choice myself, which I had done many times before, I reasoned that we could decide jointly and come to a mutual decision. I asked Gregory to keep those two items aside for me, and after he returned the others back to their casings, I nonchalantly inquired about the cost of each. As I held my breath awaiting his reply, I saw Beth making her way over to where I was standing. Gregory revealed the prices just prior to Beth's arrival, and I tried to remain unruffled when she returned.

"So any major decisions made as of yet?" she inquired coyly. "Funny you should ask," I encouraged. "Gregory and I were just debating over these two pieces here." She glanced over my shoulder toward the two rings remaining on the display case. Her eyes widened as her face lit up, and I could sense her delight immediately. "Wow," she exulted. "I see that you have been quite busy while I was gone... perhaps I should leave you alone more often." "Perhaps." I nodded and then put my arm around her shoulder, kissed her on the forehead, and positioned her for a closer look. As she gazed at the rings and then tried each one of them on, I could tell that she was truly enjoying the moment. Her face was radiant yet possessed an earnest and somewhat pained expression as she realized that she would need to make a choice. Seeing her indecisiveness, I queried, "I haven't seen any of your possibilities, my love. You must have seen something that caught your eye?" "Not really," she professed. "Besides, this is a hard-enough decision already." Not realizing myself that the price tags were still attached to both items, I noticed Beth slyly glance at the stickers and then turn away abruptly to conceal her discomfort. She strutted over to the full-length mirror to grasp the full picture of the jewels against her sultry reflection and then summoned me over. She asked timidly, "You have seen the amounts of each of these, yes?"

"I have," I admitted openly and then assured her that she could have whichever one that she preferred.

She moved her hands back and forth and watched the rings shimmer and sparkle against the lights. They were two very divergent pieces, but I could sense that she had made up her mind. I braced myself as we returned to where Gregory was patiently waiting for us, and tried to fathom Beth's intention. "I'll take this one please," she announced and handed him the more ornately designed ring, which I was positive was truly more her style. "Very good," Gregory acknowledged. "I will take it in the back for a quick cleaning and then prepare you invoice. How will you be paying?" "That's my department," I declared and then ushered him to the side for a brief discussion as Beth admired her new addition.

After the formalities had been taken care of and Beth and I ambled back into the faint light of the mall, she threw her arms around me and kissed me passionately. I returned the kiss warmly and then raised her chin so that I could look into her misty eyes. "I love you with all my heart and want you to have everything in life that you deserve," I confessed. "I love you too, my baby," she replied and smiled so enchantingly that my heart melted right on the spot.

The walk back toward the main intersection was longer than I had anticipated, but with Beth by my side, nothing seemed to matter. It then occurred to me that I had gone almost an entire day without any drugs, alcohol, or even gambling; and while I was still functioning, albeit barely, I had managed to negotiate all of the day's events. I began wonder if it was actually possible for me refrain from all of my vices for an extended period of time. Was it possible that Beth's presence was the true answer to filling the deep void within me? Was she really a guardian angel sent to me to cleanse my soul and to return to me the moral character and integrity that once dominated my life? Could it be so?

I turned my head sideways ever so slightly to gaze upon her out of the corner of my eye and snickered to myself, marveling at her being and how she possessed everything I ever wanted in another person—strength, courage, faith, determination, and an unassailable will to live all packaged in the most magnificent beauty I had ever witnessed. She was flawless to me in every way. Just being around her elevated my existence to a high-minded state of consciousness, and I knew that I was a better person since she had entered my world. The thought of a life without her in any way brought on a feeling of dread and deep despair. Yet I could not tell her the truth about my addiction, my deceitfulness, or the utter lack of moral conviction that presently permeated and dominated my mind and body. I was back to square one, and while my initial design for my demise had been quashed, I knew now more than ever how I needed to proceed.

My alcohol and drug use had gone from recreational to habitual to full-out abuse and dependency seemingly in a flash. I was numb to the negative consequences my health, my emotional well-being, and especially my relationships had all taken due to my continued daily usage. Not to mention the dire financial issues and the legal implications that my last few months of malfeasance had brought down upon me. The degree of my compulsion was now so intense that I spent all of my time either getting, using or thinking about these substances as they had become the most important aspect of my life. All my plans and schemes centered upon who I was going to deceive and manipulate in order to get my fix and achieve my high. That became the only way that I could stomach myself and what I had become. I went from being the fun, outgoing life of the party to a scared, paranoid, and anxiety-ridden shell of a man who could only ease his pain by inflicting more and more harm on himself. It was a vicious cycle of annihilation that could not be halted no matter how hard I tried.

Unfortunately, Beth was just an innocent bystander to my decay. She in no way could have comprehended the levels of frustration and remorse that I was experiencing. When we were together, I was legitimately happier than I had ever been, but those moments were still somewhat fleeting as I was still torn between my devotion to her and my responsibilities to my existing yet crumbling family situation. This dichotomy wreaked havoc with my emotions as the constant upheavals and betrayals were literally driving me insane. The only solace I found to cope with this turmoil were the same compulsions that continued to cripple me and pound me into submission. And now, knowing that I was to return East still alive and kicking, the panic began to consume me all over again. I never imagined that I would be right back where I started, especially after all of my meticulous planning and clandestine maneuvering. It was all too much to bear, and as I tried to shake the thoughts from my head, Beth gave my hand a firm squeeze and said, "A penny for your thoughts." I just smiled back at her sublime glory and replied, "I am just so glad you decided to stay," placating her yet again rather than coming clean.

CHAPTER 13

The Best-Laid Plans

Monday morning

BETH AND I BOARDED OUR plane right on schedule Monday morning and began our venture back to the East Coast. Unfortunately, between the hours flying and the time difference, you lost the entire day, and therefore, we were not intending to arrive until after nightfall. Normally, I would have taken the last red-eye flight out closest to midnight; but obviously, when I booked my return trip, I was not concerned with the details as I was not actually planning on being aboard. Only due to Beth's last-minute decision and change of plans were we now travelling together hand in hand. I could easily discern her exhaustion and knew that she would sleep most of the way home, so I tactfully requested a blanket and pillow from the stewardess and let her snuggle up against me. As I sat there cuddling and holding her firmly, I began to ponder what my next course of action was going to be. I solemnly closed my eyes, began to drift off, and tried to recollect the previous days' joyful events.

Ironically, the preceding day was a truly wonderful one filled with fun, frolic, and romance, one in which you were just happy to be alive. The daytime excursion with Beth was pure bliss, and the evening turned out to be quite remarkable as well. Jack had joined us at our hotel for dinner, and we were treated to a very special meal with all the bells and whistles. In addition, we also had the pleasure of meeting several well-known and legendary sports figures and coaches who were still in town, enjoying the conclusion of the first week's tournament activity.

While Beth's dubiousness toward these celebrities' identities was apparent, she still exuded her usual upbeat and enthusiastic demeanor and shared in my overall delight and excitement. Jack was his usual composed self throughout the festivities as this scene was second nature to him, and he graciously introduced Beth and me around and included us in all of the conversation. The food was classic five-star quality, and each of the professional waitstaff, as well as the head chef, also came out to greet us. After finishing our exotic coffees and scrumptious desserts, the three of us returned to the suite for our final farewell. Beth immediately excused herself in order to change and get comfortable, thereby allowing Jack and me some time to review the weekend numbers and to settle our accounts. While I was extremely curious to ask him how much the dinner had cost since no bill was ever presented and I was dying to know, I let it go and just listened attentively as he calculated the figures. When all was said and done and after all fees, costs, and expenses had been accounted for, there was still a little of over $125,000 which I was due. I had a ballpark idea of where I stood, but I believe that Jack was exceedingly generous this time around due to all the success and kudos which was lavished upon him. Of course, there still remained my personal tab with Jack, which had now been running for over twenty years and which was periodically settled up when the time was right. I knew that this was one of those times and accordingly told him to keep $75,000 toward my current negative total, which he greatly appreciated. I then instructed him to keep an additional $25,000 for me to utilize for my plays for the rest of the tournament, which still had a full two weeks of action remaining. That left approximately $25,000, $20,000 of which I could keep and another $5,000. which I could liberally distribute to my crew for all of their various winning wagers over the past week. It had all seemed to work exceptionally well, and I knew that everyone involved would be pleased with their takes.

Once the necessary funds changed hands, meaning that Jack gave me three small stacks of bills totaling $25,000, his cell phone rang, and I heard a familiar voice on the other end. I had neglected to think about Romeo over the course of my hectic day, but hearing him now made me smile, and I was glad to have the chance to say goodbye. Jack handed me the phone, and after a short yet ardent conversation with my longtime pal, we said farewell for possibly the last time. Strangely enough at that time, I did not presume that I would never speak to him again, but now, as I sat clutching Beth resolutely, the realization dawned upon me, and a somber wave of emotions passed through my core.

After shaking free from those thoughts, my attention returned to the previous night and my last few interactions with Jack, which, as always, were both serious and jovial at the same time. We bantered back and forth on a number of topics including Beth, Ann, The Prince, and of course, the remaining tournament games. I also understood that since Romeo was not making an appearance, I would need to package up the remaining "goods" and paraphernalia for Jack so that he could return all to Romeo for me. There was obviously no need for me to transport any of the leftovers back with me, and my usual arrangement with Romeo was for me to consume whatever I derived and then return the unused balance.

I excused myself for a moment, went into the bedroom, and then reappeared with my bag of goodies. I could see Jack's apprehension immediately as while he was able to overlook my usage, he was still very averse to any direct involvement with my narcotic endeavors and especially toward becoming a common "bagman." He watched anxiously as I sectioned off a few small portions of buds, powder, and assorted pharmaceuticals and then bundled up the rest and secured it back into the small black leather handbag. I kept a lighter and the small inexpensive water pipe for my convenience and concealed them with the rest of my stash in a nearby end-table drawer until later. Finally coordinated, I passed the bag across the table of Jack, who smirked and then chided sarcastically, "Always a pleasure to be of service, my boy," continuing, "Is there anything else that you will require?" "No, I think I'm good at the moment," I replied, "but check back with me before bedtime."

I smiled pensively to myself as I adjusted my seat to a more reclined position and stretched out my aching legs. Just then, I was startled out of my meditative state by the loud clanging of the approaching beverage cart. Beth awoke briefly, glanced around to orient herself, gave me a quick peck on the cheek, and then repositioned herself comfortably on my arm. I watched her intently fully engrossed by her delicate mannerisms and seemingly unalloyed happiness and tried to imagine what it would be like to be at total peace with oneself. She was so true, sound, and virtuous to herself and to her innermost principles, and her sincerity and simplicity were truly infectious. Just being in her company for even a moment lifted my spirits and brought a tranquility to my life that I had never previously experienced nor would again until much later on. I lowered my face, gave her a tender kiss on the top of her head, and tried to visualize what our life would be like together, knowing full well, of course, that it would never come to be.

As I snacked on a few pretzels and sipped on my diet ginger ale, I once again began to recall the prior evening's happenings and envisioned Beth and I sharing several warmhearted conversation and heartfelt embraces. Somehow she was able to alleviate all of my ongoing self-deprecating tendencies and make me feel worthy. I had felt inadequate and "less-than" for so long that I could not even remember the last confident instant that I had experienced. Yet with Beth by my side, anything seemed possible. Life once again meant something and appeared to have some purpose. The proverbial "glass" was beginning to loom half full rather than half empty, and my search for confirmation and approval was fading away. But unfortunately, the dice had already been cast, and I had "crapped out" long ago. There was no way to turn back the hands of time or to charge what had occurred in the past. The only thing left to do now was to formulate a new plan and prevent anyone or anything from standing in my way.

Upon my arrival back to my affluent suburban town, I instantly fell back into the revolving door of dismay that had punctuated my existence the past few years. Beth had departed, and the desires for physical and emotional security once again started to ravage my consciousness. The delusions of grandeur and exaggerations of deficiency were commonplace as I gloated over praise on the one hand and mourned over criticism on the other. I calmed my fragile nerves by medicating them by the hour with both drugs and alcohol, thereby mitigating life's up and downs and numbing my emotions. This, however, only perpetuated the fantasy world of irresponsibility and vast in accountability that I had created. My need to control everyone and everything in order to elicit the outcomes that I desired continued to grow and rankle. The more I demanded complete adherence and compliance to my affairs, the more chaos and absolute confusion I produced. I had to maintain my chimerical status quo even though it was all an illusion fabricated in my own mind. My sanity was slowly slipping away, and I commenced on a period of isolation and personal destruction as never before. I retreated into the deep despair that I was accustomed to, and the culmination of all my cruel, callous, and desperate actions beckoned to me daily. The time had come; it was now or never.

I awoke some thirty-six hours after my initial admittance into the emergency room. Ann had tried to arouse me on several occasions, but when I was unresponsive to her prodding, she hurriedly called 911. It took me a while to grasp where in fact I was, but once I heard the customary hospital noises and sounds and viewed the tubes and wires attached to my body, the scene began to take shape. There was no bright light to walk into, no sightings of dead people, and no pictures of my life flashing before my eyes. Rather, there was just the beeping and pinging of the machines monitoring my vital signs. A deep feeling of shame and remorse came over me. I wasn't supposed to be alive. What now?

The room began to fill with both hospital staffers and medical assistants alike, and I sensed that this was only the beginning of the inquisition still to come. As they processed all the necessary readings and data, one particular nurse tried to engage me in dialogue, but my mind was extremely cloudy. I managed to ask where Ann and The Prince were, and another nurse responded, "Your wife and your brother are outside but we are waiting for you to get stable prior to admitting any visitors." I thought to myself, *Stable! Is she kidding? I haven't been mentally or emotionally sound for months, let alone stable.* I struggled to sit up and gather myself; however, I was restrained by the various cables attached to my chest and arms and fell backward helplessly. I was told to relax and to stay comfortable and that the doctor would be along shortly to see me. I closed my eyes, sank into the bed, and attempted to comprehend what had transpired over the last few days.

The truth was that I had basically given up long ago, and my new mantra had become, "What's the difference anyway?" Unfortunately, I never conceived the notion that I could or would survive this attempt, nor had I comprised a plan B for such an outcome. I just pined for the anger, guilt, self-loathing, and recurring anguish to cease, and that desire blinded me toward everything else. Now, however, I understood that all of my secrets and lies would be uncovered, if they had not been already, and that epiphany rechanneled all of my fears and hopelessness yet again.

After dozing off for a minute, I was brought back to consciousness by the touch of something against my forearm. A doctor had entered the room with several other official-looking hospital personnel, and a nurse was holding my arm and readjusting my attachments. The dialogue between them was barely audible, and I was only able to make out of bits and pieces of their conversations. I did realize, however, that I had been in a comatose state since my arrival and that these were my first lucid moments in almost two days. I desperately tried to decipher the words being spoken, but my brain was still recuperating from the latest abuse it had endured.

Finally, the doctor approached me and began quizzing me with a series of simple and concise questions. Basically, it was a standard laundry list comprised of my name, my age, my birthday, who the current president was, and of course, did I know where I was and why I was there. I replied to the inquiry to the best my of ability and watched as the physician hastily scrawled notes in my medical chart. He then assured me that I was going to be fine and that he would be back to examine me further later that evening. As he departed, he motioned to one of the older well-groomed women in the room, and she followed him out into hallway. A few minutes later, she returned alone; and after dismissing the rest of the staff present, she sternly turned her attention toward me and made her way over to my bedside.

Upon formally greeting me and introducing herself as the senior hospital administrator of patient affairs, the woman pulled up a chair and sat down. She possessed an air of authority about her, and her poise was quite strong and demonstrative. I sensed that she had a specific agenda, but as she cleared her throat and began to address me, I was unsure of her intentions. Her speech became more direct, and her tone more serious as she continued to expound upon my current condition and the circumstances therein. I started to discern that my situation was tenuous and not at all commonplace for this facility, and henceforth, I was going to be treated with extreme tact and caution. While I remained in the dark as to where the discussion was headed, I noticed that her dialect had changed from a medical concern to one which possessed much more legalese. It had gone from compassion to candor rather quickly, and when I heard the words *psychiatric evaluation*, it dawned on me that the proverbial cat was out of the bag.

I strove to compose myself and to keep my emotions in check, but my anxiety got the best of me, and I became difficult and defensive. She stood up abruptly to regain control of the situation and then self-righteously stated, "We all know what you endeavored to do. Therefore, we can either proceed the easy way or the hard way. The choice is yours." I shifted my position, trying to restore some assurance, but my confidence was shaken, and my regression was inevitable. I lashed out with a barrage of unsavory remarks and established my posture of *nolo contendere*, not being willing to either confess or concede to anything. This only exacerbated matters and created more tension in an already volatile setting. She implored me to understand the consequences of my actions and to yield to the reality of the facts at hand. "Please," she beseeched, "for the sake of yourself, of your family, and of everyone else who us involved… please reconsider your stand and reexamine your viewpoint." While I attempted to stay resolute, I found some softening in my zeal and realized that my compliance was, in fact, necessary. I had already caused an inordinate amount of pain due to my recent nefarious acts of cowardice, and it became evident that I was no longer able to manage my own affairs.

Once I had agreed to forsake my intentions and acquiesced to follow the hospitals procedures, this settled down, and all returned to order. The nursing staff reappeared and were given specific instructions for my care and then commenced the required preparations for my transfer to a separate mental facility in a neighboring county. Nevertheless, while I was able to interpret all of that interplay around me, I still had no idea where I was headed or what was to transpire. My head and mind remained flushed with discomfort, and my faculties had yet to be fully recaptured. I requested to see the doctor as well as my family, but my pleas fell on deaf ears, and the crew just continued their assignments in quiet fashion.

Finally, about an hour or so later, I heard some recognizable voices in the hallway and then waited sheepishly as Ann and my brother, Hal, begrudgingly entered the room. I will never forget the look of shock and sorrow that was impaled upon their faces. They moved cautiously toward me, first Ann and then Hal; and when Ann peered bleary-eyed down at my lifeless body, I saw tears begin to well up as she reached over and clasped my hand. She asked if I could hear her and if I knew who she was, and I nodded affirmatively, trying to stay unruffled. "You gave us quite a scare," she cried, hoping to elicit some response from me, but I quickly glanced away in order to conceal my shame.

Before much else could be conveyed, the doctor resurfaced and guided Ann and Hal out to the corridor for a family consultation. While they conferred together, I wondered how they were all able to surmise the details and purpose of my plan, especially since I had covered my tracks so carefully. There were no signs of alcohol, narcotics, or any other mischief afoot at my residence, so how did they conclude that this was, in fact, a suicide attempt? Clearly, it could just have been an accidental overdose or simply an overindulgence of substances that went awry, so why the certainty that I was suicidal and deliberately attempted to end my life? I was truly puzzled by this inexplicable leap of faith, but unfortunately, as I tried to sort through the events of the last few days, my mind was virtually incapable of remembering anything. Where had I possibly slipped up? Had Ann discovered something incriminating? I searched desperately for some answers as I drifted back into a state of slumber, only to finally recognize that it didn't matter one way or another. I was still alive, and that was a contingency that I had not accounted for.

My next cognitive moment was being brought out of the hospital on a gurney and placed inside an ambulance for transport. I overheard the driver and his associate discussing the route to our destination and one of them stated that the trip should take about forty minutes. I shut my eyes and tried to relax my mind and body as I pondered what was going to happen next. I knew that both Ann and Hal were following behind us and that they would be present whenever my joyride ended, but I still had no idea of that location.

The roads were dark and desolate as it was well after nightfall, and the speed of the ambulance along with the glare from the surrounding landscape created a strobe-light effect which intermittently blinded me every few seconds. This recurrent distraction only heightened my discomfort and I lost my concentration and my train of thought rather quickly. I fiddled along the edges of the metal stretcher and flexed my legs repeatedly in order to alleviate the pain from the restraints and to mitigate their confinement. Finally, I just abandoned those efforts and stayed motionless, awaiting my fate.

When we approached the complex, I could hear the rain cascading upon the vehicle as it slowed down and prepared to enter through the gates of the asylum. We passed by the initial checkpoint and then advanced toward a small guardhouse occupied by the two security officers. It was difficult to see much else due to my locality and the dreary and dark condition and I struggled to get a glimpse of my new surroundings. Plainly, this institution was more guarded than a typical medical hospital and I began to have doubts about the standards of care that would be administered in such a facility. Once we were cleared to proceed on the final stage of our journey, the driver pulled up directly in front of the large fortified entrance, and both men exited their doors and walked swiftly to the rear cabin, whereupon they readied for my departure.

After making several mechanical maneuvers, I was carefully dislodged from to the ambulatory device, and wheeled into the lobby. "A new recruit for admittance," declared one of my caregivers. "Fresh out of ICU." A voice responded out of the intercom, "Okay, Harry, I will buzz you in." The thick metal door made a loud humming noise, and the barrier unlocked itself upon a firm tug of Harry's arm. We entered a small vestibule where a woman behind a reinforced plexiglass booth waved Harry over and asked him for my paperwork. Harry passed the documentation through the narrow slit in the windows and then stepped backward, anticipating his further instructions.

Once the information was reviewed by the female attendant and she verified all the necessary data, the door opposite the entranceway buzzed open, and the intercom bellowed, "Please continue on inside. The orderlies are prepared." Harry returned the pronouncement with a quick salute and a nod and we all made our way inside. The antiseptic odor and staunch sterility of the ward struck me immediately and a wave of comfort infiltrated my being. The safe haven of hospitalization rather than the unstable nature of incarceration registered into the threshold of my mind and my whole body eased in gratification. There was only a minimal visible police presence and while it was evident that no unnecessary chances were being taken, rehabilitation and recovery seemed to be the goals here, rather than reprehension.

CHAPTER 14

The Cuckoo's Nest

The next few weeks

MY ESCORTS AND I WERE met by two of the night-shift nurses who immediately prepared my intake sheet and recorded my vital signs. Afterward, I was transported to a wheelchair and led into the day-room for an informational briefing regarding the facility and its workings. Harry and his cohort said their farewells, wished me luck, and then excused themselves, leaving me alone with my newfound observers. Directly thereafter, a call came in over one of the nurses' walkie-talkies; and before I knew it, Ann and Hal were being ushered inside toward me. "You have thirty minutes for this initial visit," Nurse Kelly advised us, and she then pledged to return shortly with a gown and slippers for me to change into. Nurse Johnson followed her into the hallway, and they stealthily disappeared. Ann and Hal both positioned themselves in chairs facing me, took some deep breaths, and peered in at me, awaiting some kind of explication.

The next several weeks dragged by at a snail's pace as I was mentally and physically evaluated on a seemingly hourly basis. It became apparent quite early on that my release was only going to be granted upon my displaying marked improvement with regard to my emotional state. Accordingly, I was not only examined by the nurses and medical doctors, but in addition, I was also assigned both a personal psychiatrist and social worker who worked with me on alternating days. The crux of this treatment was to ensure that my depression had dramatically subsided and that I was no longer a threat to myself or to others. While I was never diagnosed as being homicidal, I was given the tag of possessing a major depressive disorder, and therefore great caution was being utilized concerning my recovery plan. Knowing this all to be the case yet still believing that I was smarter than everyone whom I was dealing with, I initially acquiesced to the barrage of therapeutic sessions and daily interrogations. I remained restrained to some degree due to my own fears and trepidation, but after a few days, I began to relax somewhat, and I became less inhibited. I started to speak more honestly about the factors that led to my demise and realized that my candor was entirely necessary for my recuperation. After all, regardless of the conditions that precipitated my breakdown, I certainly desired to be free of my current situation and to be discharged back into society. The real question, however, still remained: what was going to occur once, in fact, I was actually released?

My room was a shared twelve-by-twelve-foot cubicle which contained a central desk flanked by two standard-issue cots. There was a barred window above the desk that allowed some sunlight to infiltrate the space and an open closet with shelves which was situated directly opposite the window and adjacent to the doorway. The door leading to the corridor needed to remain fully open during the day and at least slightly ajar in the evening and at bedtime for safety purposes. It was all quite plain and simple and allowed at all times full disclosure of the activities taking place therein.

Unfortunately, however, there was neither a sink with running water nor a toilet for relieving oneself as these were communal in nature and also segregated by gender. The shower situation was similar, and there was a strict schedule and time frame when it came to bathing availability. In addition, all these venues were kept under rigid lock and key and usually had a security guard posted outside for the protection of all concerned. With all the different personalities, temperaments, and dispositions packed into such intense surroundings, the need for continuous round-the-clock surveillance was definitely necessary in order to keep decorum at all times. For if a lack of propriety arose and even one of the inmates was to lose his senses and emotionally implode, then the rest of the group would likely follow suit, and the resulting tumult could prove to be cataclysmic.

The cry of "RISE AND SHINE, IT'S MEDICATION TIME" echoed throughout the ward every sunrise. The call usually came just before 6:00 a.m., and each of us would stumble our way over to the mobile nurses' station for the morning dispensation. Not only was medicine conveyed, but also temperatures were taken, blood pressures were monitored, and sugar levels were measured to ensure that proper health and maintenance was being sustained. I myself received the vast pupu platter of treatments as I was constantly in need of a full-body check in order to keep my mind and body stable and functioning. In addition, I was prescribed several mood-altering antidepressants to help relieve the deep depression that continued to haunt me and also to prevent me from dwelling on all my past transgressions. After all, the therapeutic community existed to assist me with the healing process and to improve my mind-set rather than to allow me to wallow in my previous malaise. Accordingly, I diligently followed instructions and obeyed hospital procedure in order to remedy my dire condition.

Once all the drugs had been distributed and all the numbers had been recorded, there was still usually time prior to breakfast for everyone to utilize their personal hygiene items and to prepare for the day. Each patient was given the requisite plastic Tupperware container to store their belongings; however, the receptacles could only be accessed by imploring a staff member to render them as they were stowed in a locked linen closet outside of the latrines. Ann brought me all the necessary accoutrements including shampoo, skin lotion, deodorant, and a toothbrush with toothpaste, all of which passed inspection, were labeled with my name and bed number, and then placed on a shelf inside. Extreme care was provided for these intimate incidentals since they were personal in nature and while pilferage was strictly forbidden and dealt with harshly, items frequently went unaccounted for. A code of ethical behavior needed to be adhered to so as to parallel the societal mores and values that were prevalent in the outside world. Clearly, the reprogramming of our minds to conform to reality rather than to illusion was the paramount ideal regularly strived for.

Within just a couple of days, I had already adapted to my new surroundings and the daily mundane routine. Mealtimes, morning meetings, and afternoon activities were all craftily scheduled, and the weekly calendar of events was clearly displayed on the exterior cafeteria wall. While the actual meals and activities varied somewhat, the timetable and sequence always remained the same. In between the specific gatherings, there was freedom to read, watch TV, play board games, or just relax back in your cubicle. It was explained to me that sharing in the community setting took precedence over being alone and that keeping to one's self was actually frowned upon. I, however, needed periods of both throughout the day as my willingness to participate would often wane and cause me to retreat into solitude. Most of my difficulties stemmed from the extreme guilt and remorse that I felt due to my previous actions, but that was compounded further by the fact that I had shut down mentally and was devoid of any emotion whatsoever. I could not yet wrap my head around the actuality that I was alive and basically well and that all the nightmares which I had tried to escape from were back and now more prevalent than ever. And while the group therapy did allow for the dissemination of ideas and concepts for all to reflect upon, many of the theories seemed unsound for my rehabilitation. After all, I wasn't a drug addict or a violent criminal. To the contrary, I was just a confused soul who had made some poor decisions and needed a brief respite, or so I thought.

Colleen O' Malley was a twenty-five-year-old Irish lass whose appearance matched your initial stereotypical snapshot. She had curly auburn hair, sparkling green eyes, a round face, and a robust, full figure which she tried to downplay by dressing conservatively. As I sat in the locked padded enclosure where all the individual therapy sessions were held, I wondered how forthright I could be with a total stranger. With a series of legal charges pending on the horizon, as well as many personal and private hang-ups, I was unsure what I could actually divulge and what needed to be withheld. After all, honesty was not my best policy as deception and trickery had become all too commonplace in my daily life. I would constantly declare, "If I ate lunch at Burger King, I would tell you that I went to McDonald's instead." Factual information was neither a part of my repertoire nor something that I could express willingly. I had lived so long in my own world of lies and duplicity that I could no longer distinguish between what was true and what was fantasy.

Once inside the rubberized chamber, Ms. O'Malley retrieved my chart from her briefcase and began reviewing my file. After a moment, she took out a small memo pad, jotted down a few notes, and then turned and looked me in the eyes as if searching for my genuine spirit. "Good afternoon," she began, "why don't you tell me why you are here." "Not sure really," I nonchalantly replied. "I guess it's because they think that I tried to kill myself." She nodded and then earnestly espoused, "Well, according to your paperwork, you were admitted due to a blatant suicide attempt induced by a self-inflicted overdose of alcohol and opiates after committing a number of felonious acts. In addition, a note was found at your residence in your handwriting asking your fourteen-year-old son for forgiveness and conveying to him your unconditional love."

A lump formed in my chest as I tried to keep my emotions in check, but hearing the past events put so plainly and matter-of-fact really left me enigmatically engulfed. I cleared my throat and composed myself as I listened to Ms. O'Malley recite the remainder of my recent history. "Gambling, drugs, liquor, and an ongoing clandestine affair were all vices which led to your degeneration. That, coupled with the crash of the local real estate market, and therefore the deterioration of your many speculative investments and money-making schemes, left you on the verge of both moral and financial bankruptcy. With nowhere left to turn and millions of dollars in life insurance proceeds, which would be distributed even if the cause of death was self-imposed, you hid your intentions until the culmination of sequences finally brought you to your knees." Colleen paused momentarily to take a sip of water and to regather her thoughts and then glanced my way to see my reaction. I caught her eye as I quickly looked up, biting my lip and struggling not to show my distress. Quivering with anguish, however, I broke down in tears and released my pain.

After taking an instant to calm my sensitivity and to regain my posture, I belligerently retorted Ms. O'Malley's claims and pointed out that all of her information was not only suspect but was also nothing more than hearsay and pure conjecture. Without neither firsthand knowledge nor my testimony of what occurred prior to my meltdown, how could she be certain that her data was accurate? My truculence intensified as I changed the subject and continued by claiming that she was just another pawn of the powers that be who were working to keep me confined. She responded calmly, "Now why would I do that? What purpose would that serve?" And then she continued by reminding me that she was only there to help me through this ordeal and to assist me back to health. Perhaps my egotism and paranoia were working overtime, yet I felt the need to establish my position and proclaim my soundness of mind.

Still unconvinced of Ms. O'Malley's true role in my recovery, I left the meeting and joined the rest of the crew in the cafeteria for a session of afternoon arts and crafts. I found an empty chair and grabbed one of the plastic lunch boxes which contained the various supplies. Ms. Linda, the arts and crafts instructor, was already giving instructions for the day's project, which was to create a paper mask that would display our current emotions and present mental state. My existing consciousness remained full of both skepticism and distrust, and therefore, my artwork elicited those feelings and became a two-faced creation with dual meaning. On the one hand was the clean, pure, innocent face of a good-natured companion, and on the other hand was the soiled, obscene, guilty look of an evil pagan. Now, while the negative connotation behind my design was initially analyzed solely by my thoughts of the time, later on, while reflecting upon it back in my dorm room, I saw the deeper and more profound message. My opinion of myself had split to such a degree that I could no longer envision my essence as an individual being. Rather, I was two separate and distinct entities: good and bad, moral and satanic, Dr. Jekyll and Mr. Hyde. I asked myself, *When did this happen? How had it come to this?*

This realization of my internal dichotomy became all too clear and cast me deeper into my depression and derangement.

Accordingly, I began to distance myself from the group and to fall back into my world of escape and isolation. Ideas flooded my brain and were coming a mile a minute, and I could not stop the inundation of negativity. Even worse was the dawning of the knowledge that I would now have to deal with these issues on my own and without the aid of my old friends "Mary Jane" and "John Barleycorn." Not having my accomplices to help get me through my difficulties, my notions quickly returned to detachment, desolation, and destruction.

It was then that I met Kelly, a young single girl in her early twenties who was under daily "PC" or personal confinement and who was only allowed out of her nook with a chaperone and in the presence of constant supervision. She too was on suicide watch and previously had bouts of self-reproach where she would slash and mutilate herself as a way to punish and chastise her inner demons. Addicted to heroin and other assorted "dry goods," Kelly had recently attempted to leap from a highway overpass but was halted by a plainclothes police officer who happened to be passing by. Now not allowed to be left to her own devices and under twenty-four-hour observation, she became ostracized by the community and labeled a dangerous freak by the other inpatients. Considered somewhat of an anomaly myself, as a middle-aged white-collar professional who was more like a father figure than a compeer, I was often branded as an outcast and intruder as well. Consequently, it seemed destined that our paths would cross and that Kelly and I would begin a mutual relationship based on our seclusion.

At the inception, we would go off to a corner of the dayroom and speak softly to each other while the others watched music videos or played cards. Eventually, we were more open with our dialogue and found that we could converse anywhere as the rest of the community continued to migrate away from us. I learned quickly that Kelly had been misused as a child and that she was currently involved in an abusive kinship with another addict who regularly beat her. Even throughout her recent pregnancy and the subsequent delivery of their baby, the torment persisted, until one day she became so run-down that she ended up overdosing. Upon her release from the hospital several days later, and without anywhere else to go, she returned home and to her persistent perpetrator. Then one morning, she awoke disoriented and bleary-eyed to find herself alone and without any sign of her either daughter or her adversary. After several calls and inquiries around the neighborhood failed to evoke any results, she chose to score some crack and to get high in order to ease her concerns. A few hours later, she was taken into custody and removed from the highway shoulder.

As Kelly completed her tale of woe, I noticed that she had clawed open a wound on her arm and was trying to conceal the damage from her matron. Unfortunately, much to Kelly's dismay, the woman perceived her discomfort; and when she probed Kelley's body, she immediately discovered the injury. That was the last time I saw Kelly for quite some time as she was placed back into solitary confinement and observed round the clock. While I was sad to have lost my new friend, I had time to reflect on our prior discussions and came away with a new sense of gratitude for my own situation. I knew that I was far from being cured, but my mind began to settle somewhat, and a bit of sanity had begun to seep in. Then Beth came to visit.

Barely an hour before my encounter with Beth, I was summoned to the therapy bunker for a brief meeting with Colleen O'Malley. She asked very generic questions about my mental and physical health and spoke in a precise and straightforward manner regarding my rehabilitation plans. However, once she detected my uneasiness, she changed her candor to a more sympathetic tone and inquired why I seemed more tense than usual. I explained about Beth's pending arrival and how my self-hate and censure had reemerged. I really hadn't thought about Beth in the past couple of days, yet the thought of her presence elicited waves of emotions that were uncontrollable. There was a dread that consumed my disposition, an agonizing sense of sorrow. I knew that I had betrayed her in the worst ways. Not an infidelity of the flesh but rather a violation of her vulnerability and an abandonment of confidence, of love and of trust.

My body writhed in grief as the awareness of loss all but punctured my heart. They say that a man can only be heartbroken if he has truly been in love before, and as my extreme anguish exploded within me, it was only then that I recaptured the unadulterated rapture that we had shared. Since the day I first saw her sparkling eyes, illuminating smile, and the grandeur of her essence, I was totally captivated, and my life was changed forever. She had a face that, once seen, was unforgettable, and my adoration for her was completely enthralling. I cogitated deeply about our harmony with each other, and I knew that we were kindred souls who had been brought together for a specific purpose. Still, somehow, my uncontrollable self-centered motives and priorities stole that all away from us, and now I had to confront her and try to convey how and why it had all occurred. I only wished that I knew the answer because, as of now, I had no idea.

Growing up, I had been instilled with all the proper moral values and standards, and I was fortunate to have the best role model in the world when it came to both character and ethics: my dad. And thinking back, I always seemed to have the will and the desire to do what was just. Unfortunately, however, the performance to carry out that purpose was often lacking, and I failed to achieve many of the goals I sought out to accomplish. My virtues were on a lofty plane, but I did not have the strength, courage, or perseverance to follow them through. Sometime much later on in my metamorphosis, during a period of intense self-analysis with a renowned therapist, I came to realize that after my father's death, I lost that conviction of doing the "right" thing. Instead, I began doing what was outwardly appropriate, yet inside my motivation was sheerly erroneous. My actions were purely self-seeking and were carried out only to satisfy my expanding ego and to draw the kudos from those around me. Perhaps that's where my mother comes in.

My mom grew up in a meager household that was not only devoid of wealth and material possessions but also of tenderness and compassion. This lack of affection led her to feel alone and empty inside, and she responded by obsessing over the desire to fill that vacant hole within her. Initially, she turned to food in order to satiate her craving, but even becoming a compulsive eater could not cure her voraciousness. She felt worthless and unattractive, and as she continued to emphasize her physical appearance more and more, she fell further and further into self-degradation and opened the door for the onset of an even deeper inferiority complex. These issues not only plagued her throughout her adolescent years but also carried over into her adulthood. I remember vividly as a child watching as my mother would incessantly clean and redecorate our home for no apparent reason other than her unwarrantable exigency for all to look suitable and up to par. It was those wants and extreme needs that often paralyzed her and gripped her with panic and fear. And while she managed to still be a loving and caring maternal figure for both Hal and me, the daily trepidation that existed was allowed to run amok and pervaded our consciousness.

Subsequently, I was lucky enough to discover that my experiences as youth unequivocally shaped and molded me into the person that I became. The environment was clearly an essential aspect of my adult makeup as well. Lessons learned, wisdom imparted and insights conveyed all contributed to my debilitating disposition. Just like recalling my dad's voice when he told me to look both ways before I crossed the street, I also recollected my mom's whisper that a little white lie was always acceptable, especially if it wasn't going to hurt anyone. Looking back, that simple expression led me from childish fibs to blatant lies in order to get my way and achieve my goals. Lying become second nature to me, a means to an end, and oftentimes it was much more intriguing than the truth. Certainly, a little embellishment was always welcome, and so-called fudging came to be the norm.

However, sitting in the cafeteria waiting for Beth to appear, I was totally absent of any understanding regarding my recent deficiencies. That knowledge had yet to be gained, and I felt incompetent in every area of my life. My depression and remorse only worsened as I tried to grasp the concept that my immemorial insurance policies of drugs and alcohol were no longer accessible. Beth had been the most important individual in my life over the past four years, and I was acutely aware that she was planning to spend the rest of her existence by my side. I could not begin to even fathom the shock, bewilderment, and devastation that my failed suicide had brought upon her, and now I was going to have to attempt to transmit all of my thoughts and reasons. It all seemed surreal as I watched the visitors entering through the corridor. I retrieved an old memory of legendary football coach George Allen discussing his team's Superbowl loss the following Monday, "Losing the Superbowl is worse than death," he ascribed, "because with death, you don't have to wake up the next morning." I trembled with terror as I pondered the rationale for my decision, and then she was there in all her splendor.

Beth sat down across the table from me, and I could see the sadness and perplexity in her angelic face. Nothing was said for what seemed like an eternity, and then she cleared her throat and started asking questions. Afterward, she disclosed what the last few days had been like for her, as well as all the uncertainty and worry that she had faced. She was truly shaken by the revelations of what had occurred and could not comprehend the scenario that had played out. However, as the mosaic began to fashion in front of her and my admissions began to pour forth, a horrific realization dawned upon her. The person whom she loved, trusted, and admired the most in the world had deluded and abandoned her. Her face morphed into a mass of astonishment and anguish as the veracity of the situation persisted to pound her. All I wanted to do was to ease her pain. But unfortunately, the trauma that I had caused with my abhorrent behavior could not be displaced. There was nothing left that I could do. We held hands and wept together, wondering silently what was next.

CHAPTER 15

Let Freedom Ring

Release day

I WAS HOPEFUL WHEN I awoke that damp Tuesday morning that I would be released from captivity and allowed to return to society. My wish came true a few hours later when the cry, "Bed 8 on the discharge," echoed throughout the ward. I had learned during my stay that the "outtake" procedures were both long and arduous, and therefore, I began to prepare myself immediately for the task at hand. There were to be mountains of paperwork pending, final decrees and directives coming, and of course, one last administrative session awaiting. I organized and packed up my scant belongings and readied for the fun to begin.

The supervising nurse informed me that the process would commence right after lunch and that once the necessary documentation had all been properly signed and consented to, a meeting would be held in the small conference room located adjacent to the outside lobby. In attendance at that gathering were to be both my medical doctor and my psychiatrist, as well as Ms. Colleen O'Malley, Ann, and myself. While I certainly had nothing left to conceal at that point, I was still somewhat apprehensive of the discussion which was to follow. Thankfully, the joyous atmosphere in the lunchroom attributed to my imminent departure was able to distract my attention and allowed me to enjoy my last few minutes with my fellow psychotics. There were hugs and well wishes all around. By the time

I was summoned to the discharge area, I was feeling fairly relieved and relaxed.

The initial documents were pro forma in nature, and there was nothing contained therein that was either surprising or suspicious. I signed and acknowledged them all where necessary and was then escorted to the holding pen to await my destiny. After a few minutes, the conference-room door opened, and Colleen O'Malley asked me to join her inside. Ann was already present, and she was seated in one of the three available chairs surrounding a small circular table. She rose as I entered the room and then came over to greet me with a hug and a peck on the cheek. "Please have a seat," Ms. O'Malley instructed. "This shouldn't take very long." I nodded in agreement and sat down timidly next to Ann. "Your wife and I have been discussing your out-patient plan and what you should anticipate over the next few weeks," she continued. I looked up curiously and asked, "Shouldn't I have been here for that? After all, it is my life we're talking about."

Ann grasped my arm as if to calm me down and said, "Colleen was just giving me some basic information regarding when and where you will need to report, that's all. And I took some notes down, as well as some addresses and phone numbers in order to help." "We had some time to kill before you arrived," Ms. O'Malley pointed out. "And it was just a bit of underlying data that was passed on, nothing inordinate." Still somewhat paranoid and unsettled, I changed the subject and inquired, "What about my medical charts and diagnostic reports? Am I finally going to receive copies and to learn the find-ings?" Ms. O'Malley smiled. "The doctors will be along shortly to apprise you of their treatment strategy, and I am sure that you will be fully informed of their conclusion as well. Why? Is there some-thing on your mind?" I shrugged and sarcastically replied, "On my mind…no. What could possibly be on my mind?" Then I reminded her, "No one in this facility has yet to disclose any of the factors that have led to their decisions concerning my psychoses, nor have they been forthright with any answers. So why should I expect anything different now?"

This time, Ann tugged on my shirt sleeve in an effort to assuage my indignation, but when she saw the outrage in my eyes, she loosened her grip and quietly placed her hands on her lap. Colleen observed Ann's movements and assured her, "It's all right, Ann. It's only natural for the patients to feel combative, especially when it comes to their diagnosis. It often takes a longer period of time than they envisage, and this leads to mistrust and frustration." Ann shook her head and looked at me sympathetically while I continued to seethe internally and tried to craft my next reply in a judicious manner. "Yes," I began, "the patient frequently does feel combative, especially when his caregivers are inaccessible most of the time, and his therapy more often than not involves prescription narcotics rather than personal interaction." I also let her know that inundating mentally and emotionally unsound individuals with medication rather than metaphysics only leads them further into the abysmal world of doubt and denial, thereby perpetuating their self-criticism and self-torment. A kind word, a smile, and some basic knowledge certainly would go further than a pill or an injection." Colleen sighed and then admitted, "The system is not perfect, but it does work." Then there was a knock on the door.

Colleen rose to answer the unexpected interruption and then stepped outside to confront the messenger. Apparently, the doctors were going to be delayed for a few minutes, and Ms. O'Malley was going to seize the opportunity to make a quick call. She excused herself politely and left Ann and me alone. It was the first time in several days that the two of us were secluded together, and as I turned to look at her, I couldn't imagine what she was feeling. The events of the past fortnight had not only unhinged her universe, but they also cracked the very foundation that she had always relied upon. The life she had been accustomed to was never going to be restored, and in fact, things were probably going to get a whole lot worse before they got better. Yet somehow she seemed composed and also confident that all would be transformed and that the turmoil would pass. And while I truly believe that she was totally blindsided by my addiction, depression, and criminality, I had the impression that deep down she was aware of my disloyalty. After all, our marriage and love for each other had dissipated over the years, and now they existed more out of convenience than passion. I had always been faithful, however, until

Beth entered my life, but now I was an adulterer and someone who could no longer be trusted.

Communication between Ann and me had been our most problematic issue, and it was extremely evident that the situation still existed as we sat side by side in eerie silence. It was, though, a different kind of stillness, one of apathy rather than contempt. There remained ongoing strong feelings toward each other, yet the indifference had clearly begun to outweigh the charm. For me, this change has taken place several years earlier, but for Ann, it was presently more apparent than ever. You could sense the bitter struggle within her as she battled the emotions that oscillated between her heart and her mind. She was torn between trying to save her family and trying to save herself, except as far as she was concerned, there was no real discernible choice. Ann's family was her lifeblood; without that, there would be no preserving herself.

Luckily, before we even had a chance to work up a dialogue, my physician barged into the chamber and started his soliloquy. He bellowed out his name, rank, and serial number as he shuffled through the various file folders in his possession. Upon locating the specific one of interest, he glanced up and was immediately taken aback. "Where's O'Malley?" he inquired. "Is this not the scheduled discharge proceeding?" I mockingly replied, "I certainly hope so, Doc. I have several appointments to keep today, and I hate being tardy." He peered at me, completely dumbfounded, reexamined the open chart before him, and began to fidget in discomfort. It was obvious that he was both unprepared and uninformed regarding my case and that without Colleen's input, he would be totally ineffectual. Accordingly, he hurriedly made his way to the door and went back into the lobby searching for answers. Within a few seconds, he and Colleen returned side by side with my shrink in tow, a triumvirate ready to rule.

I tried to remain unruffled throughout the twenty-minute interlude and conceded to the fact that it was all part of the necessary procedures. Ann listened in attentively to all that was put forth and nodded along with each speaker as she diligently scribbled in her notebook. It was truly just a dog-and-pony show for effect, one last chance for the system to prove its value and confirm its merit.

Afterward, the two doctors said their brief farewells and then hastily went back to business, leaving Ms. O'Malley behind to close the deal. I ruminated for a moment and thought about all that had occurred during my stay. I also reflected back on my behavior and personal conduct over that period. Undeniably, I had been hardheaded and difficult to bear at times, especially with Colleen, but I assumed that aspect came with the territory. Obviously, her job description championed patience, care, and understanding, and I was certain that she had dealt with patients far more abusive and sicker than me. Yet throughout it all, her demeanor stayed invariably pleasant and professional, and that was still the case as she concluded her perfunctory chores. Once finished, she paused a moment to stretch and sigh, and I noticed a variance in her posture. She pensively stood up, shook hands with Ann, and then turned her focus on me. I froze momentarily as she unexpectedly embraced me and whispered several warm salutations in my ear. I hugged her back and thanked her sincerely for all of her help, and then she disappeared from my life forever. I rotated back toward Ann and quickly quipped, "Let's get out of here before they change their minds."

The sky was gray and overcast as we made our way out of the hospital and over to the guest parking area. I was absolutely relieved to be exiting the facility, but was also both physically and emotionally drained from my sojourn. I stared ahead until we passed through the security gates and then closed my eyes in exultation. Ann allowed me a few moments to decompress and then alerted me to our itinerary for the remainder of the day. The journey was to be comprised of an initial visit with my legal team, followed by an introductory meet and greet with my new think tank, and then finally a quiet dinner with The Prince. While I was already considerably weary from the day's goings-on, I was well aware of the importance of the forthcoming agenda and attempted to regain my concentration.

I must have drifted off because the next cognitive concern I secured was the car jostling over the raised speed bumps as Ann entered the underground garage of my attorney's building. She pulled into the first available space, turned off the ignition, and prepared for the venture ahead of us. I watched as she adjusted her hair and makeup in the foldaway mirror and then collected my thoughts with regard to the impending conference. "Ready?" Ann proposed. "As ready as I guess I'll ever be," I responded. And with that, we left for the elevators.

The office waiting room was plush and fanciful, and we were greeted eagerly by a young lithe receptionist. She told us that they were expecting us and to take a seat momentarily until she could announce our arrival. The chairs were soft, comfortable, and expensive; and just as I began to ease myself back into one, I heard our names audibly over the intercom. About ten minutes later, we were shown inside to the firm's main epicenter where three men in finely tailored suits calmly awaited our entrance. I immediately recognized one of them as a former colleague of mine whom I had previously worked with on numerous occasions. Apparently, Ann had utilized our network of contacts to employ counsel who were not only experts in the field but who would also have a personal stake in the outcome. I softened my stance and naturally relaxed a bit, knowing that my best interests would truly be sought out. We welcomed one another, commiserated for an instant, and then got down to the business at hand.

Considering that I had yet to be criminally charged with anything officially, the tenor of the meeting was more cordial than accusatory. I agreed to have Ann document my hospitalization since she had taken extensive notes and had undeniably paid greater attention to detail than myself. She conveyed in elaborate specificity the terms of my release, as well as my diagnosis of major depressive disorder, a dangerous psychological condition. The doctors had concluded that my fragile state of mind, coupled with the onset of my rigorous drug and alcohol abuse, created a toxic situation which culminated in my attempted self-destruction. In other words, I was already suffering from severe depression, and the addition of chronic depressant use on top of that simply pushed me over the edge. It was the classic "straw that broke the camel's back," and in my instance, it was the logical conclusion to my addictive state.

We left the meeting feeling somewhat optimistic about my circumstances, yet we also realized that there was quite a long road ahead. The future was tenuous at best; however, Ann and I were both hopeful that our next stop would be the impetus for my recovery. I had never partaken in any type of private psychiatric care prior to this upcoming experience, and as such, my anxiety and apprehension increased as we approached the treatment center. The less-than-impressive building was located on a busy commercial thoroughfare in one of the seedier sections of a nearby town. There was no private parking, only metered spaces on the street, and I mused silently as Ann circled the block looking for a spot. Once inside, the interior lobby also left much to be desired, but somehow the shabby decor and scant surroundings had an appeasing effect. The workmanlike atmosphere and the good-natured staff added to the safe and secure aura contained therein, and I felt myself begin to relax and unwind as I undertook the task of completing the admittance paperwork.

After concluding with the dozen or so pages of the questionnaire, I passed the clipboard through the opening in the plexiglass window and returned timidly to my seat. Within no time, a cheerful middle-aged woman surfaced and introduced herself as the nurse-practitioner who would be handling my intake process. She informed us that the procedure would take a couple of hours and advised Ann to return around six o'clock as it was already approaching 4:00 p.m. Ann looked at me for approval, and I just shrugged and said, "I guess I'll see you later. Please give The Prince a big hug for me." She patted my shoulder tenderly, told me to behave myself, and then disappeared outside, leaving me alone to face my new inquisitors.

I was gingerly guided out of the lobby, past the intimidating doorkeeper, and down a long corridor into an examination room. The initial interrogation centered around my physical traits—height, weight, blood type, allergies, medication, and the like—and also included a standard swift physical once-over. After my bodily data was entered and recorded, the nurse set the chart on the counter, washed her hands, and informed me that someone else would be with me shortly. I sat patiently on the edge of the cushioned lounge wondering what was going to occur next and why it was going to take another hour and a half of my time.

When the door opened again, two therapists joined me and cautiously began to expound upon the psychotherapy that would be utilized for my treatment. It was to be an eclectic approach comprised of individual and group sessions, as well as an educational seminar once a week. While I remained skeptical toward their strategies and how they planned to remedy all of my ills, I know that they were certified specialists in dealing with these matters, and I also knew that I still was in need of considerable help.

The next several minutes were devoted entirely to the history of the recent month's events and the orchestration of my attempted demise. We covered all aspects of my life including my drinking, drugging, gambling, cheating, and lying as well as all the personal and legal issues stemming from those vices. It was a veritable hodgepodge of depravity, and as I painfully portrayed both my objectives and my mind-set. I felt my rectitude slipping away. I was neither proud of my previous actions nor arrogant concerning my newfound worth. Instead I found myself more or less adrift, craving someone or something to grasp on to. I was visibly longing for some sort of guidance, a new purpose and direction for my existence, and I hoped that I could find that at the threshold of my recovery. I professed, "I am willing to do anything in order to rectify my spirit. I am in your hands utterly and completely." The two healers smiled, glanced at each other then toward me, and then one spoke, saying, "That's all we wanted to hear. Welcome aboard."

Subsequently, Ann returned and was asked to take a part in a final recapitulation of the day's session. After clarifying a number of points and confirming the proposed game plan and method of attack, it was time to head home and to start on my transformation. The process had to commence at the core level and work its way outward and the logical onset was within the familiar confines of my abode. I needed to return to the basics and reconnect with my deep-seated convictions and with my family. Yet the fundamental question still remained, how was this miracle going to occur? Clearly, my greatest defect had been my lack of foresight, and I was so accustomed to gobbling up anything and everything for immediate gratification that I was truly unsure where to begin. But when the garage door rose and my little black puppy bounded outside to meet me, the first wave of unconditional love struck my heart. That, coupled with a long affectionate hug from The Prince, enhanced my mood and made me hanker for more.

I had been living an empty, meaningless life where I chased the wrong things and substituted materialistic items for a sense of love, compassion, and benevolence. And while I was so eager to absorb all the positive energy being emitted, I had to quell my enthusiasm and realize that an overnight panacea was not immediately available. I needed to understand that years of abuse were not going to be retracted in a manner of minutes or hours or even days. It was going to take a series of actions, one step at a time, to achieve the desired results. One of the first adages I learned in my rehabilitation was "Time takes time," and more accurate words have never been spoken. However, as we sat in the den eating our dinners together in front of the TV, a feeling of normalcy reemerged. Unfortunately, little did I know that my circumstances would never be normal again.

CHAPTER 16

The Greatest Gift of All

The next day

I AWOKE LATE AND GROGGY, and it took me awhile to comprehend where I was. As I struggled to gain my senses and grasp my surroundings, little Fifi yelped twice and then leaped on top of me, and I instantly realized that I was safe and sound in my own bed. I pondered whether it could all have been just a vivid nightmare, an eerie *Christmas Carol* like dream. Unfortunately, however, as I hugged and snuggled with man's best friend, the actuality of all that occurred became all too clear. The bedroom was in total disarray and surely not in the condition that I would have consciously or even unconsciously left it in. In addition, there were stacks of pads, loose papers, bills, phone numbers, and sticky notes covering the night table and overflowing onto the floor below. Apparently, Ann had been busy organizing our affairs in my absence, and her system was somewhat haphazard. Regardless of that fact, she had done a superb job keeping it all together and managing the household over the past few weeks. While I wrestled to clear the cobwebs from my mind, it dawned on me that I neither had anywhere to go nor anything pressing to do, so I took a long, deep, cleansing breath and lay back against the headboard. It was the first day of the rest of my life, and I was puzzled over where to begin.

First off, I knew that I was alone as both Ann and The Prince had already left for work and school respectively. I had not planned a full schedule of daily chores as it was the seminal day of my evolution, and I did not want to overburden myself. However, in the same light, I did not want to pussyfoot around either, so I jumped out of bed and commenced my morning hygiene routine. Once freshened up, I established a few small goals for the afternoon hours, leaving ample time to both eat and to take Fifi for a nice, long, leisurely walk. It was a beautiful spring day with all of nature's glory in full bloom, and I hungered to bask in its resplendence. I had been cooped up long enough of late, and I needed time to just enjoy the scenery. There were still many serious consequences that I was going to have to confront, but since these were not going to dissipate anytime soon, I was undeniably entitled to a few moments of peace, especially after yesterday's deluge of activities. My rationalization skills were still sharp as ever, yet this time I truly felt valid in my justification.

In spite of that, the one item that could not be overlooked under any circumstance was locating a nighttime AA meeting to attend somewhere nearby. I had been instructed that an essential piece of my recovery puzzle was to incorporate a 12-step program into my daily course of action and that this should be done immediately and not postponed or delayed. As such, I referred to the pamphlet I had been furnished with and began my search of the local Alcoholics Anonymous meetings in my neighborhood.

The mid and late day passed by rapidly, but I was able to accomplish the small number of things that I had set out to do. The most peaceful interval was spent on my walk with Fifi as she pranced around the community exploring all of the sights and smells of the region. It made me hanker back to the time when The Prince was a toddler, and he would strive to absorb his surroundings as a sponge does water. It was a pure innocence, a simplistic curiosity, and one I yearned to retrieve again. Now, however, as a teenager, much of this naivete had perished, and his credulous nature had transmuted into one of vigorous inquiry and investigation. This was all too apparent when he and Ann came to visit me during my hospital stay, and he peppered me with nonstop questions: "So why are you here, Dad?" "Do you know when you will be coming home?" "How come everyone here looks different than you?" "What do you do all day long?"

They were normal questions to normal feelings and reactions, yet I knew that the answers had to be made in a precisely prudent and tactful manner.

Neither Ann nor I had told The Prince the truth about my hospitalization. Instead, we stuck with the story that I was overwhelmed and depressed more than usual and thus required a brief respite. While initially we both believed that we had him fooled, it became evident as time went by that he was no longer buying our canard. In addition, as the frequency of his visits increased, so did his insatiable thirst for gaining the truth. At one point, Ann chided him, saying that it was neither the time nor the place to discuss our private family matters and that if he had further inquiries, she would address them later at home, even though I know she never did. After all, there was no reason for him to learn the exact cause of my confinement or the conditions that preceded it. We needed to keep him in the dark concerning the gory details and also to keep his spirits up and in a positive light. I would be home soon and would be better and stronger than ever, or so we feigned. In actuality, neither one of us could predict the outcome of my treatment plan, yet we were optimistic that it would be a success. As long as I was no longer suicidal, then there was plainly a light at the end of the tunnel, a glimmer of hope rather than one of despair.

Evening emerged and it was time for me to venture out and to experience the next phase of my repentance. I had discovered that there was an AA group just a couple of miles away from my house, and I was determined to get there for the 7:30 p.m. assembly. Naturally, it was situated within the confines of a local church, and I knew the destination well as I had driven past it on numerous occasions. Tonight, however, there was a different stake at risk, and one which I sincerely needed to restore my sanity.

Dusk had fallen, and my eyesight began to diminish as I approached the enormous Catholic cathedral. It was truly a vast array of buildings and structures, and I had no idea where among the shapes and shadows I would discover my goal. I pulled into a small obscure parking lot which was virtually vacant and continued my journey on foot. I found the seminary, the rectory, and the main worship center, but no one was visible in any of those locations. As I strolled throughout the compound, nervously aspiring to attain my purpose, it seemed more and more distinct that failure was in my future. As darkness eclipsed the last remaining strand of daylight, my probe had become virtually impossible, and I returned sullenly back to my car. I sat for a minute trying to calculate a course of action, and as I closed my eyes in disappointment, a tear ran down my cheek.

Ann was surprised that I had returned so soon, but after I conveyed to her my experience, her shock turned into compassion. I was obviously upset and annoyed by my lack of achievement, and my composure was evaporating rapidly. "There will be another meeting tomorrow," Ann assured me, continuing, "Don't beat yourself up over it…you tried your best." I mused anxiously and then pointed out that I had devoted my entire focus to attending tonight's gathering. Then I let her know, "I am going to find the right place tomorrow by hook or crook, even if I have to leave an hour early." "Perhaps there is a meeting at a more modest site that might be easier to reach," Ann suggested. "Maybe," I replied. "I'll make some calls in the morning and try to verify one for sure. It's my obsession now."

I spent most of the succeeding morning phoning various houses of worship and researching the possible options. While there were quite a number of choices available, it was difficult to obtain any useful data. Most of the responses that I received were similar in nature: polite, sympathetic, but uninformative. The receptionist and staff that I spoke with knew vaguely about the meeting but were unsure about the exact times or the program schedule. I understood the AA meant Alcoholics Anonymous, but I was vexed by the lack of facts that were accessible. Finally, I narrowed it down to a specific unassuming venue and then instinctively decided to do a quick drive-by just for good measure. The small Presbyterian church was situated on a scenic overlook that conveyed a welcome aura of peace and tranquility. Moreover, it was nothing similar to the massive enclave that stared at me the previous night, and I had a good feeling that I would accomplish my mission. I returned home full of anticipatory angst, yet also comfortable that I had made the proper selection.

Not certain if the commencement was either at 7:30 p.m. or 8:00 p.m., I timed my departure so that I would arrive promptly at 7:15 p.m. The sun was slowly fading over the distant horizon, but there remained enough daylight to make my resolve visible. I tentatively made my way to the central entrance, and as I drew closer, I noticed that there were also stairwells on each side of the building leading to subentries as well. Having no firm notion where to proceed, I made the decision to follow the path toward the main entranceway. As I reached for the large ornamental door handle, I was startled by a noise off to my right, which reverberated like footsteps descending into the night. My inclination was to follow after the sound, but since I was already at the front doorway, I tried to pull the door ajar. It shifted a bit but was clearly bolted from the inside, and I realized that I should have followed my initial impulse. Redirecting my steps toward the northern staircase, I noticed a well-illuminated vestibule containing a tiny sign displayed in the window. As I approached farther, I saw that it was the AA insignia, a triangle within a circle and the words *unity*, *service*, and *recovery*. I knew then, for truly the first time, that I belonged.

Once inside, I maneuvered my way through the maze of corridors until I reached a moderate-sized auditorium. In the center of the sparse hall were a dozen or so chairs positioned in a circular manner, each of which possessed a thick hardcover book carefully centered on the seat cushion. The room had an air of coldness about it, and while it lacked any real charm and allure, I could sense a plenary presence within. Just then, a languid older gentleman appeared and deliberately paced his way toward a small table cluttered with various leaflets and handouts. The man shuffled through the papers, seemingly unaware of my existence, until he glanced up and saw me peering at him. Eventually, he straightened up and then barked, "Hey, young fella, I didn't hear you come in. My name is Herb, and I'm an atheist. Welcome to AA."

I chatted with Herb for the next few minutes as he put the finishing touches on the preparations for the upcoming eventide. He explained that tonight's group format was to be an "anniversary meeting" and that there would be three celebrants sharing their experience, strength, and hope with the rest of the fellowship. Accordingly, there was to be a special cake, as well as decorations, which need to be arranged properly and with precise know-how. Herb took these trusted assignments quite seriously, and he diligently went about his duties until he was satisfied that everything was just right.

Every so often, a group member would arrive, deliver Herb a salutation, and then methodically take his or her customary seat in the circle. I tried not to be conspicuous, so I busied myself by assisting Herb in setting out the necessary accessories comprised of plastic forks, plates, paper products, and of course, the compulsory coffee. As the clock approached 8:00 p.m., most of the chairs were occupied, and I apprehensively located an empty spot to sit. Now appropriately seated, I felt a flow of immense invigoration course throughout my body. Something special was going to happen this night, yet I had no idea that it would alter my life forevermore.

The meeting opened with the oration of the AA preamble followed by a series of informational announcements. Herb had taken up the place next to me and was cleaning his eyeglasses as he recited the introductory phrases and urged me to join along. After the precursors had concluded, a most unexpected and unsettling question was brought to the floor: "Are there any new people here with us tonight?" Herb shot a gentle elbow into my arm and whispered, "You're up, kid," and I swallowed profoundly before choosing my words. "Good evening," I began. "It's my first time participating in a group like this, and I am hopeful that I will learn a great deal from the experience." Cries of "Welcome" and "You're home now" and "Keep coming" resonated throughout the room, followed by a moment of thunderous applause. I couldn't help from restraining a brief smile as I gestured back in acknowledgement and sank down lower into my chair. *Perhaps this might work*, I thought encouragingly, and that's when the real revelations started to emerge right before my eyes.

The proceedings continued with each of the anniversary speakers providing his or her own personal story about their unique journey. One by one, they stood up and told tales about what they were like, what happened, and what they are like now. It was an enlightening experience which culminated with an extraordinary "share" expressed with extreme articulation and command. This particular member's voice rang out like it was directly channeling God's word and conveying His message. It was a powerful, robust and melodious tone that filled the atmosphere with hope and optimism. One could not help but be mesmerized by the sheer omniscience of his wonder. And while the man himself was neither overly impressive nor visually pious-looking, once he summoned his instrument from within, it was clear that he possessed the aura of God.

My connection with Francis seemed almost instantaneous and I felt my spirit begin to ascend. I related to everything that he said and felt as if he was talking directly and solely to me. Afterward, I had the opportunity to introduce myself, and he graciously spent a few minutes with me extolling the virtues of the program. When all was said and done, I left with a new attitude and outlook on AA, its participants and on life in general. If all these people could emerge from their hopeless states of both mind and body, then I certainly had an opportunity to do the same. It was that glimmer of hope, coupled with the unbridled enthusiasm which brought the group together, that made me desire more. I wanted what these people had—sobriety, serenity, and most of all, joy—all things that I had lacked most recently. Their bonds linked them in a unity of understanding and camaraderie that I aspired to become a part of. It was not only that these men and women had lost urge to drink and become abstinent, but it was also how they had changed their whole way of thinking. Love and tolerance of others was now their code and it was supremely manifested in both their behavior and appearance. While I was relying on AA to resolve my drinking problem and to relieve me of my anguish, I never imagined that it would make me a better person as well.

The next morning I awakened to the roar of my dinosaur alarm clock and I immediately felt coherent and alert. I had set the timer for 9:00 a.m. which gave me just over an hour to shower, dress, and grab some joe at a local coffeehouse. Today I was headed to the morning discussion meeting of Alcoholic Anonymous at a temple in a nearby hamlet. Yes, it was true, the meeting was taking place in a temple. That fact mollified my earlier audacity that perhaps AA was some sort of anti-Semitic Christian-based cult that surreptitiously held gatherings in churches in order to exclude other sects and specifically Jews. After all, I had previously discovered only certain houses of worship devoted to a particular religious faith and practice which allowed these events to be convoked. In addition, the night before, both the literature displayed and the liturgy expressed showed distinct devoutness toward Christianity and principles based on biblical scriptures. Of course, being an agnostic for the better part of my life left me ignorant regarding the Bible and its doctrines, yet somehow the godliness of the proceedings seemingly steered me away from the precarious position.

My undergraduate studies at the university led me to major in philosophy, and my final thesis had been an essay centered on theology. While my adolescent years had been also devoid of any divinity, as I matured, I found myself asking many metaphysical questions. Accordingly, I sought out an area of study that would enrich my mind and expand my horizons. I enjoyed that the theoretical discussions and intimate lectures that the courses provided, and I established a good working relationship with most of the professors. Furthermore, even though the department itself was quite diminutive and was actually abandoned for lack of interest just prior to my graduation, I could not have imagined a better path for rediscovering my true essence. The logic, reasoning, and judgement skills that were taught allowed me to reach levels of thought that I had previously never conceived of. There was no other field of study that ever stretched my imagination the way the philosophical postulates and arguments did. And for me, a person already fully embedded in the early stages of addiction, it permitted and even invited my continued alcohol and drug use as a means to further enhance my knowledge and experiences. However, even with all the rhetoric and instruction, it was still impossible for me to consign to certain notions and hypothesis.

The leading tenet that I struggled with the most was the existence of a Supreme Being, some godlike manager of the universe who created the world and all its reality. I was leery about such doctrines and was swayed more by the words of the early skeptics than those of, say, St. Anselm and Thomas Aquinas. The ontological and teleological arguments seemed easy to dismiss, or at the very least, extremely flawed. Now, however, a large number of years later, it appears clear to me that trying to utilize reason and logic to confirm the existence of God is as senseless as trying to change the past. Faith and spirituality are based on belief and love, not facts and formulas. It took me a long time to grasp that concept and to learn to live more with my heart and less with my head.

As I pulled into the long driveway fronting the temple, I wondered whether this encounter would be as stirring as the night before. The parking lot was already crowded with various upscale vehicles ranging from BMWs to Mercedes to even a few Bentleys. I parked between a small sporty Mercedes convertible and some type of large expensive SUV and stared out the window, waiting for a sign to proceed. People were moving to and fro, and then an older-model classic van pulled into one of the designated handicapped spots in front of the synagogue walkaway. I watched as the driver helped an elderly woman into a wheelchair and how, almost instantaneously, a crowd grew around her. She was showered with kisses and warm embraces, and I later learned that she was the matriarch of this particular group and that she had been absent as of late due to a chronic illness. At the time, however, I just remember feeling a sense of comfort as I witnessed the heartfelt scene play out. It was enough to arouse my emotions and to thrust me into action.

The bright morning sunshine had begun to heat up the day and I squinted as I removed my shades and stepped out of the car. I tried to act casual and to blend in with the others, but by the time I entered the classroom where everyone was mingling about, it was obvious that a newbie had invaded the arena. I was greeted with an abundance of fervent interest and encircled by several of the male figureheads. Afterward, one of the more zealous fellows ushered me toward a seat near the lectern and began to bestow upon me various informational pamphlets and literature. I informed him that I had attended my first meeting only last night and that I was currently searching for somewhere to call home. "Oh, I think you'll like it here," he replied. "Just try to relax and absorb the message." And with that the room came to order and the formalities commenced.

The overall tenor was very similar to yesterday's doings, however, the enthusiasm and ardor that were present were much more conducive in nature. This morning AA session was actually tailored for beginners like myself, and although all were welcome, the fresh and novel attitudes of the newcomers created a very poignant scene. I listened as member after member raised their hands, announced their names, followed by the words "and I'm an alcoholic," and then revealed to everyone their current day counts. It was particularly moving to witness the emotions on the people's faces as they proudly recited the number of days sobriety they had attained, and also to hear the loud rounds of encouragement that followed. I was captivated, drawn in by the happenings, and when I spoke of these feelings afterward, I was told that "AA is a program of attraction rather than promotion," and also that "people don't care how much you know until they know how much you care." Those two phrases stuck with me throughout the next few weeks, and little by little, I become enthralled by the program and its insights.

As I attended additional meetings at the temple, I got into a rhythm regarding both the structure and the schedule of the gatherings therein. In addition, I also continued to meet Herb and Francis at the weekly Thursday-evening church group, and I developed a nice balance between the two associations. While the early daytime undertakings provided a broad spectrum of knowledge, as well as a broad-minded approach due to the large number of attendees, the nighttime encounters were more intimate and serene. Each, in their own style, embodied the true crux of the AA message: "WHAT WE COULD NOT DO ALONE—WE COULD ACCOMPLISH TOGETHER." We are all "sick" and "suffering" people, and we need the "experience, strength, and hope" of others in order to heal ourselves. There is a certain mystique that binds people to one another and that also produces a mutual connection and consolation. AA seemed to have captured that essence, and the union of its souls was powerful indeed.

CHAPTER 17

Serenity Now

Thirty days later

THE PREVIOUS MONTH HAD BEEN filled with examples evinced, ideals imparted, and lessons learned. I had achieved all of my precursory goals including obtaining my thirty-day coin, attending over sixty AA meetings and acquiring a sponsor to help guide me along my journey. In addition, I had also commenced to both studying the program literature and working "the steps." The fog had steadily lifted from me, and while I knew that I still had a long way to go, my self-assurance was increasing daily. More importantly, I was actually glad to be alive, and the precarious mood swings that had previously plagued me were slowly dissipating. The process and change from my life of debauchery to one free from moral turpitude was well on its way.

Thankfully, my new comrade Francis had agreed to mentor me, and his counsel and advice were already permeating my consciousness. He explained to me that AA's formula for recovery was really a very simple plan of action and that as long as I gave it my all, I would espy "prodigious results." We would often meet at a local diner or coffee shop and converse for hours about life and about dealing with "life on life's terms." Many of these new notions and concepts were foreign to me, and it was as if I was trying to learn a new language. Luckily, Francis had the patience and repose to cope with my ignorance, even though he repeatedly insisted that I keep a volitional attitude and one free of preconceptions. He dropped "jewels" and "pearls of wisdom" regularly, and I attempted to retain as much of this knowledge as possible. Phrases such as "contempt prior to investigation" and "a closed mouth does not get fed" were expounded daily during our dialogues. The numerous AA mottos and slogans became a fabric of our sessions and I gobbled them up with alacrity. The input I received made me thirst for more, and I grasped all that I could with great resolve. I was informed painstakingly that "half measure avail us nothing" and that "it only works if you work it," so I was aware that I had to give it my all. I was compelled to; there was no other choice.

Sensing my eagerness to succeed, Francis proceeded accordingly and taught me the basic principles necessary to be successful. He alerted me to the three most indispensable tools of the Alcoholic Anonymous program: honesty, open-mindedness, and willingness and he used the acronym HOW to convey their significance. He then continued by stating, "Without being totally honest, first with ourselves and then with others, without liberating ourselves from prior misconceptions, and without also surrendering to unaccustomed ideas, we would be lost forever." Next, Francis sincerely next asked me the sole question that truly needed to be answered: "To what lengths are you willing to go in order to recover?" He followed that query with a subsequent interrogation that culminated by him asking, "And are you willing to do whatever I suggest irrespective of your fears and apprehensions? For if you are, then join me on the Broad Highway to repentance and let's start the real pursuit."

Already pumped up from my regular rendezvous with Francis, I simultaneously threw myself into the outpatient phase of my treatment and began to abide by all the guidelines therein. I had been assigned a licensed and certified therapist for my individual care and was also enrolled in both an educational seminar as well as a weekly group assembly for alcohol and drug offenders. While I was not mandated by the authorities to attend these courses, it was subtly insinuated that I would benefit from their precepts. This mélange of treatments, interwoven with the assistance of my 12-step support groups, maintained a daily commitment of recovery that kept me directed on the appropriate pathway. I fully immersed myself into the clinic's gamut of guidance and found the added instruction to be both informative and therapeutic. Furthermore, I had previously learned from my recent hospitalization and my interaction with Colleen O'Malley that in order to undergo a proper metamorphosis, I had to be absolutely frank with the caregivers who were aiding me. After all, being dishonest and deceitful had already brought me to my knees, and it was now time to stand up, become trustworthy, and convey my genuine sensitivities.

It was during this early stretch of time that my counselors informed me how imperative it was to maintain my current status quo and not to make any material changes. Due to the tenuous resources that I currently possessed, it was essential that I kept my immediate surroundings as stable as possible. Accordingly, I had remained living at home with Ann and The Prince and attempted to carry on in a state of resoluteness. Of course, returning to the scene of my past misery was quite unsettling, and it took all of my determination to assuage my discomfort. There wasn't anything tangible that I could actually put my finger on, but the atmosphere in the house certainly possessed an eerie tenseness. Neither Ann nor The Prince was sure how to behave in my company, and this only added to the discomfort. I tried to be both amiable and scrupulous each and every day in order to assuage their concerns about my health and welfare, yet they still persisted to timidly walk on eggshells. Consequently, I found myself spending less and less time at home and more and more time delving into my rehabilitation. I had to establish a cautious yet firm balance to ensure that all involved could heal appropriately. Emotions were running high and a backlash could surface at a moment's notice.

Unfortunately, my lifestyle only proceeded to conform lethargically as I remained adverse to relinquishing control of myself and of those around me. I was still learning how to subvert my desires, how to conquer my fears, and how to do the next right thing. Manipulation and machination had been my sources of sophistication, and this required an immediate about-face. I had always tried to play God, to manage the world, and also to regulate people's emotions. Forcing my will and inflicting my expectations into every situation in order to achieve the outcome which I craved had become my deepest compulsion. In fact, it became so debilitating that I would often physically flush and tremble as waves of hysteria crashed down upon me. These "panic attacks" were occurring far too frequently and the ensuing battle to thwart them was far more difficult than I had imagined. Moreover, my longing for Beth had begun to mount as well, and I was slipping backward into a state of self-deception and self-denial due to my constant fervor. Fortunately, Francis called for a timely intervention to clarify my intentions and to keep me focused on the proper objectives.

The informal interlude was attended by Francis, his sponsor John and myself. I reiterated my tale of woe for John, and he assured me immediately, "Kid, I've heard it all," and then reminded me that "if they already have a name for it, then someone else has already done it." He went on to say that while we all believe that we are unique and that nobody else could share our afflictions, this could not be further from the truth. Rather, both he and Francis understood my ordeal far too well as they had lived through and endured the pain just as I had. In fact, their stories mirrored my own much more than I had anticipated, and I began to realize that sharing my experiences with people who had "been there and done that" was a truly liberating phenomenon. It was just the right tonic to get me back on track, but then the hammer really fell.

No booze, no drugs, no gambling, and no Beth either—it was an impossible task. I was told that I would have to go cold turkey with regard to all these depravities if I wanted to see results. Total abstinence from every evil was the only way that I could overcome my addictions. Furthermore, I had to foremost fully accept that I was an addict and that I was in a state of dependency. It was clear that my life had become "unmanageable," but I was not yet ready to admit that it was attributable to my obsessions. Denial is a powerful deterrent, and my sagacious ability to rationalize away my difficulties was still lingering about. There were the central issues that I needed to remedy if I was going to advance to the next stages of recovery, and I soon understood that I could not cure them on my own. It was then that the concepts of *acceptance* and *surrender* were introduced to me.

Having become overwhelmingly obvious that once I stopped trying to shape life into what was comfortable for me and started accepting life for what it was, then and only then could I achieve a state of peace and tranquility. I was told over and over that "position determines perspective" and that until I altered my thinking accordingly, I was destined to fail. But how was I to let go of all the fears and reservations that I had carried for so long? The solution was to surrender unconditionally. I had already abandoned all of my honor and integrity in favor of satisfying my immediate gratifications, but now it was time to reverse that condition. Surrender was not the process of giving up, instead, it was the decision to give into the moment or the circumstance that was upon us. My drinking, drugging, gambling, and cheating had stolen my identity, and I desperately needed to rediscover who I actually was. Enlightenment and self-awareness were the indispensable tools that were required here. Without securing more clarity, paying more attention to those around me and acquiring the essential listening skills to be more present, I would never reach the elevated plane of consciousness necessary to achieve satisfaction.

Beth was the purest example of someone who possessed that inner solace and I suppose that was what melted my heart right from the get-go. Her presence always lit up the room when she entered, and she had a notable talent to make everyone around her feel special and important. However, even her ability to exhibit those traits and to shower me in her splendor, was not enough to impact my perversions. It was going to take a Higher Power to rescue me, one whom I had previously cynically discounted.

With that in mind, I turned to "Step Two" in the AA manuscript "Twelve Steps and Twelve Traditions" in order to move forward. The final paragraph of that essay professes that "step two is the rallying point for all of us... True humility and an open mind can lead us to faith and every AA meeting is an assurance that God will restore us to sanity if we rightly relate ourselves to him" (p. 33). I ruminated whether such a simple spiritual writing could elicit such returns, but I only had to go back to the text to receive the answer. The entry presented the explicit view that I had pondered: "This AA business is totally unscientific," "This I cannot swallow," "I simply won't consider such nonsense." But the proof was in the proverbial pudding. The author writes, "Then I woke up. I had to admit that AA showed results, prodigious results. I saw that my attitude regarding these had been anything but scientific. It wasn't AA that had the closed mind, it was me. The minute I stopped arguing, I could begin to see and feel. Right there, Step Two gently and very gradually began to infiltrate my life" (p. 27). Amazingly, this made sense, and I was able to fathom the notion of a "power greater than myself."

The morning daylight illuminated the small outdoor café as I patiently awaited Francis's arrival and our next spiritual session. It was 10:12 a.m. and my trepidation was slowly increasing. I debated whether or not I should text him, but instead I hesitated for moment, closed my eyes, and turned my face skyward to bask in the sun's soothing rays. It was almost Memorial Day and the heat of the upcoming summer months had already made its appearance. Right then, my cell phone exploded in excitement, and I saw Francis's name flashing on the display. I activated the call and heard Francis bellow, "Yo, sorry for the delay. I will be there in five." "No problem," I replied. "I was just relaxing and enjoying my iced coffee." "Good, man," he blurted back. "See you in a minute."

Relieved by the news of Francis's imminent approach, I tried to collect my thoughts and to realign my frame of mind. I watched as his big SUV negotiated through the vast parking lot and pulled into a spot right in front. As he strolled toward me, he gave me a broad smile and his familiar laconic greeting, and then sat down beside me. "Can I get you something to drink?" I inquired. "No, I'm good for now," he answered and changed the subject by asking, "So what's on your mind today? You seem preoccupied." I explained that I had been battling with both my spiritual intolerance and my meager existence and that I was trying to reconcile those issues. "Well, well, well"—he snickered—"perhaps it's time that we enter the realm of the Holy Spirit and discuss His omnipotence and omniscience." He continued by admitting, "I wasn't sure if you were ready yet, but evidently you're now disposed to accept His gifts." "I'm not really sure what I am," I mumbled. "But I am striving to remain open to every aspect of the program…including the God thing." Francis then pointed out, "The God thing, as you like to call it, will be your salvation. In fact, he has already shown you His mercy. Now it's up to you."

The true perplexity for me was trying to comprehend a lifeline that was founded on faith rather than on fact. I grimaced and asked Francis, "How can I completely rely upon something that is indiscernible with my own eyes?" He paused for a moment, moved in closer toward me, and then delivered a sermon that I would never forget. The gist of his message can be summarized as follows: "It doesn't really matter what or who God is as long as you remember that it's not you." He continued, "The greatest gift that anyone can receive is life. God brought you into being, recently saved you from yourself, and now wants you to consider His brilliance. Invite Him in. He will appear to all those who seek Him out." I thought deeply about those humble words and how uncomplicated they actually were. It was frightfully apparent that my elementary way of life was not working and that a change was definitely required. Could faith and a belief in Supreme Being be the solution? I had always been afraid of the unknown, and generally, when faced with a decision to risk confronting my fears, I had always cowered and crumbled in despair. Yet now, for some inexplicable reason, I felt the ability to extract the courage and to muster up the strength to oppose my demons.

The next phase of my spiritual development arose out of the notion of giving rather than receiving, and I flung myself into AA "service." In actuality, performing the daily duties indispensable for the sustenance of all AA's activities was not only strongly suggested but rather was often clearly compelled. The selection of assignments were numerous in nature and ranged from greeting the members upon their arrival at the meetings, to brewing the coffee and preparing the snack station, to collecting the chairs and cleaning up afterward. My initial involvement came from my selection as the Wednesday-morning "greeter." This was a perfect role for me as it allowed me to both informally meet all the membership and also to become more known throughout the fellowship. Accordingly, I faithfully arrived at the synagogue early, ensured that the classroom was accessible, and then took my position out in the hallway. In addition, I always properly dressed for the occasion, making sure that I looked presentable and carried an air of respectability. I had previously been advised by one of the "old-timers" that when you are given a task and assume a "commitment" to the group, it is vital to look the part and to provide a good impression for any beginners who may show up. I was told over and over again that "the newcomer is the most important person in AA," and also that the program is one of "attraction rather than promotion." I knew that was the case from my own personal experience and therefore made certain that I emitted the appropriate poise in order to welcome all who arrived.

As my three-month term proceeded, I began to get more and more comfortable with my status, which in turn permitted me to be more creative with the morning salutations. I initiated several new formats including a "word of the day," as well as "morning mottos" and "Wednesday witticisms." Upon the entrance of each parishioner, I would bestow my gospel; and inevitably, I would receive a smile and a warm embrace in return. The kinship that this evoked was remarkable and invigorated me to want to do more. This unfamiliar rush of sensations and sentimentality which I gained from helping others allowed me to undergo an even greater fundamental change than I had ever anticipated.

Experiencing an increased sense of enthusiasm and compassion, I found myself easing from my constant state of self-reproach. I evaluated my recent conduct and behavior and quickly realized that I was making significant strides. I learned that no man is beyond redemption as long as he strives to conduct himself in a redeemable fashion. Knowing is not enough; being willing is not enough. Rather, you must apply the principles and put them into practical use. We all have the capacity to better ourselves and to locate the absolute truth that resides within. Unfortunately, however, this truth can be sometimes hidden so deep inside our limits of comprehension that only a profound cleansing will elicit the necessary expulsion. For me, this only commenced when I broke down my walls, removed my barriers, and began to share my sincerest emotions with my fellow alcoholics.

I had heard on a number of occasions that "a problem shared is a problem lessened," yet the sheer vulnerability needed to accomplish this feat had always escaped me. That was the case until I finally acquired enough confidence and composure to raise my hand and join in the discussion. I remember the thumping in my chest as I stood up and poured out all of the pain and suffering that I kept locked away for a seeming eternity. Luckily, the regulations of the morning group limit each participant's "share" to a period of three minutes, so I knew that I had to keep my comments concise. Nevertheless, as each second passed, I encountered tremendous relief as all the oppressive burdens began to lift and vanish. I watched the veterans nod their heads in approval, sympathy, and understanding since they had already been there and done that. It was a truly liberating feeling and one that would persist as I continued to vent daily and to communicate my thoughts and emotions. I found it astonishing that the humble conveyance of my vexations could remove the long-term turmoil that I had suffered with. It was revealed to me that "it's a simple program of action—not easy but simple," and that as long as I kept coming back, my chances of enlightenment would greatly increase.

While my recovery progressed day by day and week by week, so did the interminable remorse that continued to plague me and hold me back. The process of introspection had alleviated much of my fear and pain; however, I was still haunted by my past indiscretions. I could not shake many of the images from my memory, and even worse, I did not know where to begin to try and extract these loathsome impressions. My nights were consumed with reflections and visions of regret, and I often awoke in bouts of horror. Gratefully, I recognized that neither alcohol nor drugs would cure my ongoing sorrow, but my mind continually retreated backward into lapses of self-pity and fantasies of self-destruction. I called on Francis, as well as a few of the elders in the group, and implored them for help and guidance with my struggles. Unequivocally, again and again, I received the same anticlimactic solutions that "time takes time," and that, "this too shall pass." I was also told that TIME stood for "things I must endure" and that until I advanced further along the road to redemption, I needed to have patience and to be kind to myself. After all, I was just in the beginning stages of my transformation, and much more was yet to be revealed.

CHAPTER 18

It's a Wonderful Life

One month later

THE SUMMER SOLSTICE ARRIVED, THE school year ended and The Prince departed for sleepaway camp all in the matter of a couple of days. In addition, it had become immediately apparent that my relationship with Ann would be sorely tested over the next two months as the already tense atmosphere in the house increased exponentially. The buffer which had appeased my angst, my adoring son, was now absent, so I needed to look elsewhere for another suitable outlet. Thankfully, it came in a little four-letter word. No, not Beth. It was *golf.*

In the past, I had always hit the links for either fun with the boys or as a light way to conduct business, but now it became more of a respite and a way to mollify my moods. Not only did I play on the weekends as a way to escape for a whole day, but I also teed off at least once a week with my AA foursome in order to enhance my mental magnitude. Those encounters were like holding a program meeting on each hole as Francis, John, myself and Father Sean toured the course in search of pars and panaceas. The therapeutic value of these contests were beyond recognition at the time. However, in hindsight, they truly proved to satisfy both my longing for acceptance and my need for companionship. While the quality of play was often far from exceptional, the comradeship gained by my participation was paramount. I finally "fit in" somewhere, and I was no longer the square peg trying to force myself into the round hole.

Besides all the male bonding and incorporeal instruction, being outdoors and present with nature also allowed me to feel closer to my Higher Power. I became conscious of my surroundings, really aware and alert; and for the first time in a long while, I was able to listen uninterrupted to the world around me. Previously, my senses and perception had been hijacked by my addictions, but now as the fog lifted from my mind, I began to see clearly again. My present-day occurrences became so strong and so intense that they commenced to obscure my past and all of its hardships. I discovered that most of my evil tendencies had arisen from a lack of consciousness and an inability to separate fantasy from reality. We all create our own realities, and what seems real to us may not seem real to others. In actuality, there had been nothing genuine in my life. It was all a facade with no true clarity or understanding whatsoever.

Moreover, when we have a prolonged history of failure and misfortune, often it is very difficult to imagine our own success. As the literature provides, "Even though we are not doing what we always did, we still expect to get what we always got," and, "We have to learn that all things can really change for us if we are willing and have faith." These realizations, along with the knowledge that God does not love us because we change but rather He loves us so that we can change, catapulted me into the next dimension of my spiritual journey. The key component to this newfangled way of thought was to nurture positive thinking and to stay motivated. Unfortunately, I had always possessed a predisposed negative outlook of life. The glass was invariably "half empty" and I needed to find a way to stay confident and to focus more on the pluses in my life as opposed to the minuses. I had to put up a "good fight" and realize that there is no dishonor in falling short, only dishonor in giving up because we are afraid to fail. Deficiency, however, is part of the deal, and no one really ever succeeds without failing at some point. I was reminded that "we are only responsible for the effort, not the outcome," and that we cannot let ourselves get discouraged. Handling rejection, being resilient in the face of frustration, and overcoming all of our obstacles and disappointments had to be our purpose. And finding faith, a faith that works, and wholeheartedly trusting in that faith was the only way to remove the shackles that bound me.

The first step toward achieving that goal was to clear a pathway of communication between myself and my Higher Power. Prayer and meditation were the two most natural routes available to both direct my thinking and to channel God's will for me. I needed to establish a true and meaningful relationship with Him and to fully understand that He provides us resources rather than resolutions. God wants us to utilize our power of know-how and the gifts that He has provided us so that we can choose wisely and discipline ourselves. Yet we still need the assurance of things hoped for and not seen, and this leap of faith can oftentimes be a difficult one indeed. However, without faith, prayer, and meditation, there are no guarantees in life; but with them, you can secure God's love, guidance, and support. The choice was overwhelmingly evident and I have not looked back since.

My initial venture into the realm of pure prayer occurred early on during my AA orientation. Every one of my AA meetings concluded with all the members joining hands, forming a large circle, and reciting either the serenity prayer or the Lord's Prayer, it was a powerful and moving experience to witness and to be a part of, and the message it conveyed was, "What we cannot do alone, we can all do together." Unity was a focal point of the AA doctrines and was interwoven throughout the program's structure. The prayers themselves asked for serenity, strength, and salvation and the wisdom, the wit, and the worship to bring them to fruition. These innocent utterances stoked my inner fire and sparked my salient curiosity until I could no longer resist their allure. They became an everyday activity, and I began praying everywhere and forevermore. Then when I joined those supplications with a period of quiet mediation, the transcendent tranquility that I achieved was incomparable.

Still being a novice at the prayer and meditation game, I sought advice regarding the composition and character of these constitutions. I continued to be unsure of the conforming methodologies of prayer, and meditation remained an even more foreign enterprise entirely. While I knew that theology and its counterparts were totally subjective in nature and that each of us has our own travails to negotiate, I needed a helping hand to keep me on course. The short answer to my inquiries identified prayer as "talking to God" and meditation as "listening for the response." In broader yet similar terms, the definitions were expanded to mean the continual search for God and then the complete clearing of the mind in order to exclude anything but His grace. These concepts became easier to grasp through practice and repetition, but just like trying to hit a golf ball without first knowing the basic swing components, I wanted to avoid the confirmation of any bad habits. Therefore, still searching for additional enlightenment, I turned to the pages of "Alcoholics Anonymous" for further instruction.

The main text of the AA program titled "Alcoholics Anonymous" is affectionately referred to as the "Big Book" by all of its readership. Not only do its contents divulge the history, teachings, and disciplines of AA, but they also contain numerous personal stories of recovery from people who have been rescued from their own "seemingly hopeless state affairs." This combination of scholastic knowledge, coupled with the real-life stories of hope and triumph, gives the reader a true holistic approach for the appropriate model of rehabilitation.

As far as the debate regarding prayer and meditation, the writings avow that "Step 11 suggests prayer and meditation. We shouldn't be shy on this matter of prayer. Better men that we are using constantly. It works, if we have the proper attitude and work at it" (p. 85–86). They continue by relaying a fitting fashion of expression and advising that "we ask especially for freedom from self-will, and are careful to make no request for ourselves only. We may ask for ourselves, however if others will be helped. We are careful never to pray for our own selfish ends. Many of us have wasted a lot of time doing that and it doesn't work. You can easily see why" (p. 87). Moreover, with respect to meditation, the phrases connote that,

> "As we go through the day we pause, when agitated or doubtful and ask for the right thought or action. We constantly remind ourselves we are no longer running the show, humbly saying to ourselves many times each day, 'thy will be done.'

We are then in much less danger of excitement, fear, anger, worry, self-pity or foolish decisions. We become much more efficient. We do not tire so easily for we are not burning up energy foolishly as we did when we were trying to arrange life to suit ourselves. it works—it really does. We alcoholics are undisciplined. So we let God discipline us in the simple way we have just outlined" (p.87-88).

Much to my surprise, once I began to incorporate these objectives into my daily routine and established a firm schedule, they became rote and a permanent part of my everyday lifestyle. I started and concluded each day with a series of prayers that I had memorized and also set an hour aside every afternoon for a period of peaceful meditation. In addition, I located several guided audio meditations online and regularly selected a different theme in order to expand my experience. After a while, I gained a handful of favorites, which I rotated accordingly based on my disposition at the time. These intervals of quiet contemplation allowed me to both relax and also to attain some desperately needed introspection. Furthermore, I was careful to avoid the proverbial "foxhole prayers," asking God specifically for some self-centered wish or desire and instead adhered to the words of Step 11 by asking Him "only for knowledge of His will for us and the power to carry that out." After all, as it directs us in the final paragraphs of Step 3, "It is when we try to make our will conform with God's that we begin to use it rightly. To all of us, this was a most wonderful revelation. Our whole trouble had been the misuse of will power. We had tried to bombard our problems with it instead of attempting to bring it into agreement with God's intention for us." (Step 3). The problem now, however, is attempting to decipher exactly what God's will for us is. However, this source of vexation turned out to be much more acquirable than I imagined. It had been hidden within me the whole time.

There is no right way to do the wrong thing, and whether they occurred intentionally or accidently, our misfortunes are only elicited by ourselves. Unfortunately, most of the ongoing torment that consumed me came from my deep-seated pangs of doom and my unhallowed thoughts of what the future might bring. I was terminally unsatisfied with my life, and I could not comprehend how to stay in the moment and to live life "one day at a time." I was told that true happiness was "wanting what you have, not having what you want," but my unrealistic expectations and sense of entitlement led me to search for more, always more. I needed to extract that poison from my mind, set boundaries, and simply return to a fundamentally moral foundation of values. My existence was lost in a vacuum and I had to reestablish the notion that there are certain self-evident truths that are either simply right or wrong. True redemption is when guilt leads to good, and once I began to do the next "right thing," all the pieces of the puzzle aligned in perfect harmony.

Soon thereafter, Francis invited me to spend an afternoon with him poolside to soak up some sun and some AA acumen. As I approached the palatial old-world estate where he presently resided, I wondered what new insights would be infused into today's instruction. I parked in the designated visitor's parking area below the main house and followed the upgrade past the manor and into the lavish gardens. I heard voices as I entered the gated cabana enclosure and found Francis holding court with several other AA brethren. Initially taken aback by the grandeur of the surroundings and the spectacle of the moment, I surreptitiously maneuvered my way toward the enclave. Francis was lecturing the men on the virtues of humility and how it was an absolute necessity to humble oneself if they desired prosperity in the recovery process. As he noticed me approaching, he paused momentarily, glanced my way, and then continued with his discourse. I quickly pulled over a vacant chaise lounge and took up a place on the outskirts of the circle. He proceeded on briefly but then ended abruptly as he had to take an incoming call from another fellow. The group seized the moment, disbanded rapidly, and gathered up their belongings as they exited the compound. Suddenly I was all alone and uncertain what to do next, so rather than look for trouble, I made myself comfortable, lay down, and awaited further direction.

I was startled from my doze by a large splash and the spatter of water on my face and torso. Looking up, I observed Francis swimming toward me, and I sat upright to greet him. He surfaced, shook the excess moisture from his face, and bellowed, "Glad you could make it. Better late than never!" I reminded him that I had an earlier engagement and also that I had texted him to advise him that I would be tardy. He then continued, "It's time we have a meaningful discussion regarding your progress. Go grab a drink and meet me under the umbrella. I'll be there in a minute." I nodded in compliance, followed his orders, and made my way over to the shady corner to await my fate.

Once Francis joined me and got himself situated, I tried to ease into the upcoming conversation by inquiring about the property and its history. He concisely gave me a vague account of the real estate's chronology and then reiterated that we had a lot of work to do and needed to get started. Pulling no punches, he commenced his interrogation by asking, "Are you glad to be alive today? Are you glad that God spared you?" Caught off guard by the brusque nature of the questions, I responded, "Excuse me!" and took a long gulp from my can of soda. "It's a pretty straightforward query," he pointed out, continuing, "Are you pleased that your suicide attempt failed and that you are still with us in the here and now?" I tried to answer with my first thought, which was, *Sure, of course*, yet something inside me held me back, and I hesitated for an instant. Finally, I assured him, "Listen, I'm happy and grateful to still be walking among the living, yet I have doubts about why I survived and what my function is now." "I noticed that you wavered a bit," he observed. "What's that about?" I peered downward, crossed my arms against my chest, and then somberly retorted, "Maybe it would have been better if I hadn't outlasted myself… I mean…because of all those who I hurt and whose lives I destroyed." He sat back in his chair, took a long, hard look at me, and said, "Look, whether you believe it or not, I know that God saved you for a reason. Your soul has not yet served its purpose, so you did not die that day. He still his plans for you."

After taking a deep breath and reflecting for a moment, Francis further advised me, "Everyone's sense of harm is different, and while the gravity of your actions was certainly significant, you individually did not ruin anyone else's life." And then he said, "Remember the words of the famous quotation that states when one door closes, another one opens, we just need to stop staring at the shut door so that we can see the new one which has been unlocked for us." Those words hit me like a ton of bricks, and I envisioned a long corridor with doorways becoming accessible and revealing new and wonderful opportunities. But how could I overlook what I had done and all the suffering that I had caused? How could God just forgive me and allow me to move on? How? Those answers again came from Francis when he voiced the following expression: "God doesn't rescue people from drowning in the ocean just so He can beat them up when they get to the shore. If God can forgive you, then you can forgive yourself. God wants us all to find him, so He places things in our lives that we cannot manage in order for us to seek out His guidance. It is then that He wants us to call upon Him. This is your opportunity to command the here and now, to shift your perceptions, and to find your true master."

It was certainly a compelling argument. After all, I did still exist. I was improving daily and I had begun to discover and accept convictions about many things that used to elude me. Maybe I had been too hard on myself, too harsh, too unforgiving. I had hoped and longed that someone would come and rescue me from my despair. I was ashamed of most of my life and clearly needed aid. However, I never realized that a spiritual solution would be the cure. I had always looked in the wrong places.

It was customary, ever since he was a toddler, for The Prince and I to have breakfast out one morning each weekend. In the early years, I would load him into his car seat, and we would trudge our way to the local Mickey D's for pancakes and eggs served in the familiar Styrofoam platters. After a few years of destroying my innards therein, we moved up the ladder and began heading to IHOP or Denny's for our local fare. I can vividly recall The Prince's first experience at the Pancake House, where he remarked, "Dad, this is really good. How come you kept taking me to that other place that sucked?" Inevitably, we graduated to several local dinners for our weekly rendezvous, and we also began mixing up our menu selections. Regardless of where we went or what we ate, it was a special and precious time for us together, a true father-and-son event, and one that has continued right up to the present day.

On one particular occasion, just a couple of weeks after my poolside chat with Francis, we chose one of our usual joints and headed out accordingly. There was nothing out of the ordinary that day, nothing either pressing or urgent to discuss. It was a typical morning with all the normalcy of any other. But as we took our places in our accustomed fashion and settled in, The Prince appeared to be a bit out of sorts and uneasy. He browsed through the menu quickly, made his selection, and then stared blankly ahead at me, waiting for my acknowledgement. Not paying attention initially, I made some small talk until he cut in and said, "Dad, I need to ask you some things. I have a few questions, if that's okay?" "Sure... what's up?" I replied. "Ask away." "Well," he stammered, "I'm curious to know who's going to teach me how to write a check and manage my money and invest in the stock market and stuff? And about, you know, general life stuff they don't teach you in school?"

It was a seminal stage in our relationship, and even though I was surprised by his inquiry, I immediately recognized the significance of the moment. My son needed me. He needed a role model, a mentor, a confidante to explain life's various endeavors, to care for his well-being, and to foster his growth into adulthood. Clearly, that job fell to me. I began to get choked up, felt my emotions getting the best of me, and had to take a sip of water to steady myself before I could answer. "I guess that will be my job," I answered back. "It's a father's duty to impart that wisdom to his son, just as Grandpa did to me." He poured some creamer into his cup of decaf, stirred it in, and then sampled the flavor without replying. Then after a couple of smacks of his lips and a long *aahh* noise, he replied, "Okay, I was just wondering."

That seemingly insignificant and fleeting dialogue not only changed me from that day forward, but it also allowed me to buy into all of Francis's previous preaching. God was leading me out of darkness and into the light. He was converting me into a better person, father, and friend. He was doing for me what I could not do for myself. He was disclosing to me both my reason for living, as well as a way to truly love again. The love of our children is the purest way for us to escape from ourselves. It is a greater love, a love that allows a parent to take themselves away from their self-centered attributes and to restore and mend relationships with the ones they love. God also instilled in me an "attitude of gratitude," which shifted my perspective once more from what was missing in my life to what was already achieved and currently in the now. I came to realize that gratitude, faith and love can bring people together even as life has kept you apart. We all need to believe in something; if not, we are truly lost. When I was drinking, I used alcohol as my crutch, as a way to handle my problems; and while I thought that it was working, all it did was mask my emotions and mar my experiences. Whenever I became restless, irritable, and discontent or worried, sad, and depressed, I knew exactly what to do: reach for a bottle and inoculate myself. But now alcohol was no longer a viable solution, and I had to locate a fresh and more feasible answer. My recovery needed to reign over everything else, and I knew that anything that superseded my struggle would be the first thing that I would lose.

I looked at the young man across the table from me and wondered where the time had gone. Sure, I had been there physically for him, but mentally I was absent more often than not, and I had killed so many years due to my addictions. Repentance is coming to your senses, recoiling from sin, and reapportioning your priorities. That day at breakfast, I received a good glimpse at what was in store for me next, and I felt the intense desire to stop asking *why* and instead to ask, *what now?* When you want something bad enough, truly from the heart, God will hear your call and compel you to achieve your goals. I knew then that I was surely on my way.

Yet there was still one last remaining piece of the puzzle that had to be affixed. Unfortunately, it would prove to be the most elusive of them all. The absence of Beth from my life was far more debilitating than any of the other divergences that had previously distorted me. Until I met her that glorious summer evening, I had neither believed in kismet nor had any idea that true love existed for me. But almost immediately after laying my eyes upon her, I knew that she was my soul mate, my inamorata. We became so close, so intimate, that it was hard for me to distinguish where my essence ceased and where hers began. We were one being, shared one love, and existed totally for each other. My heart was hers from the very beginning, and wherever your heart is, that is where you will find your true self. This powerful adoration caused such internal shifts within me that I became completely enthralled and overwhelmed. Her intrinsic beauty, benevolence, and blithe, along with her outpouring of love, urged me to seek out my own betterment. Every time I was in her presence, a torrent of bliss surged up within me, which at times made it difficult for me to even look at her. I was amazed that she could evoke such strong feelings in me, especially since I had been so numb for so long. She was everything I could have asked for in a woman, a partner and a lover. There was no ceiling to her wonder.

In spite of that, it would all later turn to both panic and dismay as I began to recognize my hopeless inferiority next to her magnificence. Paranoid delusions became commonplace and I imagined that sooner or later Beth would sense my ineptitude and inevitably leave me for another. But rather than come clean and admit to my constant duplicity and disparagement, I just continued to wallow in self-pity while trying to project an image of plenitude. This cycle of deceitfulness was portrayed for far too long and I fell deep into a self-conflicted confinement which I could not escape. It slowly drained my spirit and then finally Beth's as well. In the end, it became too much for me to endure.

Even worse was the fact that I did not know how to deal with her highly charged emotions and that I invariably trivialized her feelings rather than giving her the sympathy and support that she required. I was always remiss in my approach and tried to fix things with logic instead of with love, with complacency instead of with compassion. I had to learn that "people don't care how much you know until they know how much you care," and even then, they may just want a hug rather than a harangue. My biggest regret is that I could neither identify nor empathize with what Beth was actually experiencing. How could I possibly relate to her needs and issues when I barely had a handle on my own? This unavailability and dereliction only led to further self-defeating behavior and enabled the merry-go-round of self-destruction to remain in constant motion.

Accordingly, in my recovery, I had to learn to distinguish between hating myself and hating my actions and to understand that I could be restored to my wholesome, caring, and good-natured state. I yearned so badly for a second chance with Beth, but I knew that she had reverted into her safety zone, into her mode of self-preservation. She needed to keep her guard up and to shield herself from further injury and vulnerability, and I wondered if or when she would ever feel safe with me again. On the other hand, I needed to realize the gravity of the damage that I had caused and also to comprehend that her forgiveness and ability to forget all that had occurred could have significant consequences for her own psyche. I had hurt her in so many ways that reconciliation, while possible, was highly unlikely. Furthermore, if it was, in fact, a possibility at all, I still required the knowledge that it wasn't going to be on my timetable or on my terms. I had to let her heal on her own schedule and in her own way. Otherwise, my incessant longing to correct that which I had marred would just make things worse and ensure a final discord.

With that in mind, I turned to the tenets of Step 3, and by "turning my life and my will over to the care of God as I understood him," I commenced the process of getting right with myself and with others. I had missed out on so many of life's happenings when my drinking took precedence, but most of all, I had missed out on myself. It was time, therefore, to take action, to make determined decisions and to follow through on my promises. I needed to do God's will, not just talk about it, I needed to begin to perform according to His plan, not mine. Once you relinquish control and allow Him to steer you, life becomes more natural, comfortable, and serene. Lucidity in recovery is one of God's many gifts, and we need to realize that doing "the next right thing" in God's world is only made difficult when we detach from Him and try to run the show ourselves.

Our exploits in obeying our Higher Power exhibit to him more love, honor, and praise than any empty words we might convey. The Bible states that it is in following God with deeds and in truths rather with vacuous vows that we honor our Lord and Savior. If we are not properly tuned in to our Holy Spirit, sin will devour us. It goes on further to explain that if you do not know what is right, sin is crouching at your door; it desires to have you. However, there is a way for us to rule over sin to face temptation and to repel the lure of immorality, that simple path is to rely upon God, and to heed his words and warnings.

So now, every day, I include a passage in my daily prayers that asks God to free me from the bondage of self-affliction and to take all the relationships in my life and do with them what He will—His will, not mine—nothing more, nothing less, nothing else. These concepts and mores have broken the chains of self-will that have plagued me over the past few years, and I now convey that authority to my Higher Power. I turn over all the things that I cannot change, focus on those that I can, and live in a place of utter gratitude, joy, and acceptance. Today I thank God for all that He has given me. I thank Him for all that he has taken from me. And I thank Him for all that he has left me. Recovery, along with peace of mind, faith, hope and love.

EPILOGUE

Home Sweet Home

Present day

TODAY AS I SIT IN my prison cell awaiting for the PA to blare out, "COURT ON THE DOOR," I understand that the last 365 days which I spent in the lockup were the most important ones of my life. It was there where I learned true empathy, sympathy and compassion and had the opportunity to transform my prejudices. While many of my preconceived notions about human nature and the flaws in society as a whole were exacerbated, the exigency for camaraderie outweighed everything else. The manner which inmates from all different walks of life banded together in a common purpose was truly remarkable. As a jailhouse novice experiencing my first "bid," I certainly entered with doubts and distrust of both the system and its inhabitants. Yet with a respectful demeanor and a kind word to all, my sentence whittled down without any major incidents. When you can stop looking for the splinter in your brother's eye…and can notice the log in your own and also practice the principles of the twelve steps in all your affairs, it is amazing how differently we can perceive ourselves and others.

Thankfully, God has helped me to Recover by, Removing my fear, Easing my pain, Cleansing my soul, Opening my heart and mind, Vowing never to leave me, Engaging me daily, and Restoring my sanity. Without His mercy, favor, and guidance, my conversion would have been inconsequential. Still, as all alcoholics surely know, the addictive blood type is "B negative" and more often than not, we let our thoughts get the best of us. Accordingly, the key for me was to stay in the *now*, to not try and forecast the future and to prevent my projections from propelling me imprudently. By concentrating correctly and keeping in concert with the precepts of the program, I not only survived but also flourished. It is true that once we navigate through troubled waters clean and sober, we commence to believe in our own resiliency, trust our recovery and realize that our success is not measured by external forces but rather by ourselves and by how high we can bounce back after hitting our bottom. Helping others, giving rather than receiving and contributing to our community are the clear constants that we need to consume us.

Consequently, I was able to help several of my fellow inmates acknowledge that there may be a better way for them to handle their lives and, moreover, that there is truly no right way to do the wrong thing. I took my leadership position very seriously and I knew that the others were looking to me for both support and direction. A role model needs to walk the walk rather than just talk the talk, and a hypocritical existence was not going to suffice. Luckily, God was on my side, and He aided me through my times of self-doubt and self-examination. It was often quite difficult and I frequently wondered in the face of adversity whether or not it was truly worth it. However, it was then that I remembered that we must do God's work without self-consciousness, haste or fear of other people's judgement. Instead, it must be done calmly, confidently and lovingly knowing that performing His will alone brings us our true salvation. And while my marriage to Ann seems destined to terminate, I am still hopeful to rediscover my friendship with The Prince, rekindle my relationship with Beth, and reconnect with my friends in the fellowship. I know that there is much more still to be revealed, but I also know that I do not intend to quit before the miracle.

Stay safe and may God bless you all.

CPSIA information can be obtained
at www.ICGtesting.com
Printed in the USA
JSHW040136170520
5719JS00001B/121